WILLIAM MONSELL OF TERVOE
1812–1894

To Colette, Alex, Anna and Michael

William Monsell of Tervoe 1812–1894

Catholic Unionist, Anglo-Irishman

MATTHEW POTTER

University of Limerick

Foreword by

GEARÓID Ó TUATHAIGH

IRISH ACADEMIC PRESS

DUBLIN • PORTLAND, OR

First published in 2009 by Irish Academic Press

2 Brookside,
Dundrum Road,
Dublin 14, Ireland

920 NE 58th Avenue, Suite 300
Portland, Oregon,
97213-3786

www.iap.ie

British Library Cataloguing in Publication Data
An entry can be found on request

ISBN 978 0 7165 2989 7 (cloth)

Library of Congress Cataloging-in-Publication Data
An entry can be found on request

Printed by the MPG Books Group in the UK

Contents

List of Illustrations

Acknowledgements

There are many persons to whom I owe a great debt of gratitude in connection with the publication of this book. I am particularly grateful to Professor Gearóid Ó Tuathaigh of NUI Galway, who supervised the thesis on which it is based as well as contributing the foreword. He was always enthusiastic, courteous and encouraging and gave me the benefit of his vast knowledge and experience. I would also like to thank Professor Nicholas Canny and Professor Paul Bew, the other members of my thesis committee, whose useful advice I have tried to embody in the present work.

I wish to acknowledge the contribution made by the staff of the various libraries and archives which I visited, including the National Library of Ireland, Dublin; the National Archives of Ireland, Dublin; Archives of Trinity College Dublin; Dublin Diocesan Archives, Dublin; Limerick Diocesan Archives, Limerick; Limerick City Archives, Limerick; Limerick County Archives, Limerick; Limerick City Library, Limerick; Limerick County Library, Limerick; Public Records Office of Northern Ireland, Belfast; British Library, London; Post Office Archives, London; Public Records Office, Kew, London; Archives of University of Southampton; Public Records Office of Somerset, Taunton; Royal Archives, Windsor Castle; the Oratory, Birmingham; Cambridge University Library, Cambridge; and National Archives of Scotland, Edinburgh.

I wish to thank Dr Dermot Roantree for allowing me to consult his doctoral thesis 'William Monsell MP, and the Catholic Question in Victorian Britain and Ireland'. This has proved to be particularly stimulating in my discussion of certain aspects of the career of William Monsell. I am indebted to various members of the Monsell and de la Poer families, including Peggy Reidy, the late Nigel de la Poer and the late Trifine Turner, who furnished me with information and materials. I am conscious of the contributions made by local historians to the study of the Monsell family, including John O'Connor, John Sheehan and in particular Mary Hanley, all three of whom are now sadly deceased. In addition, Mary's son Liam was able to provide me with a great deal of valuable information and assistance.

I want to pay warm tribute to the staff of Irish Academic Press, in particular to my editor Lisa Hyde, for the professional, efficient and courteous manner in which she has facilitated the publication of this book. I wish to express deep appreciation to the following for the use of their images: the National Portrait Gallery, London; the Earl of Dunraven, Kilgobbin House, Adare, County Limerick; the Knight of Glin, Glin Castle, County Limerick; Mr Daniel McSweeney, Ballyanrahan, Patrickswell, County Limerick; Mr Liam Hanley, Limerick City; and the late Mr Nigel de la Poer, Kilsheelan, County Tipperary. I should also like to thank Mr Michael Martin, Photographer, Upper Gerald Griffin Street, Limerick City, for photographing a number of the illustrations.

I would like to thank the following for their very generous assistance: Dr Gordon Holmes and the JP McManus Charitable Foundation Ltd; Ms Sheila Deegan, Limerick City Arts Officer and Limerick City Council; Ms Joan McKernan, Limerick County Arts Officer and Limerick County Council; Fr Thomas Morrissey SJ and the Society of Jesus; the Most Reverend Dr Donal Murray, Bishop of Limerick and the Diocese of Limerick; Mrs Margaret Dalton, Administrator, Limerick Diocesan Office; Sister Loreto O'Connor and the Sisters of Mercy and Fr Seamus Enright CSsR and the Redemptorist Community, Mount St Alphonsus, Limerick.

I want to thank my friend Declan Maguire who, together with his family and friends, extended warm hospitality to me whenever I undertook research trips to Dublin and provided me with accommodation, entertainment and nourishment, both physical and mental. My colleagues and friends in the University of Limerick, Mary Immaculate College, Limerick, Limerick City Council and Limerick City Library were always encouraging and supportive. I salute my other friends, relations and others too numerous to mention, who afforded me assistance of various kinds over the years. In particular, I cherish the memory of my friend and colleague, the late Carole Murphy of Limerick City Council, without whose assistance the thesis upon which the present book is based would not have been completed.

Finally, I would like to acknowledge the huge support, endless patience and tireless devotion of my family over many years. I should also like to pay tribute to my parents John and Mary Potter, as the former (now deceased) installed in me a love of history and the latter (who suffers from Alzheimer's disease) always joined him in believing in my efforts. My wife's parents, Mary and the late John Tracey, were also very loyal and encouraging over a long timespan. My wife Colette, our children Alex and Anna and my brother Michael are deserving of particular mention for putting up with both Monsell and I (together with our many foibles!) for many years. They always displayed unstinting kindness, encouragement and forbearance and it is for this reason that the book is dedicated to them.

Foreword

The act of union finally failed because, in an increasingly democratic Ireland (though universal male suffrage, and limited female suffrage, did not come until 1918), the persistent strength of nationalist sentiment ultimately led to a substantial measure of national self-determination being embodied in an Irish Free State, covering twenty-six of the island's thirty-two counties, in 1922. The concentration of a strong Unionist sentiment in eastern Ulster likewise resulted in Northern Ireland's six counties remaining part of the United Kingdom of Great Britain and Northern Ireland.

Narratives of nineteenth-century Irish political history written under the shadow of the ultimate partition settlements of 1920–2 frequently gave short measure to the rich varieties of Irish Unionist sentiment to be found in the other provinces, outside of Ulster, throughout the long century of the union. In more recent decades, however, a more complex presentation of the variegated support-base of Irish unionism has been emerging: its popular support in Dublin, its electoral fortunes in the period between O'Connell's movement and the polarised politics of the Home Rule era, and, most pertinent to this new study of Monsell, the élite circles in the provinces who supported the union.[1]

For some time scholars have been emphasising that 'constructive unionism' was not simply a late nineteenth-century idea or policy, prompted by the need to 'kill Home Rule with kindness' in the years following Gladstone's espousal of a devolved Irish parliament. In fact, advocates of 'constructive unionism' – that is, advocates of proactive government and of administrative measures in Ireland aimed at securing a stable society and majority support for the union – were prominent from relatively early in the union era. O'Connell's Repeal movement needed to be 'killed with kindness' as urgently as the later Home Rule demand, while the pacification of Ireland, which the Fenian scare prompted Gladstone to undertake, produced its own reform programme of a constructive unionist kind. And, all the time, individual politicians, landowners, lawyers, clergymen, pamphleteers and publicists continued to propose 'measures of improvement' for Ireland, all anchored in a determination to make the union work for the benefit of Ireland as well as for the United Kingdom as a whole.

One strand of constructive unionism, which remains relatively under-investigated, is the sentiment for union shared by influential figures and 'circles' among the Catholic élite of nineteenth-century Ireland. This Catholic Unionist sentiment is closely related to, though not quite synonymous with, the Irish sentiment for empire – a compound of conviction and careerism – which historians of the British empire have been investigating in recent decades.[2] Soldiering and other areas of service in the empire, sport and popular culture, labour mobility between the two islands, and, increasingly, a common vernacular, all might be judged as having contributed to widening the sense of a pan-British identity in Ireland in the later nineteenth century. Historical consciousness, congealing into a strong ethno-religious identity provided a major stumbling block to assimilation and political 'contentment' for the majority. The route to high legal office for Irish Catholic lawyers – and the political accommodation that accompanied and facilitated it – still awaits systematic investigation. But, 'identity politics' were complex and contradictory in nineteenth-century Ireland, and the case for socio-economic progress could be made, and was in fact made, from a variety of constitutional and political positions. It is important that this complexity be fully explored by students of modern Irish history.

It is in this context, and specifically in the discussion of the anatomy of nineteenth-century Irish unionism, that Matthew Potter's new study of William Monsell, first Baron Emly of Tervoe (1812–94), is to be welcomed. Monsell was not a 'towering' political figure of his day. But he was active in Irish and British politics for many decades, and his personal 'journey' and career sheds light on the paths to ambition and political office open to the provincial élite of Victorian Ireland. A Tory Protestant landowner by birth, but who became a Catholic in 1850, Monsell held a seat in Parliament for County Limerick from 1847 to 1874, and a succession of government offices (essentially as a Whig Irish Catholic) in the mid-Victorian decades, before being created Baron Emly of Tervoe in 1874. His conversion to Catholicism did not shake his firm Unionist faith, and he broke with Gladstone in 1886 on the Home Rule question. Monsell's background and personal development, his political career, his contacts, his relationship with 'his own place' and with the rarified world of the palace of Westminster, are brought to light in this sympathetic and well-researched study. Potter's book raises sharp questions about religious and political identity and loyalties in nineteenth-century Ireland, and rescues from long neglect a Limerick Catholic convert and firm unionist of genuine historical interest.

Professor Gearóid Ó Tuathaigh
National University of Ireland, Galway

NOTES

1. See, for example, Jacqueline Hill, *From Patriots to Unionists: Dublin Civic Politics and Irish Protestant Patriotism, 1660–1840* (Oxford: Oxford University Press, 1997), K. Theodore Hoppen, *Elections, Politics and Society in Ireland,1832–1885* (Oxford: Oxford University Press, 1984), Andrew Shields, *The Irish Conservative Party 1852–1868* (Dublin, 2007); Jennifer Ridden, '"Making Good Citizens": National Identity, Religion and Liberalism among the Irish Elite, c. 1800–1850' (unpublished Ph.D, University of London, 1998), and Paul Bew, *Ireland: The Politics of Enmity 1789–2006* (Oxford: Oxford University Press, 2007).
2. See Keith Jeffery (ed.), *An Irish Empire? Aspects of Ireland and the British Empire* (Manchester: Manchester University Press, 1996); also, Stephen Howe, *Ireland and Empire* (Oxford: Oxford University Press, 2000).

CHAPTER ONE

The Rare Bird

William Monsell, first Lord Emly, is a major figure in the history of modern Ireland.[1] Born in 1812 into a wealthy Protestant landed family, whose principal residence was Tervoe House, near the village of Clarina, about five miles from Limerick city, he was reared in an atmosphere of devotion to the union with Britain, loyalty to the Church of Ireland, and adherence to the Tory party. In the 1840s Monsell flirted with federalism and even Repeal, but from the early 1850s onwards his religious and political views remained fairly fixed for the rest of his life. Thereafter, he was always to be a staunch Unionist and broke with the Liberals over Home Rule in 1886. However, he was to give long and valuable service to the Liberal party for many years, sitting as MP for County Limerick from 1847 to 1874, and serving in several British administrations under four prime ministers, between 1853 and 1873, successively as Clerk of the Ordnance (1853–7), President of the Board of Health (1857), Paymaster-General and Vice- President of the Board of Trade (1866), Under-Secretary for the Colonies (1868–71) and Postmaster-General (1871–3). Monsell became one of Ireland's leading political figures and was a close friend of such giant figures as Newman, Cullen, Pius IX and Gladstone. In 1874 he was raised to the peerage with the title Baron Emly of Tervoe and died in 1894 after enjoying a political career of nearly sixty years' duration.[2]

That Monsell is a significant personage in the history of Ireland and even of Britain may not be easily appreciated. As a Unionist, a landlord, and an upholder of the status quo in all its essentials, he opposed the principal forces which led to the creation of modern Ireland – political nationalism, land agitation, the rise of democracy – and although he converted to the religion of the majority, he espoused a particular brand of it, Liberal Catholicism, which had no immediate future, either in Ireland or abroad. Indeed, the political and religious causes for which he fought, in Ireland, Britain, France and the Catholic Church, were all defeated, while the social milieu within which he lived has utterly vanished. Thus, the modern observer might be forgiven for considering him a minor and reactionary figure, unworthy of serious consideration by present-day historians.[3]

However, this would be a gross injustice to Monsell of Tervoe, one of the most significant Irishmen of the nineteenth century. Historians often side with the winners, but one of the reasons why a study of Monsell is of immense importance is precisely because he is one of the great losers in Irish history as defined by Ciaran Brady: a figure who operated at the highest levels in the political process but who ultimately failed and was 'worsted in the game'.[4] Monsell's entire career can be understood as a *via media* similar to the original Tractarian vision of his mentor Newman.[5] He spent most of his life in a struggle to reconcile various conflicting ideologies, and like the Oxford vision that he had embraced in the 1830s and 1840s, the attempt was ultimately to perish at the hands of its own inner contradictions and the superior strength of its more polarised opponents. This book is a study of Monsell's lifelong battle in support of his *via media*, his vision of an Ireland that was catholic, liberal, united and an integral part of the United Kingdom.

Monsell's complex and paradoxical political philosophy, a classic *via media*, informed his entire career in public life. He started out as a bigoted member of the Church of Ireland, a passionate hater of Popery, and a staunch Tory. He subsequently underwent a political conversion that took him, by way of the Peelite split and federalism, to liberalism, and a parallel journey, primarily under the influence of Newman, into the arms of Roman Catholicism. He became one of the leading lay Catholics in the United Kingdom, and one of the most powerful and influential figures in Ireland. The paradoxes of his ideology are many. His unionism was his most passionately held political belief, yet he dabbled with federalism and even Repeal in the 1840s. He was attached to the liberal connection for most of his career, yet in the crisis of the first Home Rule bill his liberalism succumbed to his unionism. His Catholicism and liberalism were also difficult to reconcile in the era of Pio Nono and the Syllabus of Errors.

Monsell was both a Catholic Liberal and a Liberal Catholic. As a Catholic Liberal, he mediated between successive British administrations and the Irish Catholic bishops. He became a leading member of the Irish Catholic Whigs, a sub-group within the Liberal party who combined unionism, liberalism and Catholicism in an interesting attempt to preserve Ireland as an integral part of the United Kingdom. The Catholic Whigs constituted a proto-élite who tried to fill the vacuum created between the demise of Repeal and the rise of Home Rule.[6] Their *via media* is paralleled in Monsell's adherence to Liberal Catholicism. One of the greatest conflicts of the nineteenth century was that between organised religion and the 'modern world', which took its most acute form in the struggle between the various strands of liberalism, and the most powerful and highly organised of all religious bodies, the Roman Catholic Church. Again, Monsell cleaved to the middle way, adhering to the French Liberal-Catholic movement, which, in Lammenais's words, wanted to 'baptise the Revolution'.[7] Monsell was the most prominent Liberal Catholic to be active in Irish or British politics, and drew inspiration from his prominent French friends, such as Montalambert and Broglie.

This, in turn, highlights another aspect of Monsell's career – his internationalism. His sense of nationality was, by present-day standards, an anomaly, as he was both a patriotic Irishman and a staunch 'West Briton'.[8] His particular brand of convert Catholicism gave him a broad worldview, while his social status, education and fluency in French gave him the *entree* to the cosmopolitan world of European intellectuals, churchmen and aristocrats. Monsell campaigned for Catholic causes throughout the world, speaking in support of the Church on the occasion of crises in the Lebanon and Italy (1860), Poland (1863), Germany (in the 1870s) and even Uganda (1893). His involvement in successive British administrations was another aspect of his internationalism, especially during his periods at the Board of Ordnance (1853–7) and the Colonial Office (1868–71). Unusually among Irishmen of his own day and since, he was a close friend of both the British and French prime ministers (respectively Gladstone and Broglie). Typically and symbolically, Monsell's chief preoccupations in 1870 were Irish (the Land Act), French (the Franco-Prussian War) and Catholic/Italian (the Vatican Council and the fall of Rome).

Yet Monsell's political base was always a local one. His career was informed by the concept of service, of *noblesse oblige* which had long formed an essential part of the ideology of the European élites and was re-enforced in the nineteenth century by the rise of liberalism, philanthropy and religious earnestness and morality. As a local notable, he served on various bodies and in local administrative offices. He was a Justice of the Peace, a Grand Juror and Deputy-Lieutenant and later reached the summit of county politics when he became in succession Chairman of the Limerick Poor Law Union, Colonel of the County Militia, and Lord-Lieutenant of the City and County. Thereafter, it was but a natural step to become an MP, and to strive for Government office. Monsell, who belongs in a tradition stretching from Gladstone to Tony Blair, which combines committed Christian beliefs and *realpolitik*, was a mixture of the selfless and the self-interested, the principled and the expedient, the moral and the materially ambitious. He often found that his own self-interest coincided with the advancement of his ideological aims, best exemplified in his attitude to the holding of office in British administrations by Catholics. Monsell always sincerely believed that Catholic office-holders would be able to advance the cause of their co-religionists and solidify Catholic adherence to the Union, while at the same time he longed for self-advancement and in particular a seat in the Cabinet. Unfortunately for him, the number of Irishmen in Government at any level was always comparatively low, even in an administration that made Ireland one of its chief priorities, such as Gladstone's first premiership.[9]

Monsell saw the holding of office as a sacred trust and, as an Irishman, additionally believed that he had a particular duty to assuage the disaffection of his fellow countrymen by promoting reform. Consequently, his political career was devoted to the advancement of civil and religious liberty and he used his various periods in office towards these ends. He served in the 1850s, 1860s and early 1870s, at the height of the period of Liberal reforms, and he confronted some of the leading administrative issues of his time – the role of Government in the economy, recruitment by competitive examination, the relationship between the political head of a department and his civil servants, and the beginnings of industrial unrest in the civil service. Monsell's record as an administrator was a mixed one and rather oddly, his performance diminished rather than improved with experience. His most outstanding successes were achieved at the Board of Ordnance (1853–7), while his period at the Post Office (1871–3) was a disaster. Nevertheless, he always strove to advance his ideological objectives – promotion of Catholics to office, advancement of Catholic education in Trinidad and elsewhere, recruitment of staff by examination.

Monsell is a representative of the Catholic gentry, an unexpectedly large minority within an Irish Ascendancy whose Protestantism is supposed to have been axiomatic. In 1871 Catholics represented 38 per cent of the total number of Irish landlords and included major figures such as the Earl of Kenmare (who owned 118,606 acres), the Earl of Dunraven (15,467 acres in Ireland alone) and the Earl of Fingal (9,589 acres). In the late eighteenth century Catholics had owned 5 per cent of the land in Ireland, but by 1871 the proportion had increased to about 15 per cent, an increase due to purchases in the Encumbered Estates Courts and the conversion to Catholicism of many prominent figures, including the Earls of Granard and Dunraven and indeed Monsell himself.[10] The Oxford Movement produced a rich crop of such recruits in County Limerick, and

Monsell was the most prominent political figure from the 'Limerick Convert Set'.[11] Indeed, Dermot Roantree has described him as 'one of the very few examples – in England or Ireland – of a Tractarian convert active in parliamentary politics, and probably the only example of one that held a series of Government offices'.[12]

Nineteenth-century Limerick and Clare produced a remarkable and closely knit coterie of enlightened gentlemen who practised *noblesse oblige* on a large scale, over several generations and over a wide geographic area. A useful collective term for them is the 'Shannon Estuary Group'. David Fitzpatrick first drew attention to them in an article in 1988.[13] Ten years later they formed the subject matter of a dissertation by Jennifer Ridden.[14] Both of these concentrated on the group in the first half of the century, and some of its leading members have also been the subject of individual studies, including Spring Rice and Sir Richard Bourke.[15] For the second half of the nineteenth century, there exists a number of works on Aubrey de Vere and William Smith O'Brien, but one was primarily a literary figure and the other became a nationalist and thus moved out of the group's political mainstream.[16]

Monsell, the most significant figure that the Shannon Estuary Group produced between 1850 and 1914, was a remarkable personality, and Dermot Roantree has rightly described him as an 'avis rara' (a rare bird).[17] His combination of the ordinary and the unusual, the local and the national, the old and the modern, all invite study. It is also remarkable in how many ways he was a precursor of contemporary developments – his internationalism, his belief in the reconciliation between religion and modern science and politics, his struggle for civil and religious liberty. The issues that he confronted – the relationship of the individual to the state, of the state to the economy, the place of religion in society – are of continuing and universal relevance. The present work is based on the belief that there is a necessity for a comprehensive contextual biography, treating of all aspects of Monsell's life and career in the context of his time.

NOTES

1. See Sidney Lee (ed.), *Dictionary of National Biography*, Vol. 24 (supplement) (London: Smith and Elder, 1909), pp.159–60; W.P. Courtney, revised H.C.G. Matthew, 'William Monsell, first Baron Emly (1812–1894)', in Colin Matthew, Brian Harrison and Laurence Goldman (eds), *Oxford Dictionary of National Biography* (Oxford: Oxford University Press, 2004), hereafter referred to as *Oxford DNB*, and Matthew Potter, 'William Monsell', in Aidan Clarke, Ronan Fanning, T.K. Hoppen, Edith Mary-Johnston-Liik, James Maguire, Maureen Murphy and James Quinn (eds), *Dictionary of Irish Biography* (forthcoming, 2009).
2. For a short introduction, see Matthew Potter, *A Catholic Unionist. The Life and Times of William Monsell, 1st Baron Emly of Tervoe (1812–94) A Centenary Essay* (Limerick: Treaty Press, 1994).

3. Good accounts of the social order within which Monsell operated can be found in Terence Dooley, *The Decline of the Big House in Ireland* (Dublin: Wolfhound Press, 2001) and David Cannadine, *The Decline and Fall of the British Aristocracy* (New Haven and London: Yale University Press, 1990).
4. Ciaran Brady (ed.), *Worsted in the Game. Losers in Irish History* (Dublin: Lilliput Press, 1989), p.3.
5. John Henry Newman, *The Via Media of the Anglican Church* (edited by H.D. Weidner) (Oxford: Clarendon Press, 1990). The term was used to describe the Church of England, a 'typically English' compromise between the extremes of the Catholic Church and of Protestantism.
6. See David Thomas Horgan, 'The Irish Catholic Whigs in Parliament 1847–74', (unpublished Ph.D thesis, University of Minnesota, 1975). This remains the only work devoted to this neglected political movement.
7. Eamon Duffy, *Saints and Scholars. A History of the Popes* (New Haven: Yale University Press, 1997), p.81.
8. The term was famously used by Thomas Spring Rice during his famous speech opposing O'Connell's Repeal motion in 1834.
9. W.E. Vaughan (ed.), *A New History of Ireland*, Vol. 5, *1801–1870* (Oxford: Oxford University Press, 1989), pp.776–7.
10. Ibid., p.740.
11. An alternative is the Tervoe Convert Set.
12. Dermot S. Roantree, 'William Monsell M.P. and the Catholic question in Victorian Britain and Ireland' (unpublished Ph.D thesis, University College Dublin, 1990), p.10.
13. See David Fitzpatrick, 'Thomas Spring Rice and the Peopling of Australia', in *The Old Limerick Journal,* 23, Australian edition (spring 1988), pp.39–49.
14. Jennifer Ridden, 'Making Good Citizens. National Identity Religion and Liberalism among the Irish Elite, c. 1800–1850' (unpublished Ph.D thesis, University of London, 1998).
15. Charlotte Mary Murphy, 'The Life and Politics of Thomas Spring Rice, First Baron Monteagle of Brandon 1790–1866' (unpublished MA thesis, University College Cork, 1991) and Hazel King, *Richard Bourke* (Oxford: Oxford University Press, 1971).
16. For de Vere, see Thomas A. Pijpers, *Aubrey De Vere as a Man of Letters* (Nijmegen-Utrecht: Dekker and Van de Vegt, 1941) and Wilfred Ward, *Aubrey de Vere – A Memoir Based on his Unpublished Diaries and Correspondence* (London, New York and Bombay: Longmans and Co., 1904). For Smith O'Brien, see Blanche M. Touhill, *William Smith O'Brien and his Irish Revolutionary Companions in Penal Exile* (Colombia, MI: University of Missouri Press, 1981); Richard Davis (ed.), *To Solitude Confined. The Tasmanian Journal of William Smith O'Brien 1849–53* (Sydney: Crossing Press, 1995) and Richard Davis, *Revolutionary Imperialist. William Smith O'Brien 1803–64* (Dublin: Lilliput Press, 1998).
17. Roantree, 'William Monsell and the Catholic Question', p.7.

CHAPTER TWO

The Making of Monsell

The Monsells originated in the ancient province of Maine in northern France and the name signifies a native of Le Mans, formerly spelt Le Mauns, one of its principal towns.[1] Philip Maunsell, who served under William the Conqueror and received English lands as a reward for his services, is the ancestor of the very numerous branches of the family, who have spelt their name variously as Maunsell, Mounsell, Monshall, Monshale, Monseall, Mansell, Monsell and (in Irish) Moinséil. Colonel William Thomas Mounsell of Tervoe (1754–1836) omitted the *u*, and thus became Monsell.[2] The name was brought to Ireland in the twelfth century by the Normans, where it has occurred ever since, most frequently in counties Tipperary and Limerick.

The Tervoe Monsells came to Ireland much later, as part of the great migration in the Age of the Plantations (1550–1700). They hailed from Dorsetshire, in the West Country of England, an area that played a disproportionate part in English overseas expansion at this time. Humphrey Gilbert, Richard Grenville, Francis Drake, Walter Raleigh and John Hawkins all hailed from the neighbouring county of Devonshire, and many of these were involved in colonisation in Ireland as well as in America. Thus the plantation of Munster brought to Ireland a great number of settlers from the West Country.[3] While John Mounsell (1547–86) was a merchant of Weymouth and Melcombe Regis (both in Dorsetshire), his second son, also John (1581–1637), became a prominent London merchant. Like many such men, he wanted to progress into the ranks of the gentry, and did so by purchasing land in the Askeaton area of County Limerick, where he lived for over twenty years (1612–34). A decade after John's return to England, his third son, Ephriam (1627–75) returned to Ireland in 1644, oddly enough in the midst of the chaos of the Confederate Wars.

However, the long Monsell connection with Clarina did not commence until after the Cromwellian conquest. The Barony of Pubblebrien, which had been the patrimony of the O'Briens, Lords of Carrigogunnell, was confiscated in the 1650s and made available to Adventurers.[4] It lies to the West of Limerick city and includes the modern villages of Clarina, Mungret and Patrickswell. The Monsells were not among the original grantees of Pubblebrien but Ephriam acquired lands near Clarina in the 1660s, while his second son and successor Thomas (died 1712) did much to consolidate the family's position in Ireland. He disposed of his remaining English property in the 1690s (thus making the Monsells exclusively Irish-based) and lived at Tervoe near Clarina, which was to be the principal Monsell residence for 250 years. Around 1690 he built the original Tervoe House (the remains of which still stand), and in 1692 he acquired the ruins of Carrigogunnell Castle plus lands in Pubblebrien for the sum of £5,200. He is the first of his family to be recorded as holding public office in Ireland, for he was High Sheriff of County Limerick in 1697 and 1698.[5] However, his period in office was controversial, as he was heavily fined for removing one of his tenants from the gallows, an illegal act, but possibly a harbinger of future Mounsell sympathies with popular causes.[6]

The rise of the Mounsells in the eighteenth century was a steady and a progressive one. They were hard-headed merchants as well as landowners who used marriage as one of their principal means of advancement. Thomas's grandson, William (1705–72) was the first of four successive Williams who were masters of Tervoe, from 1735 to 1894, and in 1751 he married, as his second wife, Dymphna Pery (died 1794), a member of one of the leading families of County Limerick. In addition to land in counties Limerick and Clare, the Perys owned the largest estate within the borough boundary of Limerick, later known as Newtown Pery, which made them one of the most influential families in the city. The head of the family at this time was Edmond Sexton Pery (1719–1806), who has been described as 'the most notable Limerickman of all time, and also its greatest benefactor'.[7] He was MP for Limerick City from 1760 to 1785, and as Speaker of the House of Commons from 1771 to 1785 was one of Ireland's most powerful men.[8] Pery's influence on the history of Limerick city is greater than that of any other single individual, as he was largely responsible for the creation of the present Georgian city of Limerick, which was named Newtown Pery in his honour.[9] His brother William Cecil Pery (1721–94) was successively Anglican Bishop of Killala (1781–4) and Limerick (1784–94).[10] Edmond was created Viscount Pery of Newtown Pery in 1785 and William became Baron Glentworth of Mallow in 1790, while the latter's son, Edmond Henry (1758–1844), inherited his uncle's parliamentary seat (sitting for Limerick City 1785–94) and in 1803 was created the first Earl of Limerick. Besides Dymphna Monsell, two other Pery sisters made good marriages. Lucy (died 1793) was married to Sir Harry Hartstonge of Bruff, who sat for County Limerick from 1776 to 1790, and Diana was married to Reverend Henry Smyth, whose family dominated Limerick city from 1776 to 1841.

Dymphna Pery brought to her new family two important assets. First, as a direct descendant of King Edward I, she provided the Mounsells with the illustrious pedigree which they had hitherto lacked. Her great-grandson, the first Lord Emly, had her to thank for the many exalted ancestors with whom she had thus furnished him. These included the Kings of England, France, Scotland and Castile, the medieval Emperors of Germany and of Byzantium and even the Rurikid dynasty, who ruled Russia for 700 years to 1598. William the Conqueror, Alfred the Great and St Louis were some of his most celebrated forbears, while Henry VIII, Mary Queen of Scots and even Ivan the Terrible were distant cousins.[11] In an aristocratic age a good pedigree was an important acquisition for an upwardly mobile family of merchant origins. Secondly, William Mounsell's marriage brought him into a powerful political and social circle. There was close collaboration in business as well as in politics. In the 1750s, Edmond Sexton Pery embarked on his first major building venture in Limerick, St John's Square, as part of a consortium that included his brother-in-law, William Mounsell, who acquired one of the residences as his town house.[12]

Much more significantly, the alliance also brought the Mounsells into the mainstream of politics. From 1776 to 1841, Limerick city was dominated by a family dynasty of remarkable durability, the Smyths and the Verekers, whose supremacy was based on their control of the Corporation and of the freeman vote. They had 'numerous friends of theirs from throughout the country admitted as freemen of the city, with the power to vote in elections, while simultaneously denying the franchise to members of the local community, who should have had the right to vote'.[13] Edmond Sexton Pery and his supporters opposed this 'corrupt corporation', and founded Newtown Pery within the city boundaries but independent of the Corporation's jurisdiction. Between 1770 and 1840 a whole new Georgian city was created there that as early as 1822 contained 2,000 houses and 16,000 inhabitants, including the wealthiest and most elegant parts of the city. In 1807 the Commissioners of St Michael's Parish were established to govern Newtown Pery. In effect, Limerick city was now governed by two opposing corporations, a situation that continued until 1853, when Newtown Pery was annexed to the (by now reformed) Limerick Corporation. Edmond Sexton Pery allied himself with the 'free citizens' (also called 'independent citizens') who opposed the Smyth–Vereker clique. Limerick city returned two members to the

Irish Parliament, so that from 1760 to 1794 the representation was always divided between one Pery and one Smyth.[14]

The Mounsells had arrived politically through the marriage of William Mounsell and Dymphna Pery, but it was their son who reaped the full benefits of their alliance. William Thomas Mounsell (1754–1836) changed the spelling of the surname to Monsell, and in many other respects paved the way for the career of his grandson, the first Lord Emly.[15] He succeeded to his rich inheritance in 1772, and added to it by marrying a wealthy heiress, Hannah Strettle (died 1818) in 1776. A graduate of Trinity College, he was a non-practising barrister, a successful landowner and an entrepreneur. At one stage he had 200–300 people in the Clarina area engaged in spinning and weaving for him, under the 'putting out' system.[16] Wealthy he was by any standard. His daughter, Dymphna, was reported to have brought with her a dowry of £30,000 on her marriage to Richard Ellis of Abbeyfeale in 1804, and in 1820 he gave £7,468 to another daughter, Frances.[17] In the 1770s he built a newer and much grander mansion at Tervoe, consisting of a central block of three stories, which he extended in the 1830s with the addition of two one-storey wings on either side plus a single-storey Ionic portico at the front entrance.[18] Tervoe House, which had forty-two rooms and stood in a beautifully landscaped park overlooking the Shannon, was the country seat of the Monsells until 1951. W.T. Monsell also acquired a town house on Kildare Street, Dublin, to be used while attending Parliament and the Viceregal Court.

William also used his great wealth to carve out for himself a major political role in this, the golden age of the European aristocracies, and became the first Monsell to sit in Parliament, successively for Dunleer (1776–83) and Dingle (1798–1800). His uncle, Speaker Pery, was a strong and consistent supporter of Free Trade for Ireland and the independence of the Irish Parliament, and Monsell followed his uncle's example, supporting the Patriots with enthusiasm. During his second period as an MP (1798–1800), Monsell initially opposed the proposed union with Britain.[19] However, he was not a staunch anti-Unionist and later sold his seat for £1,500 to the Earl of Altamont, a Unionist.[20] After 1800 the anti-Unionists, including Monsell, adapted themselves remarkably well to the *fait accompli*, and indeed, he became very anxious to secure a Commons seat. In the general election of 1806, O'Dell and Windham Quin (later the second Earl of Dunraven) supported respectively by the earls of Clare and of Devon (the two most politically powerful figures in County Limerick), were returned, with Monsell coming a very poor third; in the 1807 general election Monsell stood with the support of the Masseys (led by the two family peers, Lords Massey and Clarina), but was again defeated and a final drubbing in an 1811 by-election put an end to his political activities on the national stage.[21]

Edmond Sexton Pery was a Patriot, a warm advocate of free trade, of legislative independence for Ireland and of Catholic relief, and had allied himself with the popular elements in his battle with the Smyths for the control of Limerick city. The Pery popular tradition was continued primarily not by the first Earl of Limerick, but by his son-in-law, Thomas Spring Rice (1790–1866).[22] In 1776 the Smyths and Verekers had succeeded in gaining control of Limerick Corporation, and in consequence the majority of the parliamentary electorate, by refusing admission to the freedom of the city to Catholics, Dissenters, Protestant supporters of Catholic relief and allies of the Perys.[23] As a result, these elements were moulded by the Perys into a 'party' alliance on a political platform of Catholic emancipation and corporation reform. These disputes were now framed by the emergence of a new two-party system in Britain and Ireland, with Limerick Corporation, led by Lord Gort, adhering to the Tories while the Perys, Thomas Spring Rice and the merchant élite supported the Whigs. The question of Catholic emancipation also divided the parties, with the Tory Corporation against and their opponents (with the important exception of Lord Limerick) largely in favour.

The Act of Union, by reducing Limerick's representation from two members to one, made the struggle between the Perys and the Smyth–Verekers much more bitter, and it reached its most intense stage in the years 1811 to 1820, culminating with the election of Spring Rice as MP for Limerick in the latter year. However, the Vereker control of the Corporation survived this electoral defeat and came under attack in the 1830s from William Smith O'Brien (1803–64), a close friend and ally of the first Lord Emly. O'Brien may have seen Spring Rice as a role model in these 'reform' activities.[24] The final overthrow of Vereker supremacy only came as late as 1841, with the abolition of the old Corporation.

Thus the Pery political tradition to which Colonel Monsell belonged was 'popular', patriotic (though Unionist after 1800), moderately reformist and supportive of Catholic relief. His address to the electors of County Limerick following his defeat in the 1807 general election referred to his having always given 'my feeble assistance to promote every measure brought forward in favour of the Roman Catholics'.[25] His grandson was to make the obtainment of such all-party support one of the cornerstones of his own political career. In addition, Colonel Monsell seems to have been popular in his own area. Local tradition tells of how he reacted to a priest-baiter who reported a Catholic clergyman to him for celebrating Mass on a regular basis at a Penal rock in the Monsell estate by sending a message to the latter warning him to stay away and then ordering the informer to be flogged for raising a false alarm.[26] However, in 1837 Daniel O'Connell described him as an arch-reactionary.[27] In 1876, Michael Hogan (1832–99), the Bard of Thomond, a celebrated Limerick poet of nationalist sympathies, mercilessly attacked him, describing him as the 'Wolf of Tirvoe', 'a shark' and a 'carnivorous puritan'.[28] He alleged that the Colonel had brought about the judicial murder of a young man from the locality during the period of reprisals following the 1798 rebellion. However, the *Limerick Chronicle* of 5 January 1803 carried a report concerning the arrest and charging of this man, one William Regan, with committing serious agrarian crimes, and on 3 March 1803 reported that Regan had been tried, convicted and sentenced in a most impartial manner. The reputation of Colonel Monsell still remains unclear.[29] Nevertheless, he was a link in the tradition of adherence to what might be broadly described as popular and liberal causes, which continued in the Monsell and Spring Rice families into the twentieth century. Perhaps the most important legacy he passed on to his grandson William was a tradition of political activity, and also the wealth to sustain a long career in Parliament.

Colonel Monsell, the *paterfamilias* of all the later Monsells, had four sons and four daughters. Two of his sons survived to adulthood and became the ancestors of the respective Irish and English branches of the family. The eldest, William (1778–1824) followed the usual family route of Trinity College and the Bar. Nicknamed 'Black Billy', he was a notorious and unpopular figure, whose reactionary political views inspired the following unflattering poem:

> Black Billy Monsell who lived at Tervoe,
> Greatly connected with the orange and the blue.
> That infernal Tory we will put him down,
> What good did he do for country or crown?[30]

Local tradition claims that he died when in the act of striking someone, thus causing his horse to throw him against the pier of one of his own gates, but in fact his death is recorded as having occurred in Nice, on the Riviera.[31] In contrast to this turbulent figure, his brother Thomas (1782–1846) entered the Anglican priesthood and became noted for his piety and good works. From 1820 to 1846 he served as Archdeacon of Derry, and was effectively the bishop's deputy. He died on 20 November 1846, reputedly from famine fever, contracted from the hungry multitudes, amongst whom he was labouring.

On 3 June 1811 in St Mark's church, on what is now Pearse Street, Dublin, Black Billy married Olivia Johnson-Walsh of Ballykilcavan, near Stradbally, Queens County, who had been born and had spent most of her life in Dublin. Their only child William Monsell was born on 21 September 1812, in a house on Mount Street, Dublin, but spent most of his childhood in Tervoe House, where he was educated by tutors. In 1824 he became heir to the Monsell estates on the death of his father. His grandfather, the old colonel, gave the boy the best education available at the time. Breaking with family tradition, he elected to have young William educated in England rather than Ireland, so at the age of 14 he was sent to Winchester, one of England's most exclusive public schools.[32] Situated in the old capital of England, beautifully located on the River Itchen, it was redolent of England's past and future greatness. The buildings of the school itself were old and historic, but William must have been even more impressed by the nearby cathedral. Every Sunday afternoon the whole school attended a sermon in this vast and glorious Gothic edifice, which contained the tombs of the Saxon kings.[33]

Despite this splendid ecclesiastical background, the curriculum of Winchester, in common with the other public schools of the time, included very little religion. During Monsell's four years there (1826–30) his fellow Wykehamists included the future Catholic convert and writer William G. Ward (1812–82), the future Liberal Lord Chancellor, Roundell Palmer, first Earl of Selbourne (1812–95), and two prominent Liberal statesmen, Edward Cardwell, later first Viscount Cardwell (1813–86), and Robert Lowe, later Viscount Sherbrooke (1811–92).[34] It is an interesting comment on the role of the public schools in the British establishment, that the three latter were later to serve as Cabinet ministers in Gladstone's first administration, in which Monsell also served as a minister outside the Cabinet.[35] Around 1800, over 70 per cent of all English peers received their education at just four public schools, Eton, Westminster, Winchester and Harrow.[36] Thus, Monsell's period at Winchester was a formative one by helping to initiate him into the British élite and by inspiring him to become an educational reformer. One of his strongest beliefs in later life was that education and religion should be inextricably linked.

Having left Winchester at the age of 18, Monsell spent two years at Oriel College, Oxford, reputed to be the most brilliant college of the ancient university and then enjoying one of its most glorious epochs. There, he combined a lively social life with a serious devotion to duty, and it was later asserted that 'his career as an undergraduate was very distinguished and he there laid the foundations of that Classical knowledge which he preserved throughout his life'.[37] While also described as having been 'a hard reading man' at Oriel, he 'was also known as one of the boldest riders to the hounds in the university' and a 'capital rifle shot'.[38]

Monsell's education had two main affects on him. First, it made of him a thoroughly British gentleman. He was much more English than any of his immediate ancestors, who had all been educated in Ireland, while his heritage of unionism and English culture was greatly strengthened by long exposure to the powerful influences of Winchester and Oriel. Secondly, and paradoxically, it eventually led to the repudiation of one of the most significant elements in his British heritage. Oxford was a bastion of the Established Church, only Anglicans were admitted as students, and the great majority of the teaching body consisted of ordained Anglican clergymen. Yet, it was at Oriel College that Monsell encountered the Tractarian Movement, which was to lead him into the Roman Catholic Church.

Monsell left Oxford without taking a degree. He returned to Ireland in 1833 to manage his aged grandfather's properties, and came of age in September of that year. His twenty-first birthday was marked by great celebrations which concluded when 'the young gentleman gave each of his numerous labourers a fine suit of clothes to keep them warm in winter'.[39] On the death of his grandfather in April 1836, William Monsell, then aged 23, inherited the extensive family properties. The heart of the estates was the property at Tervoe and Carrigogunnell, consisting of about 600 acres. Tervoe House had only just been extended and was in excellent repair. It was filled with beautiful furniture, pictures, silverware, glassware and other *objets d'art*.[40] The rest of the estate consisted of properties in the parishes of Monasterenagh and Ballycahane near Croom, and lands at Athlacca and at Bruree, all in County Limerick. In County Clare, Monsell owned lands at Cratloe and Quin. There were also properties in Limerick city, including the house at St John's Square and the former town house in Kildare Street, Dublin, which was now used as a hotel. Monsell's annual income at the time of his succession was estimated at £3,881, which is equivalent in current purchasing power to about €400,000.[41]

Indeed, Monsell was one of County Limerick's most eligible bachelors. Jane Austen has written that 'it is a truth universally acknowledged that a single man in possession of a good fortune must be in want of a wife'.[42] Monsell had already made his choice when he inherited Tervoe, having first paid court to Lady Anna Maria Charlotte Wyndham-Quin (1814–55) in 1834. She was the only daughter of Windham Henry, second Earl of Dunraven (1782–1850) and his wife, the former Caroline Wyndham (1790–1870). Lord Dunraven was one of the richest men in Ireland, and was somewhat concerned about having the untitled and less wealthy Monsell for a son-in-law.[43] He laboriously calculated William's income, and made some effort to discourage his suit, but was eventually prevailed upon to give his consent to the happy couple. William and

Anna Maria were married in the parish church of Adare on 12 August 1836. Six days later, Anna Maria's brother Edwin Viscount Adare (1812–71) was married to Augusta Gould, his sister's closest friend.[44]

Anna Maria was a beautiful and a pleasant young woman, and she made an ideal companion for the more serious and conscientious William. In consequence, the marriage was a very happy and successful one, though greatly marred by the deaths of their children. Their first child was baptised William in Adare parish church on 9 July 1837, but died a few weeks later.[45] Their second, also William, was born on 23 March 1841, shortly after the Adares' heir (who later became the fourth Earl of Dunraven), and the village of Adare was illuminated in honour of the two births. 'Little Willie' was the apple of his parents' eyes, so his death on 12 July 1845 caused them both enormous grief. Lady Anna Maria never really recovered from this blow, and gradually became a sombre religious recluse without a great interest in life. Following a long illness, she died in St Leonards in Sussex on 7 January 1855 and was buried in the Monsell family vault in Kilkeedy cemetery, near Carrigogunnell Castle.

In 1836 these sad events were mercifully hidden from the newly weds. William and Anna Maria were part of a large network of family and friends that gave them enormous emotional security and satisfaction. They frequently visited their relatives in County Derry. Monsell's mother, Olivia, had remarried in 1833. Her second husband was John Cromie (1786–1875) of Cromore House, Port Stewart, County Derry, who had been married twice before and who was to marry a fourth wife following Olivia's death. He was a benevolent, though autocratic landlord, who dominated the town of Port Stewart, which he largely owned. He and Olivia were very happy together, and her death on 1 January 1859 filled both her husband and her son with great sorrow. Monsell's uncle, the archdeacon Thomas Monsell, lived a few miles from the Cromies at Dunboe House, just outside Castlerock, County Derry. Two of his sons were also churchmen, John Samuel Bewley Monsell (1814–75), one of the great hymn writers of the Victorian age, and Charles (1815–51), who was married to the redoubtable Harriet O'Brien.[46]

The Monsells were prominent members of the Shannon Estuary Group. In County Limerick the Monsells were particularly friendly with the Wyndham-Quins. Monsell's closest friend was his brother-in-law, Edwin, Viscount Adare (1812–71), who succeeded as third Earl of Dunraven in 1850.[47] They collaborated on many projects, and were rendered more intimate by the closeness that existed between their respective wives. The Dunraven family were extremely wealthy. In the 1870s Dunraven was reputed to be one of the richest earls in the United

Kingdom, with an income of over £35,000 a year from estates of nearly 40,000 acres, of which 23,751 were in Glamorganshire and 14,298 in County Limerick. Their principal Irish seat was Adare Manor, set in the picturesque village of Adare, about ten miles from Tervoe. Besides their immense estates in Limerick and Glamorganshire, they owned land in Kerry, Clare and Gloucestershire. Their other principal residences were Dunraven Castle, near Bridgend in Glamorganshire (from which they took their principal title), Clearwell Court, Gloucestershire, and a town house at 94 Eaton Square in London's fashionable Belgravia (which they disposed of in 1849). The Monsells visited all these palatial homes, and were especially fond of Dunraven Castle.

The de Vere family were also part of the group. They were cousins of the Monsells through a common Pery ancestry, and their country seat was at Curraghchase, on the main road from Limerick to Askeaton. Sir Aubrey de Vere (1788–1846) and his wife Mary Spring Rice had five sons and three daughters. Three of their sons, Sir Vere (1808–80), Sir Stephen (1812–1904) and Aubrey (1814–1902), were particularly close to Monsell.[48] The Spring Rice family resided at Mount Trenchard, just outside Foynes, County Limerick. Their head, Thomas, MP for Limerick City from 1820 to 1832, later first Baron Monteagle, was the most significant Limerick political figure of the nineteenth century, holding a number of senior government posts, culminating in a term as Chancellor of the Exchequer (1835–9). The Perys, Earls of Limerick, originally the most powerful family of the group, had ceased to be resident in Ireland since 1800 and had become unpopular absentees. On their occasional visits, they stayed at Pery House, on Henry Street, Limerick city, and did not again make Ireland their principal residence until the building of Dromore Castle near Pallaskenry, County Limerick in the 1860s.

North of the Shannon, the O'Briens lived at Dromoland Castle, Newmarket-on-Fergus, County Clare. Sir Edward O'Brien (1773–1837) and his wife had five sons and four daughters.[49] One of the latter, Harriet (1811–83), was married to Monsell's first cousin, the Reverend Charles Monsell of Dunboe. She became an Anglican nun after her husband's early death. Her famous (and later revolutionary) brother, William Smith O'Brien (1803–64) resided at Cahirmoyle House, near Ardagh, County Limerick. A distant cousin was Augustus Stafford O'Brien (1811–57), who lived at Cratloe Woods House, across the Shannon estuary from Tervoe House, and also at Blatherwicke House, Northamptonshire.

The Shannon Estuary Group, cultured, wealthy, politically active and related by blood and marriage, also shared a common social, religious and intellectual background. However, although they were ethnically mixed, with Irish, Anglo-Norman and English blood, they were culturally homogenous. They were a sophisticated and multi-talented coterie within the Irish aristocracy, and in this, they resembled the English Whig magnates of 1770–1830, though they were not as wealthy, prominent or brilliant as the latter. The Shannon Estuary Group, the Catholic element of which became known as the 'Tervoe Convert Set', represented the Irish landlord class at its best. In 1840, William Sewell, who had become a close friend of Monsell, Adare and other members of the group, wrote that 'an Irish gentleman, well born, well educated, and with his natural tendencies modified by English associations is perhaps one of the most perfect specimen of civilised nature'.[50]

The group included four significant political figures – Edmond Sexton Pery, Thomas Spring Rice, William Smith O'Brien and William Monsell. The literary figures included two of contemporary significance, though now largely and undeservedly forgotten. Aubrey de Vere was one of the most notable Irish poets of the nineteenth century, and numbered Tennyson, Browning and Wordsworth among his friends and admirers.[51]The third Earl of Dunraven studied astronomy for three years under his friend Rowan Hamilton, and his vast range of intellectual activity included archaeology, architecture, theology and even spiritualism. He was a leading figure in the earlier stages of the Celtic Revival and his magnum opus, *Notes on Irish Architecture*, was published posthumously in 1875–7.[52] In addition, Sir Aubrey de Vere, Stephen de Vere and William Smith O'Brien were all minor poets, and Monsell, though he published comparatively little, was a man of wide intellectual interests. The Shannon Estuary Group also made a large contribution to the built environment. The Perys inspired the construction of Georgian Limerick and were later responsible for building Dromore Castle (one of the most dramatic buildings of the Celtic Revival); the Earls of Dunraven created the beautiful mansion and village of Adare; the O'Briens built Dromoland and Cahermoyle and the Monsells constructed Tervoe House and the nearby estate village.

Politically, the group ranged from conservatives such as the first Earl of Limerick and Sir Edward O'Brien, to (moderate) revolutionaries such as Smith O'Brien, but the majority of them were liberal in the broadest sense. They played an important role in the development of liberalism in Ireland, and had a dual Irish and British identity. The Liberal alliance formed by the Perys had, under the leadership of Spring Rice (assisted by Sir Richard Bourke and Sir Matthew Barrington) won the Limerick City seat in the Commons in 1820. After 1850 the chief standard-bearer of this tradition (the origins of which can be traced back to Speaker Pery) was William Monsell, while the de Veres played a more subordinate role, and Smith O'Brien took his unlikely place in the pantheon of Irish revolutionaries.

Similarly, the dual Irish and British nationality of the Shannon Estuary Group continued (as it had in the first half) to be a feature of their outlook in the second half of the century. They 'saw themselves as British, but not English', and 'found it necessary to claim Irish identity, in order to maintain and reinforce their legitimate leadership within Ireland'.[53] Also they saw themselves as mediators, representing the needs and desires of the Irish people to the British state. Again, the compromise came naturally to Monsell and his circle. The conversion of so many of them to Roman Catholicism naturally encouraged the tendency in the group to view the British nation as 'inclusive and pluralist in religion and culture'.[54]

The Shannon Estuary Group were possessed of a strong social conscience and believed in *noblesse oblige*.[55] They were all resident and improving landlords, Monsell and Stephen de Vere in particular being renowned for their kindness to their tenants. Thomas Spring Rice articulated this view particularly well and 'the Ireland of his dreams would have contained a contented people, guided by benevolent mentors such as himself, backed up by reforming governments, disassociated from past misrule'.[56] In 1815 he wrote of

> the elevated duties of the Irish country gentleman. It is a sphere of personal privation and of personal exertion. But when a mind is awake to that first of all delights, the power of becoming extensively and permanently useful, all privations are forgotten, all labour is well repaid. A peasantry capable of improvement and grateful for every benevolent assistance, look up to the landlord as to a protector and friend. He may not only assist their distresses, but may enable them to assist themselves.[57]

This may be regarded as a virtual manifesto of the Shannon Estuary Group.

Finally, they were serious, high-minded and passionately interested in the religious controversies of their time. Indeed, the particular brand of liberalism espoused by so many of them had its roots in religious concepts and controversy.[58] They were dedicated to public duty, and to things of the mind, and did not fit the stereotype of the 'traditional hard-riding, fox-hunting, convivial country gentry'.[59] The Shannon Estuary Group continued to produce persons of the same type into the early years of the twentieth century. Monsell's son, the second Lord Emly, became a convert to Irish nationalism and the labour movement. Monteagle's great-granddaughter, Mary Spring Rice (1880–1924) was involved in the Howth gun-running of 1914. Smith O'Brien's daughter Charlotte Grace (1845–1909) became an author and supporter of the Land League. Dunraven's son, the fourth Earl (1841–1926), was a leading Conservative politician, Under-Secretary for the Colonies, and a supporter of land purchase and devolution.[60] Fitzpatrick has rightly pointed out that 'few regions of Ireland could have boasted of so dense a concentration of liberal-minded and educated patrician families'.[61] While Spring Rice was the most significant statesman produced by the Shannon Estuary Group in the first half of the nineteenth century, Monsell was to be their leading political figure after 1850.

NOTES

1. Hugh Montgomery-Massingberd (ed.), *Burke's Irish family Records* (London: Burke's Peerage, 1976), pp.849–51 and Sir Bernard Burke, *A Genealogical and Heraldic Dictionary of the Peerage and Baronetage of the British Empire* (London: Burke's Peerage, 1887), pp.506–7.
2. William W. Mansell, *A Historical and Genealogical Account of the Ancient Family of Maunsell-Mansell-Maunsel* (London: privately published, 1850), p.5.
3. See Nicholas Canny, *From Reformation to Restoration: Ireland 1534–1660* (Dublin: Helicon, 1987), pp.173–4 and Michael McCarthy-Morrogh, *The Munster Plantation: English Migration to Southern Ireland 1583–1641* (Oxford: Clarendon Press, 1986).
4. John Sheehan, *A Corner of Limerick* (privately published, Limerick, 1989), pp.36–40.
5. Maurice Lenihan, *Limerick, its History and Antiquities* (Dublin: Hodges, Smith and Co.1866 (reprinted Cork and Dublin: Mercier Press, 1991), p.744.
6. Mary Hanley, 'The Past Glories of Tervoe', a series of articles in the *Limerick Chronicle*, 7, 14 and 21 November 1953. Collectively, they are a valuable work, being particularly strong on Monsell's family background and his local activities, while extensive use is made of material that no longer exists.
7. Kevin Hannan, 'The Rich Inheritance of a Limerick Mayor', in David Lee (ed.), *Remembering Limerick. Historical Essays Celebrating the 800th Anniversary of Limerick's First Charter granted in 1197* (Limerick: Limerick Civic Trust, 1997), p.112.
8. For Speaker Pery, see A.P.W. Malcomson, 'Speaker Pery and the Pery Papers', in *North Munster Antiquarian Journal*, 21 (1973–4), pp.33–60 and David Huddelston, 'Edmond Sexton Pery, Viscount Pery, (1719–1806)', in *Oxford DNB*.
9. The family is commemorated in the city to this day by Pery Square, Cecil, Glentworth, Mallow, Henry and Sexton Streets.
10. Malcomson, 'Speaker Pery and the Pery Papers', p.55, n. 44.
11. Marquis of Ruvigny and Raineval, *The Plantagenet Roll of the Blood Royal, Being a Complete Table of all the Descendants now Living of Edward III, King of England*, 5 vols, *The Clarence Volume, containing the Descendants of George, Duke of Clarence* (London: T.C. and E.C. Jack, 1905–11), pp.565–6.
12. Judith Hill, *The Building of Limerick* (Cork: Mercier Press, 1991), pp.71–76 and Kevin Hannan, *Limerick Historical Reflections* (Limerick: Oireacht Press, 1996), p. 189.
13. Lee, *Remembering Limerick*, p.131. Their total dominance lasted from 1776 to 1841.
14. For a comprehensive account of Limerick Corporation at this period, see Matthew Potter, *The Government and the People of Limerick. The History of Limerick Corporation/City Council 1197–2006* (Limerick: Limerick City Council, 2006), pp.183–284.
15. For a brief profile of W.T. Monsell, see E.M. Johnston-Liik, *History of the Irish Parliament 1692–1800: Commons, Constituencies and Statutes 1692–1800*, 6 vols (Belfast: Ulster Historical Foundation, 2002), Vol. 5, pp.272–3.
16. Sheehan, *Corner of Limerick*, pp.60–1.
17. See Robert Cussen, 'Caleb Powell, High Sheriff of County Limerick, 1858, sums up his Grand Jury', in Etienne Rynne (ed.), *North Munster Studies, Essays in Commemoration of Monsignor Michael Moloney* (Limerick: Thomond Archaeological Society, 1967), p.414.
18. Mark Bence-Jones, *A Guide to Irish Country Houses* (London: Constable, 1988) p.272.
19. For the public declaration against the Union, see Lenihan, *History of Limerick*, p.397. It is

even thought that Speaker Pery bequeathed his private papers to his anti-Unionist nephew Monsell rather than his pro-Unionist nephew Edmond Henry Pery as a result of his annoyance with the latter. See Malcomson, 'Speaker Pery and the Pery Papers' , p.36.

20. See G.C. Bolton, *The Passing of the Irish Act of Union* (Oxford: Oxford University Press, 1966), pp.120–1 and 168–9, and Patrick M. Geoghegan, *The Irish Act of Union. A Study in High Politics 1798–1801*(Dublin: Gill and Macmillan, 1999).
21. See P.J. Jupp, 'Irish Parliamentary Representation 1801–20' (unpublished Ph.D thesis, University of Reading, 1966), pp.320–3.
22. For an overview of Spring Rice, see Ellis Archer Wasson, 'Thomas Spring Rice, first Baron Monteagle of Brandon (1790–1866)', in *Oxford DNB*.
23. Ridden, 'Making Good Citizens', p.146.
24. Davis, *Revolutionary Imperialist*, p.68.
25. 'Election Address of W.T. Monsell', 1807, in Dunraven papers (hereafter DP) in Public Records Office of Northern Ireland (hereafter PRONI).
26. Hanley, 'Past Glories of Tervoe'.
27. *Limerick Chronicle*, 26 June 1837.
28. Michael Hogan, *The Seventh Number of Shawn-na-Scoob by the Bard of Thomond* (Limerick: Privately Published, 1876), pp.4 and 18.
29. *Limerick Chronicle*, 5 January and 3 March 1803.
30. Sheehan, *Corner of Limerick*, p.118
31. *Limerick Chronicle*, 27 March 1824.
32. Lionel James, *A Forgotten Genius, Sewell of St Colombas and Radley* (London: Faber and Faber, 1945), pp.20–1.
33. Ibid., p.20.
34. Palmer, *DNB*, Vol. 15, pp.150–4; Cardwell, *DNB*, Vol. 3, pp.952–4 and Lowe, *DNB*, Vol. 12, pp.197–201.
35. Sir Robert Ensor, *England 1870–1914* (Oxford History of England, Vol. 14) (Oxford: Clarendon Press, 1962), p.16.
36. See Linda Colley, *Britons. Forging the Nation 1707–1837* (New Haven and London: Yale University Press, 1992), pp.164–77.
37. See Monsell's obituary in *Munster News*, 21 April 1894.
38. Ibid.
39. *Limerick Chronicle*, 5 October 1833.
40. See the entry in the diary of Caroline, Countess of Dunraven, 8 August 1836, DP, D3196/E/2/40.
41. For an estimate of Monsell's income made by his future (and at that time unenthusiastic) father-in-law, the second Earl of Dunraven, see DP, D3196/E/10.
42. Jane Austen, *Pride and Prejudice* (Harmondsworth: Penguin, 1933), p.1.
43. DP, D3196/E/10.
44. For an account of the wedding of Anna Maria and William, see the entry in the diary of her mother, Lady Dunraven, 12 August 1836, DP, D.3196/E/2/40.
45. *Limerick Chronicle*, 26 July 1837.
46. For J.S.B. Monsell, see D.J. O'Donoghue, revised Leon Litvack, 'John Samuel Bewley Monsell (1811–1875)', in *Oxford DNB*.
47. See G. Le G. Norgate, revised Michael Herity, 'Edwin Richard Windham Wyndham-Quin, third Earl of Dunraven and Mount Earl (1812–1871)', in *Oxford DNB*.
48. For brief profiles of the most important figures in the family, see Elizabeth Lee, revised M.C. Curthoys, 'Sir Stephen Edward de Vere (1812–1904)', and Robert Welch, 'Aubrey Thomas de Vere (1814–1902)', both in *Oxford DNB*.
49. Grania R. O'Brien and Hugh Weir, *These my Friends and Forebears: The O'Briens of Dromoland* (Whitegate, County Clare: Ballinakella Press, 1991).
50. William Sewell, 'Romanism in Ireland', in *Quarterly Review*, 67, 133 (December 1840), p.121.
51. Sr M. Paraclita Reilly, *Aubrey de Vere: Victorian Observer* (University of Nebraska Press, 1953; Dublin: Clonmore and Reynolds and London: Burnes, Oates and Washbourne, 1956).
52. Edwin Richard Wyndham-Quin, third Earl of Dunraven (edited by Margaret Stokes), *Notes on Irish Architecture* (London: G. Bell, 1875–7).

53. Ridden, 'Making Good Citizens', p.204.
54. Ibid.
55. See Horace Plunkett, *Nobless Oblige – An Irish Rendering* (Dublin: Maunsel, 1908).
56. Fitzpatrick, 'Thomas Spring Rice and the Peopling of Australia', p.40.
57. Thomas (Spring) Rice, *An Inquiry into the Effects of the Irish Grand Jury Laws* (London: privately published, 1815), p.12.
58. See Ridden, 'Making Good Citizens', chapters 2 and 3.
59. Stephen Gwynn (ed.), *The Letters and Friendships of Sir Cecil Spring Rice, A Record,* 2 vols (Boston: Houghton Mifflin, 1929).
60. See S.L. Gwynn, revised Peter Gray, 'Windham Thomas Wyndham-Quin, fourth Earl of Dunraven and Mount Earl (1841–1926)', in *Oxford DNB*, and Michael Spillane, 'The fourth earl of Dunraven, 1841–1926: a study of his contribution to the emerging Ireland at the beginning of the twentieth century' (unpublished Ph.D thesis, Mary Immaculate College, University of Limerick, 2002).
61. Fitzpatrick, 'Thomas Spring Rice and the Peopling of Australia', p.42.

CHAPTER THREE

The Dual Conversions

William Monsell's childhood and early manhood coincided with a period of great change and turmoil which affected all of Western civilisation.[1] Some of his contemporaries who emerged from the same cauldron included Isaac Butt (born 1813), John Mitchell (born 1815) and Charles Gavan Duffy (born 1816) in Ireland; Disraeli (born 1804), Manning (born 1808) and Gladstone (born 1809) in Britain; and Montalambert (born 1810), Falloux (born 1811) and Broglie (born 1821) in France. Born in the year of Napoleon's invasion of Russia, Monsell himself was a child of the French and Industrial Revolutions, which are better understood as a Dual Revolution.[2] This was a period of tremendous economic, social and cultural change. The transformative dynamics of the French and more crucially the Industrial Revolution were beginning the long, complex and continuing reshaping of what is called the modern world, in the first instance throughout parts of the Western world. Population growth, urbanisation, the mechanisation of the means of industrial production and distribution, technological revolution in the systems of energy production, transport and communications; all of these forces were operating in an evermore-integrated international economical order dominated by the 'first industrial nation', Britain, and by the economic doctrines – notably *laissez-faire* – adopted and promulgated by the élites of expansionist Britain. These were key elements of what Hobsbawn has called 'the Age of Revolution'. The *laissez-faire* doctrine held that the Government's role in the economy should be strictly limited to creating the conditions that favoured the free play of national economic forces. 'An invisible hand' guided the economy and government interference would only distort and disrupt this smoothly running mechanism.

The ideas, social structures, institutions and cultural forms that accompanied – whether as cause or effect – these seismic socio-economic changes had a predictably profound impact on the beliefs and total view of all classes of society, but especially that of the educated and articulate political classes within the more rapidly 'advancing' societies. The class and social and intellectual milieu to which Monsell belonged could not fail to register and to respond to 'the shock of the new' in nineteenth-century Britain. It was a period of change in every field of human endeavour. Socialism and communism originated at this time. It was also the age of the Romantics in the arts and philosophy and ranks as one of the greatest eras in the history of Western artistic achievement.[3]

If it was a period of dual revolution, it was also characterised by a dual reaction, as the European élites responded in two different ways to the French Revolution and Napoleon. On the one hand many of them sought to turn the clock back to 1789, and during the Restoration Period (1815–30) on the continent of Europe, the old absolutist regimes were restored and revolutionary movements suppressed. On the other hand there was also a widespread belief that it was impossible to turn back the clock, and that only timely reforms and concessions could stave off further turmoil. This response was more typical of the pragmatic British ruling classes. The struggle between the forces of revolution and reaction in various forms was to continue throughout the whole nineteenth century and well into the twentieth.[4]

A similar dual reaction to the French Revolution also occurred in the religious and intellectual life of the period. The Roman Catholic Church had suffered severe persecution during the French Revolution, but in the early nineteenth century a major religious revival got under way that soon produced two broad movements. Firstly, many Catholics wanted to restore the old order and make no concessions to the modern world. They felt that the best way for the Church to be equipped to undertake its mission more effectively was to concentrate all power in the hands of the Pope. The autonomy of the Bishops and their right to a share in Church government should be curtailed and even suppressed, and all local self-rule should be stamped out. The Pope would be absolute ruler over a church that would be standardised and Romanised throughout the world. This movement became known as Ultramontanism. Secondly, many wanted to try and reconcile the Church with the modern world and in particular with the doctrines of the French Revolution, many of which, such as parliamentary government, individual freedom, equality before the law and protection of private property, were seen to be positive and to be compatible with the teachings of the Church. This philosophy was known as Liberal Catholicism. Both movements began in early nineteenth-century France, originally worked in tandem, diverged in the 1830s and eventually became bitter rivals in the 1850s and 1860s. The Papacy tended to favour the Ultramontanes, and Pope Pius IX (reign 1846–78) finally put the struggle to an end in the 1860s when he made known his hostility to

Liberal Catholicism. Thus, the official Church and the revolutionary movement were to be bitter enemies throughout the century and beyond.[5]

The parallel revival in Protestantism had pre-dated the French Revolution. This Evangelical Revival had begun in the mid-eighteenth century and stressed the individual's conversion to Christ as well as placing a great emphasis on moral earnestness and charitable works. The nineteenth century saw Protestantism experience its largest ever expansion, greatly helped by the huge part played in world affairs by the three great Protestant powers – Great Britain, Germany and the United States of America.

Both the Evangelical and Ultramontane movements led to much greater religious antagonism, and the rival churches devoted as much energy attempting to convert each other's adherents as they did to the evangelising of non-Christians. However, the general religious revival saw an increasing emphasis on personal morality, strictness of personal conduct and a greater social consciousness. Thus the so-called Victorian ethos had already come into being before Queen Victoria had actually ascended the throne.

As an integral part of the Atlantic civilisation, Ireland was affected by all these trends.[6] The rebellion of 1798 had terrified the Irish Protestant élite into giving up their parliament, but Daniel O'Connell's campaigns for emancipation and repeal had revived their fears of the Catholic masses. In the late eighteenth and early nineteenth centuries relations between Protestants and Catholics had warmed considerably, but the 1820s saw a revival of sectarian tensions. The Evangelical Revival had affected Irish Protestants, and from 1822 onwards Evangelical elements within the Church of Ireland had begun a campaign to convert Catholics. This Second Reformation forced the Catholic Church, already coming under the influence of Ultramontanism, to become more assertive. Indeed, from the 1850s onwards Ultramontanism became dominant under the leadership of Paul Cullen (1803–78), successively Archbishop of Armagh and Dublin and Ireland's first cardinal. In the political sphere, O'Connell's mass movements had taught Catholics that they were a force to be reckoned with. Relations between the churches were characterised by fierce hostility and bitter sectarianism for the remainder of the century.[7] The angry political and religious controversies of the time took place against an increasingly sombre background, that of the serious economic crisis that gripped Ireland from 1815 onwards. This manifested itself in rapid population growth, increasing poverty, rural violence and emigration, culminating in the Great Famine of 1845–50. Thus Monsell grew to manhood in a highly charged atmosphere.

Finally, there were two main political parties in the United Kingdom, each of which was a loose amalgam of different groups rather than a tightly organised body such as the modern political party. The Tories (later the Conservatives) were the party of the Crown, the Established Church and the aristocracy. In Ireland, they often believed in Protestant and Orange Ascendancy. In England, under the leadership of Sir Robert Peel (1788–1850) they moved away from their previous policy of reaction and repression, and advocated timely reforms to preserve the essential elements of the Establishment. The Whigs (later the Liberals) were also led by aristocrats and disliked revolution, but tended to favour a greater amount of social and political reform. In Ireland, there was a third party, Daniel O'Connell and his Repealers, who because of their loathing for the Orange Tory Party were usually aligned with the Whigs.

The decade of Liberal rule in Britain and Ireland (1830–41) had produced many useful Irish reforms, including the establishment of the National Schools System (1831), reform of the Church of Ireland (1833), the establishment of a Poor Law (1838) and Municipal Reform (1840).[8] It was the Church Temporalities (Ireland) Act of 1833 which triggered off the Oxford Movement, which was to profoundly affect the Anglican Church and bring about a radical change in William Monsell's life. The Established Anglican Church in Ireland purported to be a church for the whole nation and had four archbishops, twenty-eight bishops, 2,000 clergymen, and an annual income of £1,000,000. However, only 14 per cent of the population was Anglican, and the other 86 per cent resented supporting such a vast ecclesiastic monolith. In 1833 the Whig government brought in legislation which suppressed ten bishoprics and, among other things, imposed a clerical income tax. This timely measure of reform caused great controversy. Many Anglicans in both Britain and Ireland considered the legislation to be illegal and sacrilegious and as a harbinger of disestablishment in both Britain and Ireland. The Church was seen to be a mere department of state, without the power to prevent its own mutilation.

However, fear of disestablishment would not have been the concern of the Oxford Movement (also called Tractarianism).[9] Its leaders were John Keble (1792–1866), Edward Pusey (1800–82), Horrell Froude (1803–36) and John Henry Newman (1801–90), all four of whom were Fellows of Oriel College, Monsell's *alma mater*. They wanted to restore and revive the Church of England by emphasising the elements in it which would justify its claim to be the ancient, apostolic and Catholic Church. They wished to see it detached from dependence on the state, and wanted it to be governed by its own clergy. They emphasised the importance of the sacraments and the central position of communion in the church service. These tenets were the elements in Anglicanism that most resembled the Roman Catholic position, but at this stage the Tractarians were very anti-Papist. Newman, in particular, emphasised the *via media* of the one true Church between the two extremes of Protestantism and Catholicism; but after working so diligently to revive Anglicanism, many of its leaders, including Newman, Manning and Ward, eventually became Roman Catholics.[10]

Newman emerged as the leader of the movement. He is one of the great figures of the nineteenth century, a theologian, philosopher and writer and perhaps the most significant English Catholic since the Reformation.[11] His friendship with Monsell was to be one of the most significant factors in both their lives. Newman once stated that 'indeed I have perhaps written more confidentially to Ld. Emly ab-t myself than to any other person', and he wrote to Monsell two months later that 'among my many friends, the thought of whom makes me almost cry, I believe you to be one of the most affectionate'.[12] Monsell was in Oxford at the beginning of Tractarianism, but there is no evidence that he had any contact with Newman or any of the other leaders. His first recorded meeting with Newman occurred in 1840, and they did not become close friends until 1850.[13] However, from the 1830s onwards Monsell took Newman as his spiritual guide and mentor.

The Oxford Movement in Ireland was very weak. The Church of Ireland, surrounded by a sea of Catholicism, was predominantly Low Church and more inclined to stress its Protestantism than the relatively secure Church of England, which had a large High Church element.[14] However, the early years of the century saw a revival of the 'old High Church tradition of the Church of Ireland'.[15] This was an indigenous tradition independent of the Tractarian movement, whose best-known exponent was John Jebb, Bishop of Limerick from 1822 to 1833, under whose rule 'the Diocese of Limerick became a High Church centre for both clergy and laity'.[16] Tractarians and representatives of this High Church tradition did not always co-operate, and indeed became seriously estranged later, but it is due to this heritage that County Limerick saw such a positive response to the Oxford Movement. Indeed, Tervoe House came to be regarded as its Irish centre.[17] The most prominent Irish Tractarians were Monsell, his brother-in-law, Adare, and the three de Vere brothers, Vere, Stephen and Aubrey. In addition, members of the wider Monsell family also became adherents of Tractarianism. While Archdeacon Monsell of Derry was strongly opposed, his son, Charles, (1815–51), an Anglican minister, became a zealous Tractarian.[18] Following his early death, his widow Harriet (1811–83), sister of William Smith O'Brien, came to embody another aspect of the Oxford Movement by becoming an Anglican nun. (One of the most original features of Tractarianism was the revival of both male and female religious orders within the Church of England.) Harriet became a Sister of Mercy after her husband's death, and soon after she and Reverend Thomas Thellusson Carter founded the Community of St John the Baptist at Clewer, near Windsor. The chief work of these nuns was the reform of prostitutes, and Harriet ruled the convent as Mother Superior for twenty-five years.[19] Even Gladstone himself undertook some voluntary work at Clewer as part of his long-standing work with prostitutes.[20] In 2001 Harriet was declared a saint of the Anglican Church.[21]

William Monsell was also affected by the Evangelical Movement. Indeed, Tractarianism and Evangelicalism were parallel movements, similar to Ultramontanism and Liberal Catholicism in contemporary France, moving in tandem but destined to be estranged. All his life, Monsell was a serious and conscientious individual, anxious to work in a practical manner towards the realisation of the Christian vision on earth. At this time he was rabidly anti-Catholic, a strong supporter of the Second Reformation, and longed for Ireland's conversion. In the autumn of 1840 Monsell, writing of William Sewell's visit to Tervoe, stated that 'we talked much of the miseries of Ireland, and found that, however our conversation began, however we spoke of second causes, it always ended in ascribing both their [i.e the Irish people] miseries and the difficulty of getting rid of them to Popery'.[22] In 1838 Monsell found an outlet for his evangelical zeal. He and Adare, working in tandem as was their custom, visited Ventry in County Kerry, where they were very favourably impressed by the work of the Irish Society, one of the most significant organisations dedicated to proselytising the Catholic peasants.[23] The Second Reformation was characterised by a strong emphasis on using the Irish language as a means to conversion and the Ventry mission, headed by an Irish-speaking clergyman called Thomas Moriarty, seemed to be very successful. Consequently, Monsell, Adare and the latter's father, Lord Dunraven, gave it generous financial support. The two younger men became deeply interested in the Ventry mission, and became convinced that what was most needed was an Irish-speaking clergy to convert and to minister to the Irish Catholic population.[24]

However, the direction of their plans was changed dramatically when Lord Adare visited Oxford in the spring of 1839 in order to seek the assistance of Reverend William Sewell (1804–74) in his Irish venture.[25] Fellow of Exeter College and a leading Tractarian, Sewell contributed regular articles to the *Quarterly Review*, which had so impressed Lord Adare that he resolved to meet him in Oxford.[26] Sewell was an enigmatic man, an intellectual and a man of vision, industry and vigour who was to become one of the greatest educational reformers in nineteenth-century England. Unfortunately, his many faults comprised what White described as 'sentimentality, defective judgement, verbosity, impulsiveness, snobbery, silliness'.[27] Adare's visit was a great success. Sewell quickly became interested in the incipient Irish reformation and made his first visit the following year. From July to September 1840 he toured the West of Ireland accompanied by Adare at the beginning and Monsell at the end. With the former he visited the Church Mission in Achill, and with the latter he visited Ventry. By the end of this visit the three had become firm friends, but with the older and more domineering Sewell in charge. After the Irish tour Monsell and Adare begged Sewell for ideas, and he responded enthusiastically.[28] Indeed, Sewell contributed three articles on Ireland to the *Quarterly Review* at this time.[29]

Sewell had always been interested in education, and in particular the reform movement then commencing in the English public school system. His three aims were, firstly, to effect the conversion of Catholics through the medium of the Irish language, secondly, the promotion of Tractarian principles in Ireland, and thirdly, to found a public school. With a flash of genius he determined to achieve all three through the medium of the one institution, a public school in Ireland after the model of Eton or Winchester. It was to be staffed by a body of celibate clerical teachers similar to the recently founded Christian Brothers or to the teaching body of an Oxford college (from where the titles of Warden for the headmaster, and Fellows for the teachers were both borrowed). This school would train a future generation of Irish-speaking clergymen, who would continue the work of conversion with renewed vigour. The sons of the landlords would also be educated there, and learn both the Irish language and a love of Ireland. Together, this Irish-speaking clergy and aristocracy would gain the support and affection of the masses. Ireland would then become Protestant, loyal and contented. 'Be assured we are about no less a work than attempting to make a nation, save the British Empire, and put the church again in its true position', wrote Sewell in typically grandiloquent manner.[30] His programme constituted nothing less than a conservative revolution. Sadly for him, none of these extravagant ambitions were to be realised, and even the teaching of the Irish language ceased entirely at St Columba's in 1854.

Sewell, Adare and Monsell were joined by the Reverend John Henthorn Todd (1805–69) of Trinity College, and these 'Four Founders' set about the great work with enthusiasm and energy, with Sewell at their head.[31] They secured the approval of the Anglican Primate, Lord John George Beresford (1773–1862), Archbishop of Armagh, who was to contribute a total of £6,000 to the project.[32] He was a dignified and wealthy aristocrat, and the first of the many powerful ecclesiastics with whom Monsell was to work throughout his career. Adare's father, Lord Dunraven, and Augustus Stafford O'Brien became involved at this stage, as did two other

Anglican clergymen imposed by Beresford. Funds were raised in Britain and Ireland and among the contributors were Queen Adelaide, the widow of King William IV, Gladstone (who took a lively interest in the project) and Manning. Considerable effort went into securing a site for the school, and Sewell suggested Tervoe as being a suitable location.[33] However, it was formally opened at Stackallen House, County Meath, on 25 April 1843 and was later given the name of St Colomba's. It was governed by the eight founders, who formed a Board of Governors, headed by Adare, while Primate Beresford, as Visitor, kept an eye on things from Armagh. The eight governors never seemed to have met as a body, but communicated with each other by letter, while some of them also held meetings from time to time.[34]

The curriculum at St Colomba's was remarkably broad by the standards of its time, including the staple Classics, but with the addition of Irish history and the Irish language, as well as French and Italian. Very few secondary schools of the time included any subjects beyond the study of Greek and Latin. Its pupils, who numbered only thirty-five as late as 1847 (one of whom was William Smith O'Brien's son, Edward), were drawn exclusively from the sons of landlords and clergymen. In 1849 it removed to its present location at Rathfarnham, where it grew and flourished, eventually becoming the most exclusive Protestant school in the country, 'the Eton of Ireland'. At the time of writing, St Columba's is 'a co-educational secondary school for boarding and day pupils' with some 300 students.[35] Ironically, the Catholic convert Monsell is still revered as one of the four founders and is commemorated there by a portrait and a classroom named after him, while his name is a familiar one to the student body.[36] Indeed, he never lost interest in St Columba's, even after his direct connection with it had long ceased, and in 1873 he told Sewell 'it had produced some of the best men in Ireland'.[37]

However, the eventual success of St Columba's would not have been predicted by an intelligent observer of its progress during its 'Stackallen Period' (1843–9). From the beginning, it was subject to attacks, some of which came from Catholics, but with the greater number and more vociferous coming from Evangelical Protestants whose suspicions were aroused by the Tractarianism of the four founders. In 1841 Newman had published 'Tract 90' in *The Times*, which purported to show that the Thirty-Nine Articles which defined the Anglican faith could be reconciled with Catholicism, and in consequence rocked Anglicanism. In February 1843 he resigned as Vicar of St Mary's Church in Oxford, and to many it seemed to be only a matter of time before he joined the Roman Catholic Church. The whole Tractarian movement was now suspected of being tainted by Catholicism.

The year 1845 was a time of crisis for Monsell, for the Oxford Movement and for St Columba's. In April, Monsell and Adare visited England and stayed with a distinguished and eccentric Catholic convert, Ambrose Phillips de Lisle (1809–78), a close friend of the even odder architectural genius Augustus Pugin (1812–52).[38] De Lisle and his wife Laura resided at the Manor of Grace Dieu in Leicestershire. He was a pioneer of the ecumenical movement (in 1857 he established the Association for the Promotion of the Unity of Christendom), and he and Monsell were to become lifelong friends. During their visit to England, Adare and Monsell visited many Catholic churches and monasteries. Then, on 16 July, young William Monsell died, aged 4 years, and his father took Lady Anna Maria on a holiday to Europe to raise her spirits. During this trip they met many prominent Catholics and visited several Catholic churches. Finally, on 7 October, Newman became a Catholic. These events, especially Newman's conversion, shook Monsell's position considerably, and while he remained an Anglican, he no longer believed in the inherent evil of Catholicism or the Second Reformation.[39]

Sewell was alarmed. Two of the founders and governors of a school specifically established to further the conversion of Catholics were now fraternising openly with Papists, and visiting their churches and monasteries. He decided that the Board of Governors should be dissolved and Monsell and Adare removed from the scene.[40] They vigorously resisted his demands, but Todd persuaded them to go quietly, and in December 1845 the connection of Adare and Monsell with St Columba's was severed forever. They also became estranged from Sewell, whose official connection with the college also ended at this time. He returned to England and never returned, but he subsequently established another distinguished public school, St Peter's, at Radley, near Oxford. He and Monsell met fortuitously on one subsequent occasion in the Athenaeum Club in the summer of 1873, and Sewell related later that 'I told him with truth that notwithstanding his secession to Rome, my affection for him was as strong as ever.'[41]

Although Monsell was by now a very discontented member of the Church of Ireland, he was not yet ready to make the final break and continued his spiritual journey within Anglicanism. The Tractarian Movement saw the revival of orders of brothers as well as nuns in the Church of England, and while Harriet Monsell became a nun, William Monsell joined a lay sodality or fraternity in 1844. This was a select group of Tractarian laymen known as the Fraternity of St Barnabas, or The Engagement, founded by the brothers Thomas and Arthur Acland.[42] Besides Monsell, its other members were Lord Adare, W.E. Gladstone, Roundell Palmer (Monsell's fellow-pupil at Winchester), Sir Frederick Rogers (1811–89; later the first Baron Blachford), William Butterfield

(1814–1900), the great architect, and T.H. Hadden (1814–73), a barrister who became first editor of the *Manchester Guardian* (now *The Guardian*). They worshipped in the Margaret Chapel on Margaret Street, near London's Oxford Circus, which was later rebuilt by Butterfield. The Fraternity gradually broke up, due to the drift towards Catholicism of Adare and Monsell.[43]

Monsell's political conversion began around 1845. He was a hereditary Tory, for his father had been one, and his father-in-law Dunraven having changed his political allegiance on a number of occasions had finally settled on the Tory party by 1836.[44] Monsell's active political career may be said to have commenced in 1835, when he served as High Sheriff of County Limerick; his main duty was to choose the grand jury, a committee of twenty-three local landowners and gentlemen that had both executive and judicial functions. In the former capacity they were the governing body of each county before the establishment of the County Councils in 1899. It was an important, expensive and onerous position, but it showed Monsell's potential and a Scottish visitor to County Limerick wrote that he 'is said to be an excellent person, the present High Sheriff, and likely to be a most useful man in the country'.[45]

Monsell first stood for Parliament in the year of Queen Victoria's accession to the throne. The general election of 1837 was precipitated by the death of King William IV (this was the last occasion on which a general election was triggered by a monarch's death), and Monsell stood as a candidate for Limerick City, which since 1832 had returned two members to Parliament. The sitting MPs, David Roche and William Roche, were both Repealers. Monsell had previously refused nomination to stand for County Limerick, and Augustus Stafford O'Brien had become the Tory candidate there instead, but he was to be ignominiously routed.[46] In 1837 Adare was a candidate in Glamorganshire. Both he and Monsell stood in the Tory interest but followed Peel's doctrine of the Tamworth Manifesto, and Monsell's election address spoke of his desire 'to support the constitution, and by promoting the reform of every proved abuse, to give it stability'.[47] The Limerick City election was marked by widespread intimidation and violence against Monsell and the Tories and placards were posted all over the city intimating that he was an Orangeman and a fanatical anti-Catholic.[48] It is true that he was aligned with the Vereker faction on the hustings, but even Daniel O'Connell addressing a meeting of the 'Liberal electors' in Limerick on 22 July allowed that Monsell was 'stated to be a good-natured young man, and it is stated there is no mischief in him'.[49] Monsell cut a sorry figure in this election. His new-born son died suddenly on 22 July and this personal tragedy, combined with his opponents' widespread use of intimidation, effectively destroyed his chances of election. William Roche headed the poll with 973 votes, David Roche closely followed him into Parliament with 960 votes, while Monsell received only 387 votes. The second Tory candidate in Limerick City, Thomas Maunsell Wilson of Caherconlish (Monsell's uncle by marriage) polled a mere 101 votes.[50] Lord Adare was more successful, and was returned for Glamorganshire, which he was to represent continuously until 1851.[51]

At this time Ireland's only university was Trinity College, Dublin, dominated by the Church of Ireland, and there were no facilities for Roman Catholics to acquire a secular university education in their own country. The report of the Wyse Committee on foundation schools and education in Ireland, published on 9 August 1838, proposed that a third-level college be established in each of the four provinces.[52] A campaign, strongly supported by Lord Monteagle and William Smith O'Brien, was instigated to have the Munster College established in Limerick.[53] A public meeting was held on 5 January 1839 at the County Courthouse in Limerick city to discuss the matter.[54] The majority of those present were in favour, but a strong influential and vocal minority including Lords Adare and Clarina were opposed and Monsell was their spokesman. A bitter row followed.[55] Monsell claimed that non-denominational education was wrong in principle, and particularly injurious to the welfare of the Established Church. Such remarks not unnaturally drew an unfavourable reaction, and after unsuccessfully trying to have O'Brien's resolution in favour of the college amended, Monsell and his supporters withdrew from the meeting.[56] However, they did not give up the fight, and Monsell, supported by Lords Dunraven, Adare and Clarina, organised a petition to Queen Victoria, which was signed by 5,000 people. This referred to the 'polluting influence of a proposed institution for collegiate education' which separated religion and education.[57]

Here were the fruits of Monsell's irreligious education at Winchester. This was to be a consistent theme in his attitude to education, both before and after his conversion to Catholicism. At the Limerick meeting of 5 January 1839 he spoke of himself as being one 'who could not conscientiously disassociate religion and education'.[58] Forty-five years later, in January 1884, he addressed the staff and students of the newly opened Mungret College and stated: 'No greater boon can be conferred on a neighbourhood than a college such as this, uniting the soundest moral and religious training with the highest intellectual culture.'[59] Monsell also opposed the national schools for the same reasons. He believed that the Church of Ireland should have a monopoly of education, and both he and Adare supported the Church Education Society, an organisation set up by the Established Church to provide separate education for its children, totally distinct from the national system. During this period Monsell was still a staunchly anti-Catholic and reactionary Tory and had little in common with the more enlightened elements in the Shannon Estuary Group.

The turning point in his political conversion was the Great Famine. The sheer horror and scale of the events of these traumatic times caused many hitherto staunch Unionists to question their beliefs. However, there had been quasi-nationalist stirrings amongst the Unionists since the early 1830s, when William Sharman Crawford (1781–1861), a liberal Protestant landlord from County Down, first enunciated a political doctrine known later as federalism.[60] In the years 1831–4 he advocated the establishment of a subordinate legislature for Ireland that would form a compromise between the positions of the Unionists and the Repealers. This local parliament would handle 'the local interests and local taxation of the country'.[61] Among his suggestions was that 'previous to the meetings of the Imperial Parliament, an annual session were to be held in Dublin, of a body consisting of the imperial representatives elected for Ireland' and that this 'Parliament' should have limited local powers.[62] This contrasted with the position of the Repealers, who usually demanded the restoration of an Irish parliament, equal in status to that of Britain. In 1843 a federalist movement came into existence, and Thomas (later first Baron) O'Hagan and the Catholic Bishop of Killaloe, Dr Patrick Kennedy, joined the Repeal Association as Federalists. An alliance between federalism and Repeal seemed imminent, but was dashed by O'Connell's famous Derrynane Manifesto of 12 October 1844, in which he announced his preference for federalism over Repeal. The result of this was to scare the Young Irelanders and other supporters of Repeal on the one hand, and the Federalists on the other. Each side believed O'Connell to be guilty of betrayal. O'Connell was obliged to retreat from his seeming abandonment of Repeal, and the federalist movement virtually perished before it had begun.[63]

Nevertheless, federalist and other semi-nationalist ideas continued to circulate in Unionist circles throughout the 1840s. This was the period of 'a new kind of Irish conservatism which conceded not a whit to its nationalist opponent in love of country'.[64] The centrepiece of this movement, which came to be known as 'Orange Young Ireland', was the *Dublin University Magazine*, edited successively by Isaac Butt (1834–8) and Charles Lever (1841–5).[65] The famine, the poor British response to it, and the 1848 Rebellion all combined to render this movement stillborn. Isaac Butt is the most prominent Irish example of someone whose ideology altered at this time. He began as an extreme and articulate ultra-Tory, but moved into the 'Orange Young Ireland' movement and ultimately into federalism (which he was to revive in the 1870s as Home Rule).[66]

Monsell underwent a similar political conversion, and, as with Butt, it was the famine and the inadequate British response to it which cast him adrift from his Tory moorings. It was a twofold process, the first aspect of which was the Peelite split. In 1846 the Tory prime minister Sir Robert Peel brought about the repeal of the Corn Laws, which had been introduced in 1815 to maintain the price of corn at a reasonable level. This measure was designed to lower food prices and supposedly to help the hungry Irish masses, but it had little effect in this regard. However it proved hugely controversial and brought about a split in the Tory party. Peel and his followers broke away from the official party, and this third political grouping (the Peelites) survived as a separate entity until 1859, when most of its members were absorbed into the Liberals. Among the most prominent Peelites were Gladstone, the fourth Earl of Aberdeen (1784–1860) and the fifth Duke of Newcastle (1811–64). The Peelite split was the occasion of Monsell's break with the Tories.[67] Also, Monsell had a great deal in common with the Peelite leaders.[68] They were of the same generation, their ideology was similar, they were very religious and they were possessed of great integrity and seriousness of purpose.[69] Conacher wrote that 'the term Liberal Conservative described them accurately since they were all natural Conservatives. They were intelligent enough, however, to see that the system must be made to work justly and efficiently if it were to be acceptable to the whole community'.[70] Significantly, the term *Liberal Conservative* was sometimes used of Monsell when he was elected to Parliament in 1847. Nevertheless, he was never classified as an Irish Peelite MP, and the Peelite split in Ireland was a minor affair.

The second catalyst influencing Monsell's journey of political self-discovery was federalism. If, as Hoppen has written, 'Tory renegades were among the rarest exotics of the Irish political landscape', then Monsell was an exotic among exotics.[71] He was not merely a Peelite, but also a federalist, though it is extremely difficult to pin him down as a firm adherent of either. The Peelite split had weakened the connection between the Irish landlords and English Conservatism. Nowlan wrote that 'the crisis did not destroy their Conservatism, but it turned many of them temporarily adrift and this made for greater political instability'.[72] Monsell's 'federalist' period more or less coincided with the Great Famine. He was horrified by the catastrophes of the period – disease, hunger, destitution and despair.[73] Like many of the landlords, he worked diligently to alleviate the sufferings of the people. Aubrey de Vere later stated that 'among those who worked hardest was Mr Monsell', and he later described how 'Mr Monsell burst into a flood of tears' on one occasion when he encountered a child dying of starvation near Kilkee in County Clare.[74] Monsell served on a relief committee and was chairman of the Limerick Poor Law Union from 1844 to 1845.[75] The Dunravens and de Veres were also active in famine relief work, while Archdeacon Monsell of Derry contracted famine fever while ministering to his people, and died at the end of 1846.

However, William Monsell was totally disgusted by the inadequacy of the measures taken by the British government to deal with the crisis. After the Peelite split, the government of Peel was forced to resign, and the Liberals under Lord John Russell came to power. Russell was at the head of a minority government and, under the influence of Sir Charles Trevelyan, Permanent Secretary at the Treasury, he rigidly adhered to the doctrine of *laissez-faire* in economic matters. The relatively effective relief measures applied by the Peel administration were abandoned, and a ruinous and unsuccessful public works programme formed the centrepiece of the new government's famine policy. It was believed that the Government could not give the starving people food, as this would distort the Irish agricultural system. Instead, public works programmes were established to provide employment for the destitute peasants. They could then use their earnings to buy food. It was ludicrous and ineffective, but was made even worse by the insistence that the public works could not be 'reproductive' (benefit private individuals). This led to many useless 'public' works being carried out, while potentially valuable projects, such as the draining and reclaiming of waste lands, were left undone.

Monsell believed that public works should form the chief element in famine relief (as did virtually all strands of public opinion, including Daniel O'Connell and the Young Irelanders), but disagreed with the Government's opposition to reproductive works. At the end of September 1846 he wrote to the Chief Secretary, Henry Labouchere, predicting nationwide famine by November.[76] He advocated a change in the law that would provide for reproductive works and allow agricultural improvements to be carried out. He wrote: 'never since the connection of Ireland with England has so awful a power been placed in the hands of any statesman as in yours. The whole country is, as it were, fused in your hands – on you depends the future shape which it will assume'.[77] His prescience was marked. The failure of the British authorities to deal effectively with the famine did indeed lead to a significant increase in hatred of England, and ultimately to the rise of Fenianism and of the land agitation.[78] Also, the legitimacy of the Irish landed élite was to be undermined by their ineffective and sometimes harsh behaviour towards their tenants during the Great Famine.[79]

Nevertheless, it was Lords Monteagle and Devon, and not Monsell, who led the campaign which resulted in Trevelyan and Russell altering their policy. On 5 October 1846 this was announced in the form of a letter from

Labouchere which sanctioned certain reproductive works. The effect was negligible, in practice, as financial and bureaucratic shortcomings resulted in only 5 per cent of the cost of employment schemes being spent on drainage and about 2.5 per cent of the labourers employed were engaged on these works.[80] The main significance of the 'Labouchere Letter' episode was that it showed that Monsell was now aligned with those most dissatisfied with the Government's famine policy and was in favour of what were, by contemporary standards, fairly radical measures to counter the crisis.

However, the most drastic form of 'famine relief' advocated by Monsell was emigration.[81] He correctly identified overpopulation as the chief social problem in Ireland, while the British colonies in North America, South Africa and Oceania were short of labour. He believed the authorities should promote large-scale emigration to the colonies, so that both evils could be eliminated simultaneously, and he articulated these views before the Select Committee of Enquiry into Colonisation from Ireland on 23 and 25 June 1847.[82] Indeed, assisted emigration was a favourite policy of the Shannon Estuary Group, including Sir Aubrey de Vere, Sir Richard Bourke and Lords Dunraven, Adare and Monteagle, of whom the latter was in fact instrumental in establishing the Select Committee on Colonisation from Ireland.[83] As a result, Limerick and Dublin were the chief centres of landlord-assisted emigration during the famine period.[84] It must be remembered that this policy was considered enlightened at the time, and neither Monsell nor Monteagle came in for any significant criticism as a result of their passionate advocacy of it. Indeed, a historian of the famine period has described Monsell as one of the 'most competent observers of the time'.[85]

Monsell and many others in the Shannon Estuary Group underwent considerable mental and political turmoil at this time. William Smith O'Brien had declared for Repeal in 1843, and in 1848 he was to be found at the head of an armed revolt (albeit a small and ineffective one) against British rule. Stephen de Vere travelled to Canada in one of the ships carrying emigrants to North America and later publicised the horrors that he had seen. In 1848 his brother Aubrey published a severe criticism of British rule, entitled *English Misrule and Irish Misdeeds*. Monsell himself became very anti-English. On 5 November 1846 Aubrey de Vere noted that he 'tried as much as I could to soften William Monsell's indignation against the Government' but he refused to be budged from this position.[86] By July 1847 Stafford O'Brien found that Monsell's position had hardened. He told Lady Dunraven that 'the feeblest eulogies of England have rendered me liable to be eaten up without sauce' by Monsell, and he recalled in another letter to her some years later how Monsell 'was almost morose in dislike of our [i.e. English] native island, creed, customs and constitution'.[87] Monsell himself applauded *English Misrule and Irish Misdeeds* and wrote to Aubrey de Vere:

> Tell truth they say and shame the devil, but you can't shame the English – they despise us so heartily ... I must except English Roman Catholics from this charge, they do sympathise with us very much. I believe there is only one remedy ... Let the Irish Protestants move into England, and the English Roman Catholics into Ireland.[88]

This was a radical change from his position in 1840, when he had ascribed all Ireland's evils to Popery.

Monsell's public utterances were, however, more ambiguous and circumspect. His bitter electoral experience of 1837 had taught him the value of the deliberate vagueness in political actions and beliefs practised by experienced Irish politicians.[89] The *Limerick Reporter* of 5 March 1847 carried a report concerning a series of resolutions passed by Limerick County Grand Jury that were strongly federalist in their tone and had been drawn up by Monsell.[90] The *Reporter* also claimed that 'Mr Monsell and indeed our gentry at large, are every hour approaching nearer and nearer to the goal of nationality', and indeed his earlier campaign for reproductive works was part of a growing link between the landed classes and the nationalists.[91] At this time, nationalists of all shades of opinion, from O'Connell to Mitchel, were anxious to recruit the disaffected landlords to their cause and 'it was the British government rather than the Irish nationalists who were most anxious to fix responsibility for the distressed condition of the country on the Irish landlords'.[92]

For their part, the landlords were furious with the Government, as its public works programme, financed by a rising burden of taxation, threatened them with ruin. In December 1846 the Reproductive Works Committee was established as an all-party body of landlords, supported by Daniel O'Connell and his son John, as well as several Tories and Liberals. Monsell, not yet in Parliament, was a warm supporter. The atmosphere was highly charged, and it was widely believed that the landlords as a whole would declare for Repeal.[93] On 14 January 1847 the committee organised a meeting in the Rotunda, Dublin, attended by a number of peers, gentry, twenty-six MPs and many landowners and professional men, at which the Government's famine relief policies were condemned as inadequate. As one of the four Honorary Secretaries of the Reproductive Employment Committee, Monsell played a leading part in the meeting, speaking forcefully in favour of unity of action and the necessity for 'some screw to force proprietors to perform their duty. That is the way to reach the absentee. Force him as you force the resident proprietor into his duty, or compel him to give up his property.'[94] Eighty-three Irish peers and MPs agreed to form an 'Irish Parliamentary Party', which included Whigs, Tories and Repealers, to bring the proposals of the meeting before Parliament. It seemed that the famine was bringing about revolutionary changes in the Irish political landscape and the Government might have been forced into activity by the sustained pressure of a united Irish party in the British parliament. Sadly this nascent 'Irish Party' soon collapsed and had ceased to exist by the summer of 1847.[95]

The Reproductive Works Committee survived for a longer period and in June 1847 it changed its name to the Irish Council. Among its members were Monsell, Samuel Ferguson of 'Orange Young Ireland', several Young Irelanders (John Mitchel, William Smith O'Brien, Charles Gavan Duffy, Thomas D'Arcy McGee, Thomas Francis Meagher and John Blake Dillon) and a few moderate Repealers (Sir David Roche and Henry Grattan). It was described as a non-political body, and its objects were defined as being 'to combine Irishmen of every grade and section of opinion – to watch over and assert the rights and interests of our common country – to mirror its wants and wishes – to create, foster and develop a sound Irish public opinion, irrespective of party'.[96] Initially, Monsell took a leading part in its proceedings, but it maintained but a weak existence through the summer of 1847 and he ceased his involvement by the end of the year.[97]

In the period leading up to the general election of 1847 it was widely believed that Monsell was about to declare for Repeal, though his real feelings are difficult to discern. Adare wrote to him on 22 May 1847 that 'if you can stand and come in openly unpledged you will stand in a very high position, I should say the highest in Ireland'. He went on to add that 'if you can come in as a Nationalist, as distinguished from a Repealer, you will have been of great use to the whole country'. Adare himself lamented that 'I wish I could be as much of a Nationalist as you are', but it is obvious from the context that such 'nationalism' did not imply Repeal.[98] It is unlikely that Monsell ever seriously considered becoming a Repealer. Stafford O'Brien told Lady Dunraven that if Monsell took the Repeal pledge, 'the veil will be lifted' and he would realise what it really meant, but added, 'I do not for a moment however think he will.'[99]

In the general election of 1847, held in the middle of the famine, Monsell stood as a candidate for the first time since his disastrous 1837 campaign, but this time for County Limerick (which like Limerick City returned two MPs).[100] The sitting MPs were the two Repealers, Caleb Powell and William Smith O'Brien, but the latter was the only MP who belonged to the Confederate (or Young Ireland) faction. Both contested the election, although O'Brien did not respect Powell, whom he regarded as venal and incompetent.[101] The contest that followed was confused and bitter. Monsell canvassed hard and took up a position of masterful ambiguity, as advocated by Adare. His stance was as close as possible to Repeal as made no difference, or so it seemed to many of the electorate. Nevertheless, he was still in touch with his old Peelite allies. Lord Lincoln wrote to him on 21 July 1847 that there would be no problem in his receiving financial assistance from them, as 'your opinions are in such general accordance' with their policies.[102] Monsell's electoral address was carefully worded.[103] It began by striking a note which was to recur repeatedly in his subsequent career, when he spoke of having been urged to stand by 'persons differing from one another very widely in political opinions'.[104] He always claimed to have support from every sector in the political community. He promised to work for 'practical measures', such as 'for the development of our agricultural and manufacturing resources – for the promotion of railways – for the encouragement of fisheries. In short, for everything that may tend towards relieving property from oppressive taxation, and giving to every poor man that which I believe to be his right – a fair day's wages for a fair day's work'.[105] He also declared his support for 'a system of tenant right, which will secure to the occupier compensation for permanent improvements on his farm'.[106] His gesture towards Repeal consisted of a declaration that 'much of the business now transacted in London could, with great advantage to Irish interests, be transferred to this country'.[107] Finally, he pledged himself 'to advocate the principles of civil and religious liberty to make the interests of Ireland my first objective', to work towards improving the system of government, which had produced the present wretchedness, and finally to work ceaselessly for his constituents.[108] By contrast, it is interesting to note that Caleb Powell's electoral address, appearing at the same time, explicitly called for the repeal of the Act of Union.[109]

The election itself was held on 10 August and as it approached Monsell inched closer to advocating Repeal. On the day that the candidates were nominated he addressed a hostile mob in the courthouse in Limerick city, and stated that 'in reference to the measure [Repeal] let no one suppose that if he found justice was not done to his country, he wouldn't declare for that measure'.[110] He then invoked the name of Daniel O'Connell, but cleverly used the Liberator's name in support of his own claim to all-party support. On the day of the election an appeal to the electors by Monsell's ally, Father Michael Fitzgerald, appeared in the *Limerick Reporter*.[111] Father Fitzgerald declared that

> Mr Monsell has declared to me that he is for domestic legislation perfectly independent as to all questions purely Irish – he has

> permitted me to state his opinion long since formed – that the English portion of the Imperial Parliament is not competent to deal with the questions purely Irish, particularly those connected with religion.[112]

He even claimed that if O'Connell were still alive, he 'would support him [i.e. Monsell], nay come down to Limerick to second his nomination'.[113] However, not even Father Fitzgerald could claim that Monsell was a pledged Repealer, although he stated that

> in the presence of Sir Vere de Vere, Mr Monsell communicated to me two days before the election his long considered plan that the Irish representatives to the Imperial Parliament increased to one hundred and fifty or more should, without forfeiting the national right of legislating for imperial objects at Westminster, legislate on questions purely Irish in Dublin, subject only to the Royal assent.[114]

This was to be the most extreme position in favour of nationalist ideas that was ever to be imputed to Monsell.

The election, held on 16 August, was a triumph for both successful candidates, Monsell and Smith O'Brien, who polled 588 and 482 votes respectively. The two official Repeal candidates, the sitting MP, Caleb Powell, and G.J. O'Connell, received 458 and 407 votes respectively.[115] The *Limerick Reporter*'s account of Monsell's victory succinctly and accurately analysed the reasons for his success.[116]

> We knew that he had the support of a considerable number of the catholic clergy, and that a large proportion of the Repealers would vote for him – with nearly all the gentry. His Liberal principles verging towards Repeal, his religious principles tending towards Catholicism, his popularity as a landlord, his high moral character, his great ability, his exertions on behalf of the poor, his reputation for usefulness as a public man, his industry and indefatigability in whatever he undertakes, his intimacy with the gentry of the county and the esteem in which they hold him, all combined to place him in the position he occupies in the poll. Let us add to this the early canvas that was made while the County Club (the Repealers) seemed to be asleep and the enlistment of nearly all the popular attorneys in the county as agents, and we fairly largely account for the large majority of Mr Monsell, but all this would not do were it not for the shattered condition of the Repeal movement owing to the melancholy dissentions that have divided and distracted the great party that in 1843 and 1844 commanded the admiration of the world.[117]

The report went on to mention how Repeal was tainted by the Whig alliance and the prevalence of place-hunting in its ranks. Many disillusioned Repeal voters had supported Monsell because he was a federalist. Others had voted for him because 'he is eminently calculated to be useful in a local point of view, may ere long turn out a brilliant national leader' and because his federalist position was that of O'Connell in 1844.[118] Finally 'men of every political creed voted for Mr Monsell – Tories, Whigs and Repealers of all sections'.[119] The main features of his victory – his all-party support, his diligence as a local politician and as a canvasser, his reputation as a high-minded and benevolent landlord, his liberal and reforming principles, and popularity with all classes – were to be features of his entire parliamentary career.

While Monsell was for a time a federalist, though never an orthodox Repealer, his drive towards liberalism and away from nationalism commenced almost immediately after his election. In his address of thanks to the electors of County Limerick, which appeared on 14 August 1847, he again proclaimed his adherence to federalist principles, but then avowed that 'practical measures, especially measures for the relief of the poor, are those for which I shall chiefly labour. While we have been contending about speculative changes, the people have been starving around us.'[120] He stated that it was now time to 'forget party that we remember our country. We cannot serve both at once, and I avow that I prefer the substance to the shadow – practical reforms to squabbles about speculative matters'.[121] He concluded by thanking the electors 'for having elected me unfettered and unpledged, and a representative who respects himself and has a regard for the constitution will be slow to concede what is unworthily demanded'.[122] This address illustrates his extremely subtle and skilful, not to say sophistic, means of garnering electoral support and the ambiguity of his actual position on the national question. On one point, however, he was totally clear – his determination to advocate practical reforms rather than pursue 'squabbles about speculative matters'.[123] He was never once to come close to advocating federalism or nationalist views within the walls of Westminster.

Nevertheless, Charles Gavan Duffy still considered Monsell a good prospect for Repeal, writing to Smith O'Brien that Sharman Crawford and Monsell 'would be invaluable both to the Confederation and for the purpose of bringing the gentry to see their duty as Irishmen'.[124] However, Stafford O'Brien was more perceptive. 'William is making acquaintances and alliances as the *Times* strikes off copies from its steam press, or even faster. He was thinking of speaking last night and I was rather sorry he did not, for there was a good opening and a quiet house. People are inclined to listen to him, and so to say to believe in him.'[125] Later he spoke of how Monsell 'revels, basks, rolls, toys, lives, moves and has his being in the House of Commons'.[126] He could see that Monsell was undergoing a process of acclimatisation which can be traced in his speeches in Parliament at this time. His maiden speech, delivered on 10 December 1847, was a spirited defence of the Catholic Bishop of Limerick, Dr Ryan, who had been accused by Mr Cochrane, MP for Bridgport during a debate in the House on the previous night, of using seditious and inflammatory language 'and pointing out the victims for assassination'.[127] Monsell's address was warmly supported by the Chief Secretary, Labouchere, two former Chief Secretaries (Lords Lincoln and Morpeth), his own friend Stafford O'Brien, and a number of other Irish MPs.[128] Over the next six months, Monsell spoke frequently and in relation to his chief interests.[129] Later, the Government introduced the Crown and Government Protection Bill, which 'provided that the capital offence of compassing and designing to levy war against the sovereign could be dealt with as an ordinary felony and be punished by transportation instead of death'.[130] In an important provision, the offence was, however, extended to include all persons who should promote treasonable designs 'by open and advised speaking'. This was a response to the growing fear of a rebellion amongst Government supporters. It was carried by a majority of 295 to 40 on the third reading in the Commons. The Irish members, with the notable exception of Smith O'Brien, 'remained content with formal protests'.[131] Monsell was among those who voted in favour, while those who voted against included Smith O'Brien, John O'Connell and Sharman Crawford.[132]

Monsell's political conversion was completed during the course of this Parliament (1847–52). Elected as a federalist, he steadily drifted into the Liberal camp, helped by his progress towards Catholicism and the strong support of the Catholic clergy that he enjoyed. The Repeal Movement, including its opposite extremes of Confederates and Federalists, collapsed completely between 1848 and 1850 and most of its former adherents, including the O'Connells, drifted into the ranks of the Irish Liberals. While Butt was to lose faith in the Union, and to persist with federalism until he revived it in the 1870s as Home Rule, the movement as a whole crumbled away in the late 1840s. [133]

As a man of Monsell's beliefs, who favoured civil and religious equality, reform of the landlord–tenant relationship and development of the economy, had no place within Toryism, the only realistic option was to align himself with the Liberals. An analysis of his voting pattern in 1848 and 1849 reveals him to be a staunch supporter of the Liberal government, though less so in 1850.[134] His adherence to the Irish Brigade at the time of the Ecclesiastical Titles Bill further muddies the waters, so that his definite alignment with the Liberal party can only be dated to the establishment of Independent Opposition in 1852.[135] In 1848 Monsell had been horrified by Smith O'Brien's rebellion at Ballingarry, County Tipperary, but was personally distressed by his friend's transportation to Tasmania against which he voted in Parliament. He interceded with the authorities on several occasions over the next few years, to mitigate the severity of O'Brien's sentence.[136]

Monsell's religious conversion occurred in his early years as an MP. As early as 1846 it was widely expected that he would become a Catholic.[137] In the late 1840s, as a member of the Fraternity of St Barnabas, he took spiritual guidance from Archdeacon Henry Edward Manning (1808–92). However, the latter's own Anglican beliefs were ebbing away, and he soon abandoned the task. Monsell decided to become a Catholic under the influence of Newman and to a lesser extent de Lisle. His famine experience had given him an empathy with the Catholic peasants, while his increasing association with Catholic clergy as a result of both his relief work and political activity brought him closer to their church. However, it was Newman's theological influence that was paramount. At the end of 1850 Monsell travelled to England and stayed with Ambrose de Lisle at Grace Dieu. On 12 December 1850 Monsell was received into the Catholic Church in the presence of de Lisle, his family and his servants.[138]

He was a major convert. Cardinal Wiseman, the Primate of England, congratulated him warmly.[139] The Irish Bishops, and especially Monsell's friend, Bishop John Ryan of Limerick, were delighted. Others were horrified, especially the distraught Stafford O'Brien, and Lord Adare's wife Augusta.[140] It was also stated at the time and in subsequent years that Monsell had become a Catholic to further his political career. This shabby allegation was made by, among others, Caleb Powell, and by the irrepressible Bard of Thomond, Michael Hogan.[141] It can be refuted on three counts. Firstly, an examination of Monsell's correspondence over several years will show that his conversion was a gradual and a painful process. He took his religion too seriously to use it as a means of political advancement. Secondly, his conversion was remarkably badly timed if it was designed to be a cynical political manoeuvre. The period of his reception into the Catholic Church saw Britain and Ireland convulsed by the most violent anti-Catholic agitation of the entire nineteenth century – the campaign against the restoration of the Catholic hierarchy in England and Wales. Indeed, he wrote to his mother-in-law, Lady Dunraven (who strongly disapproved of his conversion), that while he believed that his move would harm his political career, he would not allow this to deter him.[142] Thirdly, the two chief promoters of this myth were not unbiased witnesses, to put it mildly. Caleb Powell was an embittered and cynical man, and was particularly aggrieved at having lost his parliamentary seat to Monsell.[143] Similarly, the Bard of Thomond was such a rabidly nationalistic and acerbic commentator on the contemporary political scene as to render his undoubtedly entertaining characterisation of Monsell worthless as historical evidence.

Lady Anna Maria Monsell never became a Catholic, although she sympathised with her husband's position and defended him to her outraged mother.[144] Lord Adare (who became the third Earl of Dunraven on his father's death in 1850) did not convert until 1855, due to his wife's vehement opposition. Her tactic was to threaten to have a heart attack when he seemed to be about to convert. After he finally did so they became seriously estranged, and quarrelled bitterly over the education of their eldest son, the future fourth earl, who in disgust ended up an agnostic![145] Stephen de Vere had become a Catholic in 1846, and his brothers Aubrey and Vere did so in 1851. Manning converted in 1851 and eventually rose to be Archbishop of Westminster in 1865 and Cardinal in 1875 (the first Anglican convert to receive the Red Hat). Smith O'Brien and Stafford O'Brien remained members of the Church of Ireland.

Monsell's political conversion was not unprecedented for a nineteenth-century politician. After all, the great Liberal prime ministers Palmerston and Gladstone started out as Tories, and the fourteenth Earl of Derby, who led the Conservative party from 1846 to 1868, began his career as a Liberal. However, it was Monsell's becoming a Catholic that was his most drastic break with his past. In Ireland, where political and religious divisions were tending to merge, it was virtually unprecedented. It was to determine the course of his political career for the rest of his life.

NOTES

1. For an excellent account of Monsell's religious and political conversions, see Roantree, 'William Monsell and the Catholic Question', pp.17–102.
2. The term was coined by E.J. Hobsbawn. See E.J. Hobsbawn, *The Age of Revolution. Europe 1789–1848* (London: Abacus, 1977), pp.11–12.
3. Ibid., pp.307–35.
4. See David Thomson, *Europe since Napoleon* (London: Longman, 1975), pp.79–226.
5. See Roger Aubert (ed.), *The Christian Centuries*, Vol. 5, *The Church in a Secularised Society* (New York: Paulist Press and London: Darton, Longman and Todd, 1978), and Wilfred Ward, *William George Ward and the Catholic Revival* (London: Longmans, Green and Co., 1912), pp.82–129.
6. Good surveys of nineteenth-century Ireland include Paul Bew, *Ireland: The Politics of Enmity 1789–2006* (Oxford: Oxford University Press, 2007); D. George Boyce, *Nineteenth-Century Ireland: The Search for Stability* (Dublin: Gill and Macmillan, 1990); Alvin Jackson, *Ireland 1798–1998: Politics and War* (Oxford: Blackwell, 1999); and K. Theodore Hoppen, *Ireland since 1800: Conflict and Conformity* (London and New York: Longmans, 1989).

7. See Desmond Bowen, *The Protestant Crusade in Ireland 1800–70: A Study of Protestant–Catholic Relations between the Act of Union and Disestablishment* (Dublin: Gill and Macmillan, 1978) and Patrick J. Corish (ed.), *A History of Irish Catholicism*, Vol. 5 (Dublin: Gill, 1967). Other works on the religious situation at the time include two by Donal A. Kerr: *Peel Priests and Politics. Sir Robert Peel's Administration and the Roman Catholic Church in Ireland 1841–6* (Oxford: Clarendon Press and Oxford University Press, 1982) and *A Nation of Beggars? Priests, People and Politics in Famine Ireland 1846–52* (Oxford: Clarendon Press and Oxford University Press, 1994).
8. Gearóid Ó Tuathaigh, *Ireland Before the Famine 1798–1848* (Dublin: Gill and Macmillan, 1972), pp.80–116 and 170–84.
9. Olive Brose, *Church and Parliament: the Reshaping of the Church of England 1828–1860* (Stanford: Stanford University Press and Oxford: Oxford University Press, 1959).
10. David Newsome, *The Convert Cardinals. Newman and Manning* (London: John Murray, 1993).
11. Among the many biographies of Newman are Wilfred Ward, *The Life of John Henry Newman*, 2 vols (London: Longmans and Co., 1912); Ian Kerr, *John Henry Newman – A Biography* (Oxford: Clarendon Press, 1988) and Sheridan Gilley, *Newman and his Age* (London: Darton, Longman and Todd, 1990).
12. Memorandum by William Neville, 15 October 1876, in Newman papers held in the Archives of the Birmingham Oratory, hereafter referred to as NP, N/P/M/6; and John Henry Newman, *The Letters and Diaries of John Henry Newman*, 31 vols, Vol. 28, p.XX, Newman to Monsell, 26 December 1876.
13. See the Diary of J.H. Newman, 9th June, 1840, NP–6, and Roantree, 'William Monsell and the Catholic Question', p.81.
14. Peter Nockles, 'Church or Protestant Sect? The Church of Ireland, High Churchmanship and the Oxford Movement, 1822–1869', in *Historical Journal*, 41 (1998), pp.457–93.
15. Alan Acheson, *A History of the Church of Ireland 1691–1996* (Blackrock, Dublin: Columba Press, 1997), p. 153.
16. Ibid., p.153. For Jebb, see Alexander Gordon, revised David Huddleston, 'John Jebb (1775–1833)', in *Oxford DNB*.
17. Hanley, 'Past Glories of Tervoe'.
18. Revd T.T. Carter, *Harriet Monsell. A Memoir* (London: J. Masters and Co., 1884), p.7.
19. See Valerie Bonham, 'Harriet Monsell (née O'Brien) (1811–1883)', in *Oxford DNB*; Valerie Bonham, *A Joyous Service: The Clewer Sisters and their Work* (Windsor: Valerie Bonham and the Community of St John the Baptist, 1989); and Valerie Bonham, *A Place in Life: The Clewer House of Mercy 1849–93* (Windsor: Valerie Bonham and the Community of St John the Baptist, 1992). For the wider context, see Susan Mumm, '"Not Worse than Other Girls": The Convent-Based Rehabilitation of Fallen Women in Victorian Britain', in *Journal of Social History*, 29, 3 (spring 1996), pp.527–41.
20. William Ewart Gladstone, *The Gladstone Diaries* (edited by M.R.D. Foot and H.C.G. Matthew), 14 vols (Oxford: Clarendon Press, 1968–91), Vol. 3, p.XLV.
21. *Irish Times*, 11 January 2001.
22. James, *Forgotten Genius*, p.82, n. 2, extract from 'Narrative' by William Monsell.
23. G.K. White, *A History of St Columba's College 1843–1974* (Dublin: Old Columban Society, 1980), p.5.
24. Ibid., p.6.
25. See S.A. Skinner, 'William Sewell (1804–1874)', in *Oxford DNB*.
26. James, *Forgotten Genius*, pp.56–7.
27. White, *History of St Columba's College*, p. 7.
28. Ibid., p.141.
29. James, *Forgotten Genius*, pp.78–9.
30. Ibid., p.93.
31. E.M. Todd, 'James Henthorn Todd (1805–1869)', in *Oxford DNB*.
32. Arthur H. Grant, revised Kenneth Milne, 'Lord John George de la Poer Beresford, (1773–1862)', in *Oxford DNB*.
33. James, *Forgotten Genius*, p.90.
34. White, *History of St Columba's College*, p.13.
35. See the school website www.stcolumbas.ie

36. Information from Mr G.K. White, author of *A History of St Columba's College.*
37. James, *Forgotten Genius*, pp.209–10.
38. See Margaret Pawley, 'Ambrose Lisle March Phillipps de Lisle (1809–1878)', in *Oxford DNB*, and Margaret Pawley, *Faith and Family: The Life and Circle of Ambrose Phillipps de Lisle* (Norwich: Canterbury Press, 1993).
39. Roantree, 'William Monsell and the Catholic Question', pp.48–52.
40. James, *Forgotten Genius*, p.210.
41. Ibid., pp.209–10.
42. John E. Acland, *A Layman's Life in the Days of the Tractarian Movement. In Memoriam Arthur (Acland) Troyte* (London and Oxford: J. Parker and Co., 1904), pp.171–7.
43. Ibid., pp.175–6.
44. Second Earl of Dunraven to William Monsell and Augustus Stafford O'Brien, 13 June 1838, DP, D3196/C/17/2). See also DP, D3196. Introduction by A.P.W. Malcomson, 'Windham Wyndham-Quin, 2nd Earl of Dunraven (1782–1850)'. This weather-vane peer had supported Catholic emancipation throughout his career, but his slippery political manoeuvres eventually led him to support the Tories, in order to further his ambition of becoming a representative peer.
45. Henry Heaney (ed.), *A Scottish Whig in Ireland 1835–38: The Irish Journals of Robert Graham of Redgorton* (Dublin: Four Courts Press in association with the National Library of Ireland, 1999), p.30.
46. Davis, *Revolutionary Imperialist*, pp.96–100.
47. *Limerick Chronicle*, 22 July 1837.
48. Ibid., 29 July 1837.
49. Ibid., 26 July 1837.
50. Brian M. Walker (ed.), *Parliamentary Election Results in Ireland 1801–1922* (Dublin: Royal Irish Academy, 1978), p.292. See also Lady Dunraven's Diary entries for 20, 21 and 22 July, and for 2 and 3 August 1837, DP, D3196/E/2/40.
51. Norgate, 'Edwin Richard Windham Wyndham-Quin, third Earl of Dunraven', in *Oxford DNB.*
52. *Report from the Select Committee on Foundation Schools and Education in Ireland. H.C. 1837–8* (701) VII, pp.345–436.
53. For an account of this controversy, see Pat Kearney, 'Limerick's Campaign for a University 1838–45', in *Old Limerick Journal*, 26 (winter 1989), pp.26–35.
54. *Limerick Chronicle,* 9 January 1839.
55. Davis, *Revolutionary Imperialist*, p.114.
56. *Limerick Chronicle*, 9 January 1839.
57. Kearney, 'Limerick's Campaign for a University', p.30.
58. *Limerick Chronicle*, 9 January 1839.
59. Hanley, 'Past Glories of Tervoe'.
60. See Sidney Lee, revised Alan O'Day, 'William Sherman Crawford (1781–1861)', in *Oxford DNB,* and B.A. Kennedy, 'Sharman Crawford's Federal Scheme for Ireland', in H.A. Cronnie, T.W. Moody and B.B. Quinn (eds), *Essays in British and Irish History in Honour of James Eadie Todd* (London: Frederick Muller, 1949), p.238.
61. Ibid.
62. Ibid., p.242.
63. Ibid., pp.248–54. See also Oliver McDonagh, *The Life of Daniel O'Connell 1775–1847*, (London: Weidenfeld and Nicolson, 1991), pp.536–9.
64. David Thornley, *Isaac Butt and Home Rule* (London: MacGibbon and Kee, 1964), p.16. See also R.F. Foster, *Modern Ireland 1600–1972* (Harmondsworth: Penguin, 1988), pp.302–7.
65. See Peter Denman, *Samuel Ferguson: The Literary Achievement* (Gerrards Cross: Smythe, 1990); Joseph Spence, 'Isaac Butt, Nationality and Irish Toryism, 1833–1852', in *Bullán,* 2, 1 (summer 1995), pp.45–60; and Joseph Spence, 'The Philosophy of Irish Toryism, 1833–52: A Study of Reactions to Liberal Reformism in Ireland in the Generation between the First Reform Act and the Famine, with Especial Reference to Expressions of National Feeling among the Protestant Ascendancy' (unpublished Ph.D thesis, University of London, 1991).
66. Alvin Jackson, *Home Rule, An Irish History 1800–2000* (London: Weidenfeld and Nicolson, 2003), pp.10–27.
67. Newman, *Letters and Diaries*, Vol. 26, p.362.

68. J.B. Conacher, *The Peelites and the Party System 1846–52* (Newton Abbot: David and Charles, 1972), p.16.
69. Ibid., p.17.
70. Ibid.
71. K.T. Hoppen, *Elections, Politics and Society in Ireland 1832–85* (Oxford: Clarendon Press, 1984), p. 279. See also J.H. Whyte, *The Independent Irish Party 1850–59* (Oxford: Oxford University Press, 1958), p.15. Monsell is not classified by Whyte as a Peelite MP.
72. Kevin B. Nowlan, *The Politics of Repeal. A Study in the Relations between Great Britain and Ireland 1841–50* (London: Routledge and Kegan Paul, 1965), p.99.
73. For the Famine, see Owen Dudley Edwards and T. Desmond Williams (eds), *The Great Famine – Studies in Irish History 1846–1852* (Dublin: Browne and Nolan, 1956); Christine Kinealy, *This Great Calamity. The Irish Famine. 1845–52* (Dublin: Gill and Macmillan, 1994); Peter Gray, *The Irish Famine* (London: Thames and Hudson, 1995); and Cathal Poirteir (ed.), *The Great Irish Famine* (Dublin and Cork: Mercier Press, 1995).
74. Aubrey de Vere, *Recollections of Aubrey De Vere* (London and New York: Edwin Arnold, 1897), pp.250–1.
75. *Report of the Select Committee of the House of Lords on Colonisation from Ireland; together with Minutes of Evidence*. H.C. 1847 VI, hereafter referred to as *Report on Colonisation*, pp.197, 199 and 213.
76. Revd John O'Rourke, *The History of the Great Irish Famine of 1847* (Dublin: J. Duffy and Co., 1902), pp.188–92.
77. Ibid., p.191.
78. Donal McCartney, *The Dawning of Democracy. Ireland 1800–1870* (Dublin: Helicon, 1987), p.173.
79. Ridden, 'Making Good Citizens', p.238.
80. Thomas P. O'Neill, 'The Organisation and Administration of Relief 1845–52', in Edwards and Williams, *Great Famine*, p.231.
81. For an overview of the subject, see Patrick J Duffy (ed.), *To and From Ireland: Planned Migration Schemes, c. 1600–2000* (Dublin: Geography Publications, 2004), pp.79–154.
82. *Report on Colonisation*, pp.197–216 and 231.
83. Fitzpatrick,'Thomas Spring Rice and the Peopling of Australia', p.44.
84. Oliver McDonagh, 'Irish Emigration to the United States of America and the British colonies during the Famine', in Edwards and Williams, *Great Famine*, p.333.
85. Ibid., p.321.
86. Ward, *Aubrey de Vere*, p.124.
87. Stafford O'Brien to Lady Dunraven, 29 July (1847), DP, D3196/E/13, no. 108, and 2 July (1855), D3196/E/13, no. 74.
88. Monsell to Aubrey de Vere, 19 February 1848 quoted in Ward, *Aubrey De Vere*, p.138.
89. Jupp, 'Irish Parliamentary Representation', p.321.
90. *Limerick Reporter*, 9 March 1847.
91. Ibid.
92. Kevin B. Nowlan, 'The Political Background', in Edwards and Williams, *Great Famine*, p.155.
93. Nowlan, *Politics of Repeal*, p.152.
94. *Limerick Reporter*, 19 January 1847.
95. Nowlan, *Politics of Repeal*, pp.133–7.
96. *Limerick Reporter*, 4 June 1847.
97. Nowlan, *Politics of Repeal*, p.152 and *Limerick Reporter*, 9 November 1847.
98. Adare to Monsell 22 May 1847, in Monsell papers, National Library of Ireland, hereafter referred to as MP, NLI, MS 8318 (10).
99. Stafford O'Brien to Lady Dunraven, 17 July 1847, DP, D3196/E/13/14.
100. For this election, see Brian Walker, 'Politicians, Elections and Catastrophe: The General Election of 1847', in *Irish Political Studies*, 22, 1 (March 2007), pp.1–34.
101. Davis, *Revolutionary Imperialist*, p.226.
102. Lincoln to Monsell, 21 July 1847, MP, NLI, MS 8318 (12).
103. *Limerick Reporter*, 30 July 1847.
104. Ibid.
105. Ibid.

106. Ibid.
107. Ibid.
108. Ibid.
109. Ibid.
110. *Limerick Chronicle*, 16 August 1847.
111. Ibid.
112. Ibid.
113. Ibid.
114. Ibid.
115. Walker, *Parliamentary Election Results,* p.293.
116. *Limerick Reporter*, 13 August 1847.
117. Ibid.
118. Ibid.
119. Ibid.
120. *Limerick Reporter*, 17 August 1847.
121. Ibid.
122. Ibid.
123. Ibid.
124. Gavan Duffy to Smith O'Brien (late 1847), in Smith O'Brien Papers, NLI, Vol. 441, no. 2244.
125. Stafford O'Brien to Lady Dunraven, November 1847, DP, D3196/E/13/19.
126. Stafford O'Brien to Lady Dunraven , 1 August 1848, DP, D3196/E/13/29.
127. *Hansards Parliamentary Debates, Third Series,* vols 1–356 (London: T.C. Hansard, 1830–91), hereafter referred to as Hansard, XCV, 80 (9 December 1847).
128. Hansard, XCV, 928–9 (10 December 1847).
129. Hansard, XCV, 1424–5 (20 December 1847) and XCVII, 338–62 (9 March 1848).
130. Nowlan, *Politics of Repeal*, p. 200.
131. Ibid.; Hansard, XCVIII, 58–60 (7 April 1848); 128–32 (10 April 1848) and 478–80 (18 April 1848).
132. Hansard, XCVIII, 478–80 (18 April 1848).
133. John Kendle, *Ireland and the Federal Solution. The Debate over the United Kingdom Constitution 1870–1921* (Kingston, Montreal: McGill-Queen's University Press, 1989).
134. Horgan, 'Irish Catholic Whigs in Parliament', pp.128–9.
135. See Whyte, *Independent Irish Party*, p.16, for the unreliability of the Irish Liberals in general in their support of Russell's administration during this period.
136. See Davis, *Revolutionary Imperialist*, pp.291 and 318.
137. See Brendan O'Cathaoir, *Famine Diary* (Dublin: Irish Academic Press, 1999), p. 73, in which he refers to such a rumour in *The Nation* of 26 September 1846.
138. Monsell to 3rd Earl of Dunraven, 13 December, 1850, DP, D3196/F/10/21. He wrote: 'Yesterday evening, at half past six o'clock in the presence of A. Phillips, his wife and children, governess etc. good Father Lorrane, a French priest of the Order of Charity received me.'
139. Wiseman to Monsell, 16 December, 1850, MP, NLI, MS 8318 (8).
140. For Stafford O'Brien's reaction, see DP, D3196/E/13, nos. 43, 47, 55, 64.
141. Hogan, *Seventh Number of Shawn-na-Scoob*, p.4.
142. Monsell to Lady Dunraven,18 November (1850), DP, D3196/E/10.
143. Cussen, 'Caleb Powell', p.420.
144. See DP, D3196/E/10, box 1A. for several letters from Lady Anna Maria to her mother on this topic.
145. Windham Thomas Wyndham Quin, 4th Earl of Dunraven, *Past times and Pastimes*, 2 vols (London: Hodder and Stoughton, 1922), Vol.1, pp.1–10.

CHAPTER FOUR

Identity and Allegiance

For William Monsell the political and religious turmoil of the 1840s was replaced in the early 1850s by a coherent political philosophy that he retained to the end of his life. The three chief and interdependent strands of this ideology were: his sense of nationality, his Unionism and his liberalism. Similarly, his conversion to Catholicism in 1850 gave him an all-encompassing belief system that satisfied his spiritual needs for the rest of his days.[1] What is most remarkable about Monsell is his wide range of activities and interests. He was at once a patriotic Irishman, a British gentleman, an adopted Frenchman and a cosmopolitan European.

Monsell always considered himself Irish. On 1 March 1870, while addressing the House of Commons, he described himself as 'an Irishman'.[2] During the Great Famine he had temporarily become very anti-English, and had clearly defined himself as Irish, in opposition to English contempt and indifference. 'You cannot shame the English, they despise us so heartily', he told Aubrey de Vere in 1848.[3] Around the same time he wrote to Smith O'Brien that 'our whole proceedings are neither Whig, nor Tory nor Repeal, but simply Irish'.[4] While these date from Monsell's federalist or quasi-nationalist period, they are paralleled by similar avowals of Irishness throughout his life. His public utterances throughout the 1850s, 1860s and 1870s were filled with references asserting that Ireland was a separate nation from England or Scotland. On 26 July 1867 he told the Commons that the Irish and the English were 'two distinct races'.[5] A very full exposition of his theory of Ireland and Irish nationality is to be found in his address to the annual meeting of the Statistical and Social Enquiry Society of Ireland, on 22 January 1869.[6] The entire speech is permeated with the idea that Ireland is a separate country, a concept that is taken by him to be axiomatic. He speaks of Ireland as 'a country', refers to 'our population' and 'the natural character of our people', and uses the term 'we' and 'home' to refer to the Irish and Ireland respectively.[7] While acknowledging Ireland's backwardness, he does not blame it on inherent racial or religious inferiority but to the penal laws which 'found us reduced to barbaric industrial ineptitude, produced by political causes, and not by the natural character of our people'. Thus, given favourable political and economic circumstances, the Irish are capable of advances as great as those of any other civilised nation.[8]

The Irish Liberal gentry claimed Irish nationality in three ways: they resided in Ireland, and so shared a sense of place with other inhabitants of Ireland; they were resident landlords committed to Ireland as an entity; and their families had lived in the country for hundreds of years. These factors were all present in Monsell's case, and help account for his firm sense of Irishness.[9] There were two other aspects to Monsell's view of the nation that were crucial to his political philosophy. Firstly, he stressed the unity of the Irish nation, so as to emphasise the élite's authentic place within it. 'The three great classes – landlords, farmers and labourers – are bound together by links almost too minute to be discerned, but which yet no human power can sever', he stated in his address of 22 January 1869.[10] Secondly, he defined his Irish nationality 'in cultural and territorial terms but in rejecting political nationalist aspirations'.[11] This was true of the Shannon Estuary Group in general, and both Aubrey de Vere and the third Earl of Dunraven were 'cultural nationalists', indeed major figures in the Celtic Revival, while remaining political Unionists.[12] In 1847 Lord Adare had distinguished Monsell as a 'nationalist' but not as a Repealer.[13] This distinction is central to the second strand of Monsell's ideology, his Unionism.

The best summary of his sense of nationhood is to be found in a remark of his close friend, David Moriarty, Bishop of Kerry, who told Gladstone in 1868 that 'there does not breathe a purer patriot than Monsell, and what is rare in Irish patriotism, he is heart and soul attached to [the] British connexion'.[14] The concept of a dual nationality developed between the years 1707 and 1837, when a British nation was constructed from the four component countries of the United Kingdom.[15] There emerged what Linda Colley has described as 'a new unitary ruling class in place of those separate and specific landed establishments' that had existed in the four countries in early modern times.[16] However, the Scottish, Welsh and Anglo-Irish nobilities did not become absorbed into the English élite, but became British in a new and very useful fashion, while retaining their pre-existing identities.[17] Similarly, Irish Liberals insisted on both Irish and British nationality, and that membership of the British nation offered them an identity which did not make them less Irish.[18]

Monsell considered himself to be both British and Irish. On 2 January 1881 he wrote to Gavan Duffy: 'I think the entire union of hearts between the three kingdoms may be arrived at without the sacrifice of one grain of our national feeling.'[19] Any attempt to deny the authenticity of this claim infuriated him. In 1893 he angrily attacked Gladstone and his Home Rule supporters for their 'monstrous' accusation that 'because we are Unionists, of not loving our country [*sic*]' and continued:

> I confess I have a strong feeling on this subject – an intense feeling – I feel bitterly the accusation. I declare before God that from the time I first entered Parliament some fifty years ago, my earnest desire was ... to raise up my fellow countrymen that were then downtrodden, and give them every advantage and every privilege that the citizens of the rest of the United Kingdom enjoy.[20]

In short, Monsell was a Unionist *because* he was an Irish patriot, not despite it.

His dual nationality owed a great deal to his English education, for while his predecessors at Tervoe had been educated in Ireland, he was a Wykehamist and an Oxonian. This affected him in two important ways. Firstly, it taught him English culture and mores, and even how to speak the English language in the cultured 'upper received pronunciation' manner.[21] Secondly, the emphasis on the Classics in the public school system instilled in its pupils a strong British patriotism, equating the greatness of Rome with the greatness of the British Empire. Monsell was also touched by two further processes that strengthened the solidarity of the British élites. First, growing intermarriage among the four British élites resulted in a very large increase in the number of landed families with multiple residences and estates throughout the United Kingdom. Thus Monsell's first wife and closest friend and brother-in-law were the children of an Irish peer married to an Anglo-Welsh heiress (the second Earl of Dunraven and his wife Caroline Wyndham, an heiress with estates and houses in both England and Wales). Similarly, Monsell's cousins, the Earls of Limerick, and his friend Augustus Stafford O'Brien were also proprietors in both Britain and Ireland. Secondly, by transferring parliamentary affairs to Westminster, the Act of Union had made it necessary for an active Irish politician to base himself for much of the year in London.[22]

The concept of dual nationality within Irish Unionism has been clouded by the tendency of some modern Ulster Unionists to stridently proclaim their Britishness, while frequently denying their Irishness. Hence, it is instructive to compare the views of Monsell with those of another Southern Unionist, Sir Edward Carson, who shared with him a view of the United Kingdom that was to perish in the increasingly polarised and sectarian politics of the late nineteenth and early twentieth centuries.

Monsell, like Carson, was neither a Tory nor a reactionary.[23] D.G. Boyce has written that 'Carson was a Whig in politics, and since he lived in Ireland, he was an Irish Whig, not only physically, but also politically in that he believed in the best possible government of Ireland, the maximum amount of liberty for its people, just and decent treatment for all, irrespective of religion, and a progressive administration.'[24] Like Monsell, Carson was a patriotic Irishman.[25] They both stood in a tradition of Liberal Unionism that produced such notable figures as Edmund Burke, Thomas Spring Rice and William H. Lecky. 'What is the object of the United Kingdom,' Carson asked in 1912. 'As I understand it, it is that all parts shall be worked together as a whole, and with the object that the poorer may be helped by the richer, and the richer may be the stronger by the co-operation of the poorer.'[26]

Monsell articulated similar sentiments in two major speeches to the Commons in the aftermath of the Fenian rebellion. On 26 July 1867 he severely criticised British misrule in Ireland. 'All history teaches the same lesson,' he said, 'justice and equality have a binding force which nothing can destroy.'[27] The Irish were discontent because 'they are not governed according to their own wishes or feelings or requirements, but according to the wishes and prejudices of the people of England'.[28] They 'have no effective control over their government, which is controlled from England'.[29] Ireland should be governed as an equal partner in the Union, according to her own requirements, 'just as the English and Scotch are according to the requirements of their respective countries'.[30] Returning to the subject on 16 March 1868, he told the Commons that 'the Irish people would not be content with a measure of justice less complete than that which would satisfy the people of England'.[31] The United Kingdom was a union between equal countries, each of which should be allowed to flourish under the protection of the Imperial Parliament.

What particularly frustrated Monsell was that the real benefits of Ireland's membership of this great empire were being denied and obscured by these obstacles. In common with his fellow British Liberals, he believed that Britain's constitution and indeed her entire civilisation were the most advanced in the world, and wrote of the Teutonic nations that, 'to those races, the future of the world belongs'.[32] The British constitution was 'so free and liberal it was so strong to protect – so just, that unless when some obstacle such as he sought to remove, interfered, it must attach to it those who care within the spheres of its influence.'[33] Spring Rice's ideal, that Ireland be so much an equal partner that she might be called 'West Britain', was also the aim of Monsell, of Carson and of the Irish Liberals in general.[34]

Thus, both Monsell and Carson saw the Union as a two-way process.

Carson fought Irish nationalism, but also British political indifference.[35] Similarly, in the aftermath of the Fenian rebellion, Monsell feared that the greatest threat to the Union came from official British indifference and the resulting alienation of the mass of the Irish people. He deplored the misgovernment and neglect of Ireland, and roundly blamed these factors for the Fenian agitation. He told the Commons that the Fenians 'were few in number, and if the mass of the Irish people were contented, there would be no more danger to society in Ireland from Fenianism than there was in England'.[36] He went on to state that 'our danger was not from the Fenian thousands, but from the millions whose discontent went very near to disaffection'.[37] The mass of the Irish people, neither committed Unionists nor convinced separatists, had to be won over by the British authorities, and this could only be done by dealing promptly and justly with Irish grievances.

Monsell's Unionism became more defensive as the Union came under increasing attack. It was one thing to flirt with federalism in the 1840s, when even O'Connell and Young Ireland wooed the landlords and the danger of social revolution seemed remote, but it was an entirely different matter when the Fenians and Home Rule represented a far more formidable threat. Monsell strongly believed that Ireland could only suffer if she left the United Kingdom, and he opposed Fenianism in the 1860s and Home Rule after 1870 with equal firmness. In 1873, furious at the rejection of Gladstone's University Bill, he told Newman: 'you cannot speak out the truth, that Ireland is unfit to govern itself'.[38] In 1885 he told the House of Lords that 'we are still, thank God, a United Kingdom'.[39] The Fenians 'were aggregated to the secret societies of Europe, and their object was to establish a democratic republic. They were the enemies of the priests as well as landlords', Monsell told the Commons in 1868.[40] Three years later the horrors of the Paris Commune, bringing revolution and destruction to the capital of his beloved France, showed Monsell where such tendencies ultimately led. Later he regarded the Home Rule and land agitations as a continuation of this revolutionary threat. On 2 August 1880 he described the land agitation, in a speech in the Lords, as 'socialistic' and 'a wicked agitation'.[41] In 1893 he spoke of the dangers that would occur when the 'law of the Queen was superseded by the law of the Land League' and of how the establishment of Home Rule would lead to these 'gentlemen' forming 'the first cabinet who would have the control of the lives and liberties of her Majesty's loyal subjects'.[42] The Southern Unionists represented 'the great mass of property, intelligence, culture and industry in the three Southern provinces' and could not be abandoned to socialism and anarchy.[43] In the 1880s and 1890s it was clear to both Monsell and Carson that Home Rule would not merely restore the old Irish Parliament at College Green, but would result in the demise of the Ascendancy and the prevailing social system. Accordingly, the only guarantee of stability and the rule of law was the preservation of the Union.

Again, it may seem puzzling that Monsell could be a life-long Liberal and yet break with the party in 1886 and align himself with the Tories, whom he had abhorred for so long. In fact, Monsell's Liberalism and Unionism were closely intertwined, as he believed that the role of the Irish Liberal élite was to negotiate with the British state on behalf of their fellow- citizens.[44] Thus, the purpose of Monsell's major policy statements to the Commons following the Fenian rebellion was to bring Ireland's legitimate grievances before the bar of Parliament and to warn his fellow MPs that failure to deal with them would fatally undermine the Union (and the position of the Irish élite in particular).[45] Accordingly, when in 1886 Monsell had to choose between adhering to the Liberal party or to the Unionist cause, he chose the latter. He did not see himself as abandoning his Liberal principals, but rather being true to them. Liberal, loyal patriotic Irishmen were by definition Unionists, he believed, and he would have agreed with Jonathan Parry's contention that 'the Liberals were a *British* party, a genuinely *Unionist* force committed to the integration of all parts of the United Kingdom [author's emphasis]'.[46] It is significant that Monsell in 1893 was described as 'a Roman Catholic Liberal Peer', when he denounced Home Rule in a most public fashion.[47]

The third strand in Monsell's ideology was his liberalism. Liberals believed that government should be carried on with the consent of the governed, and be responsive to public opinion. The state's function was to create the conditions within which individual liberty could find its fullest expression. It was there to make laws, not to meddle in the economy, or direct people's lives. Liberals believed in freedom of speech, of worship, of association, and of the press.[48] Liberalism was the dominant political force of Victorian Britain.[49] Liberals saw government as a matter of reconciling different classes and interest groups within the political nation.[50] Monsell's whole career was devoted to realising this ideal. In 1847 he had been a member of the Irish Council, which had as its aims, 'to combine Irishmen of every grade and section of opinion – to watch over and assert the rights and interests of our common country – to mirror its wants and wishes – to create, foster and develop a sound Irish public opinion, irrespective of party'.[51] In 1861 Monsell described the principles of the Liberal party as being 'liberty; a clear stage and no favour; absolute and entire equality, civil and religious'.[52] In 1893 he declared that his political aim for half a century had been 'to raise up my fellow countrymen that were then downtrodden, and give them every advantage and every privilege that the citizens of the rest of the United Kingdom enjoy'.[53] He worked throughout his career for civil and religious equality, and upheld the classic Liberal freedoms – of speech, of religion, the freedom to engage in political activity.

Monsell adhered to all the chief tenets of British Liberalism at this period.[54] First, the Liberals were a British (and a genuinely) Unionist party committed to the integration of all the components of the United Kingdom, and of course Monsell was a lifelong Unionist.[55] Secondly, the Liberals wanted open politics, and were quick to respond to popular grievances.[56] Monsell was particularly aware of his role as the standard-bearer and representative of the Irish Catholic masses, bringing their grievances before Parliament to obtain redress. Thirdly, Liberals were opposed to government by class, a religious faith or interest.[57] Monsell liked to present himself as representing all the people, boasting of the all-party support which he always claimed to enjoy.[58] Finally, Liberalism was the party of religious pluralism. Monsell was a strong advocate of religious toleration, on practical as well as moral grounds. On 17 July 1863 he quoted the views of his friend Lacordaire in the House of Commons, which expressed his own opinion on the subject: 'the public conscience will always repel the man who asks for exclusive liberty, or forgets the rights of others, for exclusive liberty is but privilege, and liberty, forgetful of the rights of others is nothing but treason ... so Catholics, know this well, if you want liberty for yourselves, ask it for all men under Heaven.'[59]

While the Liberals claimed to represent all classes and creeds, they were not classless. Parry writes that they believed 'that the possession of property, character and wisdom was an invaluable asset in leadership, both nationally and locally ... [and] that civilisation depended on the maintenance of social ranks'.[60] Monsell favoured the secret ballot and felt that the rulers had to govern with the consent of the governed, but like Palmerston, Russell and Gladstone he was in no sense a democrat, still less a socialist. On 19 April 1856 he told Newman that 'we want Irish MPs who are gentlemen. The moral weight of a gentleman is far greater than that of an able man who is not presentable and has not moral weight'; and on 25 April 1856 he informed Newman that he had in mind 'such men as Mr Meagher and Stephen De Vere as Lord Castlerosse and Mr Devereux', who 'unlike agitators or place hunters give moral weight to our cause in Parliament'.[61]

However, Liberals also opposed the notion that possession of property alone made a natural leader.[62] Good political leadership required other qualities, including 'breadth of popular sympathy, self confidence, courage and disinterestedness, and a cultured understanding of the relation between the present and the past, developed through the study of history, literature, theology and perhaps science'.[63] In 1861 Monsell stated that the leader of a party 'has a number of earnest yet sometimes diverging convictions [i.e. interest groups] to fuse together into one whole by compromise'.[64] A leader lacking the above qualities would not be successful, nor would he long remain a leader. Monsell saw himself as being in the 'long Whig/Liberal tradition of familiarity with intellectual, scientific and theological thinking and literary and historical culture'.[65] He was one of the few Irish politicians of the time who considered himself an intellectual, but then, of course, he sprang from a particularly cultured milieu in the Shannon Estuary.[66] His speeches and writings are full of statistics, quotations from literature, both classical and modern, historical references and other signs of an educated, enlightened and modern mind at work. While he was not an intellectual in the sense that even Russell and Gladstone can be so classified, he was a well-read, well-informed man of considerable breadth of culture. A striking example of this is his membership of the Statistical and Social Enquiry Society of Ireland, which he joined in 1865.[67] Founded in 1847 as the Dublin Statistical Society, this body drew its membership from the political and intellectual élite of Ireland and dealt with subjects such as jurisprudence, social science including education, political economy, public health, sanitary reform and statistics. One of its main purposes was the promotion of social, political and law reform by means of legislation. Monsell delivered two papers to the society and served as its president from 1872 to 1875.[68]

Above all, a successful Liberal politician responded to the trends of the time and was flexible, pragmatic and free of doctrinaire or rigid beliefs.[69] Monsell was a pragmatist – reform should be continuous and gradual and problems should be dealt with as they arose. Violence and revolution were to be deplored. Monsell's pragmatism was similar to that of O'Connell. He was prepared to take what was on offer, instead of holding out for an unreasonably large concession. This pragmatism brought him into conflict with more doctrinaire figures, such as Cardinals Manning and Cullen, over such issues as education, oaths and religious toleration. Monsell was always a skilled and cunning politician. His flexibility and acute reading of public opinion brought about his election to Parliament in 1847, and kept him there for the next quarter of a century. In his article 'Catholic policy', he articulates his political realism throughout: 'generosity is not the distinguishing characteristic of political parties'; for the Irish people 'politics are no question of abstract speculation'. The important issue to them is 'whether Ireland is to be governed by the representatives of the Irish nation, or by the representatives of the Protestant squirarchy'; 'in this country, no government can long remain in office that does not represent popular opinion', and 'no party, we may be quite sure, will deal justly by us [i.e. the Irish Catholics] from any exuberance of affection for us'.[70] Among the best examples of his astute exercise of political judgement were his decision to steer clear of the Irish Brigade, and thus give himself the option of taking office under Aberdeen, and his perception that in 1874 he could no longer hold his Limerick seat and would be wise to accept a peerage.

Liberals were committed to efficient and cheap government.[71] Many were influenced by the utilitarian philosophy of Jeremy Bentham, which taught that all institutions should be subjected to searching analysis and made more efficient and economical. Liberals wanted to save money and stamp out corruption and incompetence in government. Again, this task was approached with pragmatism and common sense. Monsell believed in a *laissez-faire* economic policy in general, but was prepared to countenance significant government intervention if necessary. Thus, in the 1850s he extended the state's involvement in the manufacture of armaments under pressure from the needs of the British war effort in the Crimea. In the 1860s he became the leading advocate of the nationalisation of the Irish railways, as he believed that this would be the single greatest means of stimulating the Irish economy. He was also a passionate advocate of the recruitment of civil servants by competitive examination. Hard on the heels of the Northcote–Trevelyan report of 1853, he introduced the concept into the Royal Military Academy at Woolwich in 1855 and worked for it tirelessly in every department in which he held office. He also advocated competitive examinations in the education sphere to measure the amount of government funding that should be paid to schools (the 'payment by results' system).

Education was one of Monsell's chief interests throughout his public life. Indeed, the nineteenth century saw a huge increase in the provision of education for the mass of the people in large areas of the developed world, which led to frequent church–state clashes, especially involving the Catholic Church. Monsell approached the issue both as a committed Christian and as a Liberal. While still a Protestant, he had already made a major contribution as one of the founders of St Columba's College, but his conversion to Catholicism, if anything, made him even more determined to work for the provision of Christian teaching for everyone. In 1861 he told the Catholic Young Men's Society of Newcastle West, County Limerick that education should not exclude religion.[72] He also spoke of 'a pearl beyond all price, the blessings of an education through which, as a golden thread, religion is intertwined'; while a secular system 'has an absolute irreligious tendency', leading ultimately to a drastic decline in society's standards. 'Domestic charities will languish ... natural sympathies will be deadened, patriotism will lead to place-hunting, and a universal cold reign of selfishness will prevail.'[73]

As a Liberal, Monsell saw the spread of education as being essential for spiritual revival and social stability in society.[74] Both religious and educational institutions focused on the development of morality and social responsibility in the population. Indeed, he believed 'the extension of education to be the most important social reform of all, in helping men to help themselves'.[75] He deplored the Government exercising a monopoly in education, such as that established in France by Napoleon when he founded the *Universitie* (in effect the Ministry for Education) in 1808. 'With us, on the contrary, government interference in education is jealously limited,' he wrote in 1863, 'we love liberty too much to allow the government to give a direction to opinion ... true moral training can be given only by family or religious influences.'[76] However, the state's involvement was necessary, and indeed beneficial, as Monsell recognised when he frequently praised the Irish National Schools system. In 1874 he described the primary schools as having 'conferred greater good on Ireland than any other institution founded there by the Imperial Parliament'.[77]

Monsell believed that 'ignorance is the soil in which agitation flourishes' and that a sound, moral, religious education was the best antidote to irreligion and revolution, while simultaneously it promoted economic regeneration and social mobility.[78] He thought that the superior educational system of Scotland was a major factor in her economic growth, and Ireland had need of a much more effective industrial and technical education. Monsell believed that the mass of the Irish people suffered from educational disadvantages, which stunted the economic growth of the country, as well as causing them to be socially hampered and hindered.[79] He saw that education led to greater social mobility and equality of opportunity and praised the Scottish universities, for

> you will find among the university students in large numbers, the sons of clothiers, stationers, butchers, bakers, blacksmiths, shoemakers, carpenters, masons, farm servants, labourers; and as the necessary result, you will find Scotchmen of humble extraction thriving and prosperous all over the world. If we want to compete with them, we must imitate their example.[80]

Monsell's liberal vision of the benefits that education could confer on both the nation and the national economy has a decidedly modern look to it.

John Henry Newman was not a major political philosopher, but nevertheless he had a significant influence on Monsell's political development.[81] Newman, like Monsell, had started out as a Tory, but even though he ceased to be one, he remained a conservative at heart.[82] Nevertheless, he came to believe in many of the central positions of political liberalism, while always remaining a staunch opponent of religious liberalism, which he defined as the belief that there is 'no positive truth in religion, but that one creed is as good as another'.[83] Newman favoured freedom of discussion and of religious belief and practice and preferred the modern liberal state to any other form of government in the past or present.[84] He worshipped the British constitution and described it as 'one of the greatest of human works'.[85] He thought that the State's role should be a limited one, and that public opinion was paramount in determining legislation and the pace of reform. At the same time, he had a vision of a society with a stable class structure and considered himself to belong to the cultured, educated upper class.[86]

In all of these beliefs, Monsell resembled his mentor Newman. Whether or not their views happily coincided, or that Monsell consciously imitated Newman, is a moot point. As Kenny writes, Newman was close 'to the general political thought of his fellow countrymen at that age'.[87] However, Monsell was certainly a political disciple of Newman in some of his ideological positions. Newman was strongly on the side of the Liberal Catholics, and influenced Monsell accordingly. In particular, he played an important role in forming Monsell's attitude towards religious toleration, as can be seen in relation to Spain in 1863.[88] Both Newman and Monsell believed that religion flourished when it was not strangled by the embrace of a state church.[89] Newman placed a great emphasis on education, and Monsell was to be his close collaborator in the Catholic University in the 1850s and his supporter in the controversy over the proposed Catholic Hall at Oxford in the 1860s. It is also possible to trace much of Monsell's political pragmatism to the almost cynical realism in politics which was so typical of Newman.[90] There was a 'smack of thoroughly British empiricism about Newman' that also characterised Monsell's entire career in public life, a sort of principled pragmatism.[91]

'Newman's argument that ideas do not remain static, but develop' can be seen in Monsell's changing approach to many of his general beliefs, including his Unionism, his Liberalism and his Liberal Catholicism.[92] The federalist of 1847, the Liberal of 1868 and the Liberal Unionist of 1886 represented different phases of Monsell's ideological development. Such apparent inconsistencies, however, did not reflect any shift in fundamental principles, which is an application of Newman's 'Development of Christian Doctrine' applied to the secular sphere.[93] Finally, there is Newman's emphasis on the idea of national character, the belief that it was possible to distinguish the nation from the state.[94] This closely approximates to Monsell's conception of his own Irishness, and while it was not the origin of Monsell's theory, it powerfully reinforced it.[95] Yet, Newman and Monsell also differed, chiefly in their attitudes to social problems. Newman lacked a social conscience and was never really interested in these matters, in contrast to Monsell, who was always a social reformer.[96] It must be concluded that while Newman was the major religious influence on Monsell, he was only one of several influences on his political ideology.

Monsell's Liberalism had a different flavour to that of a British politician, due to his being an Irish Catholic. In nineteenth-century Ireland the Liberals were chiefly defined by anti-Toryism.[97] During the 1830s and 1840s they benefited from their alliance with the followers of O'Connell, and as Hoppen writes, 'after 1847, the activities of Government ministers and sporadic help from England constituted just about the whole extent of national Liberal organisation in Ireland'.[98] In an age of loose party organisations, and local autonomy in constituencies, the Irish Liberals were particularly poorly organised. Although they enjoyed a period of supremacy that coincided exactly with Monsell's period in the Commons (1847–74), their strength was illusory. In fact, the Irish Liberal party was little more than an 'official party' and survived largely because Liberal administrations were almost always in office between 1846 and 1874, and thus Liberal Viceroys and Chief Secretaries provided the electrical machinery money and patronage to keep the Irish party in existence.[99] The only periods of non-Liberal rule were the Aberdeen Coalition of 1852–5 (in which Liberals had to play second fiddle to the Peelites) and the short-lived Tory administrations of 1852, 1858–9 and 1866–8. Nevertheless, the Irish Tories were formidable antagonists, and they had a very able, tireless and efficient organiser in the person of Viscount Naas, later the sixth Earl of Mayo (1822–72). As Chief Secretary in each of the three Tory administrations of this period, he forced the feeble Liberals on the defensive, and in the 1859 general election even won the majority of Irish seats for his party. From this low point of 50 seats, the Liberals staged a recovery in the late 1860s, culminating in Gladstone's victory in the 1868 general election, when they won 66 seats in Ireland. The negative governmental Liberal party of the period 1847–67 had been succeeded by the more dynamic Gladstonian campaign of reform in the fields of land, education and religion, but even this was a mirage that soon melted away. It was always a strong probability that the Catholic electorate would eventually be diverted away from this weak party, whose only strength lay in government patronage and in the intense localism of the 1850s and 1860s, so it was not surprising that it collapsed ingloriously in the 1870s. Home Rule emerged as a much more exciting alternative, while the Irish Liberal party was deprived of official largesse during the Disraeli administration of 1874–80, the longest period of Tory rule since 1830.[100]

However, there was always a fundamental difference between the British and the Irish Liberals.[101] In the 1830s and 1840s, while O'Connell saw himself and his movement as part of the Liberal party, the British Liberals generally did not regard them as colleagues.[102] Indeed, the Irish Liberal party was overshadowed by O'Connell and his party throughout this period. Then, the Famine caused the Irish Liberals to become bitterly critical of the policies pursued by their British colleagues in office, while the British Liberals despised the Irish as unprincipled, obstructionist and corrupt.[103] Thus, the Papal Aggression crisis of 1850–1 did not create a rift between the British and Irish Liberals, but merely widened the existing gap between them.[104] In addition, the Irish Liberal MPs were notoriously undisciplined and unreliable, even by the lax standards of the 1850s and 1860s.[105]

Even during their Indian summer of 1847–74, the Irish Liberals suffered from the indifference and often the contempt of their British colleagues. The most notorious examples of this were the anti-Catholic campaigns of 1850–1 and 1859–60, which caused many of the Irish Liberals (including even Monsell to some degree) to become estranged from the British party. The only Liberal Prime Minister who proved satisfactory to Monsell and his Irish colleagues was Gladstone, and his reform package proved to be too little, too late. Nevertheless, Monsell was never tempted to desert the Liberals by their insensitive policies, although he did feel frustrated that neither of the two main British parties was really friendly to his cause. He always opposed the Tory party, as it upheld the Established Church and supported Orange Ascendancy.[106] Nevertheless, the Liberal party of the 1860s, when Palmerston was Prime Minister and the younger Sir Robert Peel was Chief Secretary, was to prove difficult to reconcile with Monsell's core beliefs. 'It is quite true that the Tories are faithful, and the Liberals unfaithful to their principles when they wrong us,' he wrote in 1861.

> Carry out the principles of the one party to their logical results and we have all we ask for, or desire – liberty; a clear stage and no favour; absolute and entire equality, civil and religious ... Tory principles on the other hand, involve privilege – exceptional favour towards the Established Church. Church and King is the idea on which the one party subsists, civil and religious liberty the very life blood of the other.[107]

It was the question of Irish university education which was to break up the alliance between the British Liberals and the Irish Catholic Church in 1873.

The Irish Liberal party comprised three main divisions: the great aristocratic Whigs, who were usually Anglican; Presbyterians and Nonconformists; and the Irish Catholic Whigs who in turn consisted of three sub-groupings – old Catholic Unionist gentry, who had survived the Penal Laws; former Repealers; and Oxford converts.[108] The Catholic Whigs emerged in the period 1846–50, following the Peelite split, the collapse of Repeal and the conversion of the Irish Tractarians, and flourished in the 1850s and 1860s, when the differences between parties were slight, party discipline weak, localism rampant and governments changed frequently. They were never a tightly organised party, but rather a connection, an interest or a loosely organised body of like-minded individuals. They were also fortunate that the period 1847–74, which was framed by the two great nationalist movements of O'Connellism and Parnellism, was marked by a strong revival of the power of the Irish landed élite both economically and politically. The landlords benefited from the mid-century economic boom, the absence of a major nationalist agitation and the dominance of localist and deferential politics. A striking manifestation of these trends was the vitality of the Irish Tory Party during these decades.[109] This Indian summer of the landlords enabled both the Catholic Whigs and William Monsell to enjoy a prominence that would have been difficult in the 1830s and 1840s and unthinkable after the 1870s.[110]

The ideological origins of the Irish Catholic Whigs may be traced to the period 1800 to 1830, when a number of leading intellectuals and political figures formulated a belief system that for the first time in Ireland combined adherence to traditional British Protestant Liberal values with staunch loyalty to Roman Catholicism.[111] These included Daniel O'Connell (1775–1847), John McHale (1791–1881), Archbishop of Tuam, Thomas Moore (1779–1852), poet and writer, and Sir Thomas Wyse (1791–1862), a prominent Catholic Whig statesman, educator and diplomat. During the ascendancy of O'Connell in the 1830s and 1840s, the Catholic political classes were divided between the powerful Repealers and the less influential Catholic Whigs, and the erudite but rigid Wyse, who was briefly and unhappily married to a niece of Napoleon, was probably the most prominent of the latter.[112] After 1847 the situation was reversed and while the Independent Oppositionists upheld the O'Connellite tradition, the Catholic Whigs (with the exception of the period 1851–4) dominated Irish Catholic politics until 1874. In many respects they were O'Connell's intellectual descendants, Repealers who did not support Repeal.

Nevertheless, they had a definite programme. They tried to improve the life of the Irish masses with modest remedial legislation.[113] Like the rest of the Irish Liberals, the Catholic Whigs saw themselves as representing the masses to the British government, and making the Union more acceptable to the Irish Catholic population.[114] The Catholic Whigs were moderate, élitist and could never rely on their numerical strength. Their chief function was to provide leadership for their less articulate fellow-countrymen. Their actions were local and usually quite informal, each constituency performing the task with a minimum of regional or national organisation.[115] Their chief strengths were that they were Irish-born and Catholic, and could therefore identify with the masses. Horgan has claimed

> that an Irish Catholic oligarchy was in the making, they identified with the Union, intermarried freely with the British and Irish Protestant aristocracy and among themselves while continually striving for complete equality. Here was a solid foundation upon which to build a genuine Anglo-Irish union – a sympathetic native élite still in touch with the aspirations of the majority, and able to interpret those demands to British legislators and administrators.[116]

Monsell emerged as the leader of the Catholic Whigs in Parliament due to two strengths: his firm power base in County Limerick, one of the strongholds of Catholic Whiggery, and his unrivalled connections with both the Irish Catholic bishops and successive British ministers. His policy was one of firmly and continuously campaigning for moderate reforms, in order to bring about full civil and religious equality for Catholics. Thus he totally opposed the policy espoused by Independent Opposition in the 1850s and Home Rule in the 1870s, of staying aloof from connection with British parties. In 1864 he told his friend and confidante O'Hagan that the idea of a separate Irish party in Parliament was 'powerless for good. It will raise expectations never to be realised, and above all, it will be a sort of protest against the sound policy that of attaching ourselves to a party in the state, making ourselves useful to it, and so getting it, not as a matter of compact or coercion, but freely and willingly to support our oaths and university question'.[117] In practice, of course, this could only mean alliance with the British Liberals.

The Catholic Whigs also differed from Independent Opposition and the Home Rule party in their attitude to office-holding. While the latter groups declined to hold office under any British administration, the Catholic Whigs (like Daniel O'Connell before them) believed that one of the most important and visible signs of the attainment of civil and religious equality by the Catholic community was their appointment to public office. For most of the nineteenth century the majority of Irish office-holders were Protestants. Monsell considered this a glaring inequality and wanted to have more Catholics appointed as civil servants, officers in the armed forces, judges and indeed Cabinet ministers. Catholics should strive to obtain as much official patronage as possible, as it both advanced their civil rights and gave them a stake in the establishment, thereby strengthening the Union. Political ambition and the advancement of the Catholic cause could thus be neatly combined. Monsell himself was very ambitious and assiduously sought office in successive Liberal administrations, but failed to realise his great ambition of a seat in the Cabinet. It is not surprising that political opponents sometimes accused him of being a place-hunter and of toadying to the British Liberals.

It is easy to overstate the potential of the Catholic Whigs to become the new ruling class in Ireland, but their political demise became inevitable after the rise of Home Rule made them as politically vulnerable as their Protestant fellow-Liberals. Their collapse in the 1874 general election was followed a decade later by their defection to the Conservatives, at the time of the first Home Rule bill. Socially, too, they were unable to survive the rise of the Catholic bourgeoisie following the Land War, and the very completeness of their failure is reflected in their almost total disappearance from the Irish historical memory. [118]

As well as being a Catholic Liberal, Monsell was also a Liberal Catholic.[119] The Liberal Catholic movement in both France and Germany had arisen as an offshoot of Ultramontanism.[120] Its founder Hugues Felicite Robert de Lamenais (1782–1854) campaigned for education free from the control of a secular state, freedom of the press, freedom of association, freedom of conscience, and devotion to Rome as the principle both of unity and of ecclesiastical liberty. His vision of an independent, regenerated church had much in common with the contemporary Tractarian movement, and in particular both groups opposed a state-controlled church.[121] Lamennais wanted to bring the laity into active defence of the Church, and he began the great task of reconciling Catholicism and democracy. However, he incurred the censure of the Papacy, and eventually broke with the Church completely in circumstances of great bitterness on both sides.[122]

Nevertheless, the movement that he founded continued to grow and prosper and his rupture with the Church was led by his two chief disciples, the Dominican priest Jean Baptiste Henri Lacordaire (1802–61) and Charles Forbes Rene, Comte de Montalambert (1810–70), who was a politician, publicist, historian and author.[123] Montalambert was a member of the French parliament for most of the period 1837 to 1857, and as France's leading Liberal Catholic political figure, campaigned on two fronts: firstly, he tried to persuade Liberals that Catholics could be loyal to the Liberal political régimes that ruled France after 1830, and secondly, he sought to wean Catholics away from their attachment to the *Ancien Régime*. Above all, he wanted to train the Catholics to win their rights by parliamentary means.[124] Around 1850 Monsell first met Montalambert, and they became very close friends.[125] Although the Liberal Catholics of France were greatly influenced by O'Connell, they resembled the British Liberal party in being 'Liberal' but emphatically not democratic.

The chief aim of the French Liberal Catholics was to obtain what they called 'free education', namely freedom of secondary education from the strict control of the *Université*. In 1846, 140 deputies supporting Catholic schools and led by Montalambert were elected to the French parliament. Following the French Revolution of 1848, which had resulted in the establishment of the Second Republic, the Liberal Catholics became aligned to the 'Party of Order', a loose coalition of the conservative forces which organised itself to fight the general election of 1849. In December 1848 the conservatives brought about the election of Louis Napoleon Bonaparte (later Emperor Napoleon III), nephew of the great Napoleon, as President of France and in 1849 the Party of Order gained 500 out of 750 seats in the National Assembly. Soon after, Frederic Alfred Pierre, Comte de Falloux (1811–86), a leading Liberal Catholic and friend of Montalambert, was appointed Minister for Public Instruction. His *Loi Falloux* of March 1850 gave members of religious orders the right to open schools without requiring any further qualification, and introduced councils with strong clerical elements to control the *Université*. The restrictions on the total number of pupils allowed to attend Catholic secondary schools were abolished. However, the *Université* retained the monopoly of conferring degrees.[126]

This stunning victory was in some ways a pyrrhic one for the Liberal Catholics. It led to a sharp split developing with the Ultramontanes, so that the French Catholics became polarised into two increasingly hostile factions. Montalambert, Falloux and Lacordaire continued to be the most prominent Liberal Catholics. They were joined by Jacques Victor Albert, fourth Duc de Broglie (1821–1901), who belonged to one of France's greatest families and had a distinguished political career. He was French Ambassador to London 1871–2, Minister for Foreign Affairs 1873, Deputy Prime Minister and Minister for the Interior (1873–4) and twice Prime Minister in 1873–4 and 1877.[127] Among the French bishops, the leading Liberal Catholic was Felix Antoine Philibert Dupanloup (1802–78), Bishop of Orleans (1849–78).[128] At the same time the Ultramontanes acquired formidable leaders. Their chief among the episcopacy was Louis Francois Desire Pie (1815–80), who was Bishop of Poitiers (1849–80) and was created Cardinal in 1879. Louis Francois Veuillot (1813–83), a fiery and uncompromising journalist and writer, became editor of the newspaper *L'Univers* from 1843, and made it the organ of the Ultramontanes in France. The disputes between the two sides centred on their opposing philosophies concerning the role that the Church should play in the political and social life of the nation. The Ultramontanes denounced the *Loi Falloux* because it seemed to them insufficient in its tilt towards the Catholic Church. This fierce quarrel bedevilled the Church in France under the Second Empire of Napoleon III (1852–70).

The Liberal Catholic–Ultramontane split soon spread to the Catholic Church everywhere. The German Catholic revival had paralleled that in France, but it on the whole kept clear of politics.[129] The essential difference was that the revival took a critical and intellectual form in Germany, while in France it was a more social and political movement.[130] The German Liberal Catholics concentrated on the study of theology, the Bible and philosophy, and they demanded intellectual freedom for Catholics. From 1850 onwards they too split from the Ultramontanes. Their centre was at Munich, and their chief spokesman was the theologian and historian Johann Joseph Ignaz Von Dollinger (1799–1890), a friend of Monsell's. The feud between the two great parties also raged in England, and, to a much lesser degree, in Ireland.[131]

The Liberal Catholic movement, which had so much in common with the Tractarian movement, had obvious attractions for Monsell and his fellow Oxford converts, the third Earl of Dunraven and the de Vere brothers. It provided them with an ideology and a model of how a Catholic parliamentary body should operate that was untainted by O'Connell's Repeal movement. The chief difference between the Irish Liberal Catholics and the Irish Ultramontanes was that the former elevated their liberalism to a principle, while for the latter, operating in a parliamentary system, it was a necessary expedient.[132] Two other aspects of French and German Liberal Catholicism appealed to Monsell and his friends. Firstly, it was strongly anglophile, and both Dollinger and Montalambert, for example, idealised the English constitution and English culture.[133] Secondly, the French Liberal Catholics had shown how a successful Catholic parliamentary agitation could win 'freedom of education' and throw off the domination of a non-Catholic state bureaucracy over Catholic schools. The parallels with Ireland, and the lessons to be drawn from this example, were obvious.

Monsell soon became Ireland's leading Liberal Catholic, and favoured the Church reconciling itself to parliamentary government, freedom of thought and worship and religious toleration. Monsell believed that Christianity could survive and prosper only by embracing the modern world, and wanted to reconcile religion and science. In 1884 he stated that

> the marvellous discoveries that are being made from year to year in steam, chemistry and electricity magnify to our sense the material world so that it is always tending to hide from our perception the spiritual world ... Do not attempt to correct this process by diminishing your attention to science. Preserve the proper proportion, not by diminishing intellectual development, but by increasing spiritual culture.[134]

Besides the de Veres and Dunraven, the other principal Liberal Catholic in Ireland was David Moriarty (1814–77), who was Bishop of Kerry from 1856 to 1877 and who was a lone Liberal voice in the Irish hierarchy.[135] They were opposed to the Ultramontanism of Cardinal Cullen, and clashes between them became frequent in the 1860s, especially over the vexed issue of Catholic education.

All of this demonstrates Monsell's cosmopolitan world-view, which was both strikingly modern and not at all typical of his time and place. After 1800 Irish politicians, with some notable exceptions, did not tend to have a strong European identity, but rather inhabited an anglophone world centred on Ireland, Britain and the USA. Also, the British élite to which Monsell belonged tended to become more isolated from Europe as the nineteenth century progressed. The eighteenth century had been the age of French cultural supremacy in Europe, of the Grand Tour and of the reception in both Britain and Ireland of European fashions in art, architecture, costume and furniture. However, the nineteenth century became the age of England's supreme arrogance and England, not Europe was the loser.[136] J.H. Plumb has written that 'the maintenance of English ways, the insistence on the superiority of English ideas, led to a withdrawal from European culture as a whole, and England in the nineteenth century developed its art and its literature almost uninfluenced by foreign examples'.[137] Amongst the Protestant Anglo-Irish, this became even more marked due to their disproportionately large service in the British armed forces and their increasingly beleaguered belief in British superiority.[138] Similarly, the rising Catholic masses had strong ties with their emigrant kin in North America, Britain and Oceania, but little contact with the mainland of Europe. The Catholic religious orders, with their links to Rome and to continental Europe, remained the strongest link with the European mainland.

On the other hand, Monsell's world-view was more reminiscent of that of early modern Ireland, when the Irish diaspora had spread throughout Europe, and links with continental Catholicism were strong. His conversion to the Catholic Church had made him a member of a world-wide organisation, in contrast to the anglocentric Church of

Ireland, while his wealth and connections enabled him to travel widely on the Continent. Despite their superiority complex and insular tendencies, the British nobility formed part of an international French-speaking aristocracy.[139] 'The polite of every country seem to have but one character,' as a mid-eighteenth-century Englishman put it.[140] Monsell was a francophile fluent in the French language, and this gave him the *entree* into the entire cosmopolitan European and Europeanised élite. Interestingly, the élites of peripheral regions, such as Latin America, Russia and the Balkans, were among the most francophile of all, and in consequence Monsell (himself peripherally domiciled in the West of Ireland) was as at home in Paris as he was by the banks of the Shannon.

Three great world cities formed the capitals of Monsell's universe. Paris was the intellectual and cultural capital of the world in the nineteenth century, and Monsell, like so many others, succumbed to her charms.[141] During his frequent visits he witnessed the spectacular rebuilding of the city under the Second Empire in the 1850s and 1860s, the greatest work of urban planning in human history. He also became a familiar figure at one of the great salons of the time, that of Madame Swetchine.[142] The salon was a very French institution, a centre of discussion on such topics as art, literature, politics and religion. Of the three greatest salons in Paris of the first half of the nineteenth century, one was hosted by the French Madame Recamier and the other two by Russians, Princess de Lieven (actually a Baltic German) and Madame Swetchine. Anne Sophia Swetchine (1782–1857) was a Russian aristocrat and convert to Catholicism who had arrived in Paris in 1816 and made it her home in 1825. She resided in a mansion on the Rue Saint Dominique, in the very fashionable Faubourg Saint Germain, and hosted her salon there for some thirty years until her death. She was a strict Catholic but she favoured a Liberal monarchy, so it is not surprising that her salon should become a centre for the Liberal Catholics.[143] Monsell's close friends Montalambert, Falloux and Broglie were regular attenders, and he met them there frequently. It is a sign of the esteem in which Madame Swetchine held Monsell that she gave him the use of her private chapel for his second marriage.[144] In addition, Monsell became a very close friend of senior French clerics, including the charismatic Bishop Dupanloup (who was the illegitimate son of Prince Camillo Borghese, brother-in-law of the great Napoleon), the flamboyant Cardinal Charles Lavigerie (1825–92), who became Archbishop of Algiers and Primate of Africa, and the influential Cardinal Pie (perhaps somewhat surprising, in view of his Ultramontanism). The intellectual brilliance of Monsell's French friends was notable, as four of them were admitted to the forty-member *Academie Française*, the most prestigious cultural institution in

France, which at the time of writing has had only a total of 710 members since its foundation in 1635. These were Montalambert (1851–70), Dupanloup (1854–75), Falloux (1856–86) and Broglie (1862–1901), and interestingly all four were simultaneously members from 1862 to 1870.

Rome was another city that Monsell grew to love. He often stayed there for months at a time, and his familiarity with the city was such that he could casually remark in a letter to Newman, concerning a mutual acquaintance, that 'he does not speak French well enough to enjoy Roman society thoroughly'.[145] Also, he befriended the Pope himself.[146]'He was very intimate [with] Pius IX,' Aubrey de Vere told a correspondent at the time of Monsell's death, 'who often sent for him, and had long private conversation with him, without any ceremony.'[147] The troubles of the Pope and of the Church were matters of high priority for Monsell. In 1860 and 1861 he spoke on a number of occasions in Parliament, condemning the massacres of Christians in the Lebanon.[148] In 1863 he denounced Russian oppression of Catholic Poland.[149] Indeed, one of his last public interventions was a letter to the *Times* in 1893 concerning the slaughter of Catholics in Uganda.[150]

The third great city with which Monsell was familiar was London. As an MP, he was obliged to spend half of each year living there. The sittings of Parliament commenced in late January or early February, and continued until late July or early August, but sometimes there were additional sittings in October, November and December.[151] Monsell did not possess a town house in London, so he was obliged to live in rented accommodation during parliamentary sessions. At the beginning of his time in the Commons, he lived in Eaton Square, Belgravia, but in the late 1850s and the 1860s he found Mayfair (convenient to Parliament, and to the aristocratic heart of London) congenial.[152] Parliament usually met at 4.00 p.m., and sittings tended to last from seven to nine hours. The glittering London Season coincided with the sittings of Parliament, but Monsell was not a dedicated socialite, unlike his kinsman, the fourth Earl of Dunraven.[153] He did appear at Court in both London and Dublin, where the Castle Season attempted to emulate its London counterpart in pomp and splendour. Living in London for such long periods was very expensive, particularly as MPs were not paid an official salary until 1911. During his English sojourns, Monsell would meet his many friends there, including Gladstone, successive Dukes of Norfolk (particularly the fifteenth duke) and the successive Archbishops of Westminster, Wiseman and Manning.

However, Monsell did not allow these heady considerations to distract him from local affairs. A politician of the nineteenth century, like his modern counterpart, had to possess a strong local base, and Monsell never forgot this. He carefully cultivated his constituency, his correspondence is full of references to patronage, and he was not above pork barrel politics either. During his term as Postmaster-General (1871–3) he ordered the building of a new general post office in Limerick city. 'He also accelerated the local post, saw to it that the English mail reached Limerick between 12 and 1 o'clock instead of in the evening, and extended the telegraph throughout Ireland.'[154] Also, 'it was whilst he held office as Postmaster-General that he succeeded in getting us the first "fast train" we enjoyed between this [i.e. Limerick] and Dublin, and which for long years afterwards was known as "Mr Monsell's train"'.[155] As a popular and resident landlord, he was assured of a considerable personal following. In an age of open voting prior to 1872, the esteem of the Catholic clergy, and of neighbouring landlords, was of vital importance. Lord Dunraven's tenants were always turned out in large numbers to vote for his friend and brother-in-law Monsell.[156]

Monsell was also active on the local political scene.[157] He was a member of the Board of Superintendence of Limerick County Jail and of the Committee of Limerick County Hospital. He was one of the governors of the District Lunatic Asylum. The Poor Law Union and the Grand Jury were the most significant local authorities of the time. Monsell sat on the Board of Guardians of the Limerick Poor Law Union and served as chairman from 1844 to 1845 and from 1857 to 1882. He was frequently a member of the Limerick Grand Jury. He was appointed a Magistrate of County Limerick in 1840, and of County Clare in 1847, both appointments being for life. He was High Sheriff of County Limerick in 1835 and a Deputy Lieutenant from 1848 to 1871. Later he was to ascend to the heights of Colonel of the County Limerick Militia and Lord-Lieutenant and Custos Rotulorum of the city and county. His multiple incumbency of the most senior positions in local government confirmed his status as the leading figure in County Limerick for several decades.

It is instructive to examine Monsell's attitude to Ireland's social problems. In the 1840s he agreed with the prevailing economic wisdom (and the subsequent verdict of history) that the country's gravest difficulty lay in its huge poverty-stricken population. As already mentioned, his solution was to promote emigration to the British colonies.[158] This would have the twin desirable effects of clearing Ireland of its excess people, while providing Canada, Australia, New Zealand and South Africa with the labour force that they needed so greatly. Ireland's difficulty was the Empire's opportunity.[159] When the surplus millions were thus removed, it would be possible to consolidate the many smallholdings in the country into economically viable farms. At the same time, a major investment would need to be made in Irish agriculture. Monsell saw the Encumbered

Estates legislation as providing the means by which this would be brought about. Like many other commentators at the time, he entertained unrealistically high hopes of the benefits that these measures would confer on Irish agriculture.[160] He was also a strong advocate of agricultural education, which he promoted in the National School attached to his property at Tervoe.[161]

In 1844 Monsell told the Devon Commission then investigating Irish landlord–tenant relations that a land agent's duties 'upon a well managed estate consist in looking after the condition and welfare of tenants'.[162] He was always a benevolent and improving landlord who resided among his tenants.[163] He firmly believed that there should be a partnership between landlord and tenants, although the latter would naturally have a subordinate role. He practised the three Fs (fair rent, fixity of tenure, and free sale), which were the standard demand of tenants' groups, until the 1880s saw the demand for peasant proprietorship come to the fore. With regard to the first F, he did not increase his rents at all between the 1830s and the 1880s.[164] His tenants enjoyed fixity of tenure, for he evicted no one during his entire fifty-eight years as owner of the Monsell estates.[165] Finally, he allowed his tenants to sell their farms, subject to his own approval. He tended to give his tenants 31-year leases, rather than the more common one-year tenancy agreement.[166] During times of distress, he forgave arrears of rent, and took it upon himself to repay Board of Works loans for improvements taken out by his tenants.[167]

Monsell preached enlightened landlordism as well as practising it. He wanted the Government to promote the three Fs by encouraging landlords to grant long leases and by legislating for tenant right (which usually meant compensating tenants for improvements carried out on their farms when they departed from same).[168] However, he did not believe in the abolition of the landlord system, of which he himself was a part. He was horrified at the Land League Campaign in the 1880s and 1890s, which demanded the division of the landlords' estates among their tenants, which he regarded as little better than communism.[169] However, he did favour a limited amount of peasant proprietorship in the event of a sale of an estate, and wanted to see some estates sold to the tenants, so as to give a greater proportion of the population a stake in the status quo. However, he did not see this as leading to the complete disappearance of the landlord system.[170] Nevertheless, he was a harsh critic of tyrannical landlords, and in 1861 he fiercely condemned the notorious Glenveagh evictions in County Donegal.[171] He believed that it was the misconduct of a minority of abusive landlords that had created the necessity for Gladstone's Land Acts of 1870 and 1881.

It was alleged by Alexander Somerville (1811–85), a Scottish writer on social reform who had spent time in Ireland at the time of the Great Famine, that Monsell was a bad landlord who had cleared many tenants from his estates, resulting in their livings as paupers in Limerick city.[172] Somerville was a respected witness, whose comments cannot be lightly dismissed, but on this occasion his information was based 'on the authority of a poor-law commissioner', who is not named.[173] Significantly, the evidence to the contrary is overwhelming, as the unanimous testimony of Monsell's contemporaries, including nationalists and tenants' representatives, was that he was a kindly and benevolent landlord. The folk memory of Cratloe, County Clare, records that during the famine he 'gave seven pounds to each householder who left [1852 and for years after] [*sic*]. If they remained, he did not press them in any way or leave a process at any man's door.'[174] In 1880 William Bolster, a tenant of Monsell who was also an active member of the Land League, testified to the Bessborough Commission that 'Mr Monsell was always in favour of the tenant.'[175] In addition, he is still remembered as a 'good landlord' and an honoured figure in the folk memory of his native Clarina.

Monsell's strong devotion to the Catholic Church dominated his entire life.[176] He attended Mass daily and had a private chapel in Tervoe House, where the Blessed Sacrament was reserved, by special permission of the Pope, a rare honour that had also been conferred on Daniel O'Connell. When in London, Monsell assisted at Mass each morning in the fashionable Jesuit Church, on Farm Street in Mayfair. He belonged to several religious sodalities, including the Third Order of St Francis. His zeal manifested itself in his many charitable acts. In Clarina he granted a house to the local Catholic curate, and he took a close interest in the local National Schools, which he had built and of which he was manager.

His influence on the religious life of Limerick city was enormous.[177] He was a close friend of three successive bishops of Limerick: John Ryan (who held office 1828–64), George Butler (bishop from 1864 to 1886), and Edward Thomas O'Dwyer (who ruled from 1886 to 1917). The first two were Catholic Whigs (although Butler was later to reluctantly declare for Home Rule), while O'Dwyer, though he always declared himself a Home Ruler, was also perceived to have much sympathy with the Ascendancy.[178] Dr Butler was appointed co-adjutor Bishop of Limerick in 1861 and succeeded Bishop Ryan in 1864. Roantree has drawn attention to the important role that Monsell played in Butler's appointment in 1861, by making representations in his favour to Archbishop Cullen and Cardinal Barnabo, Prefect of the Congregation for the Propagation of the Faith.[179] Bishop Moriarty of Kerry was also a close friend and a convinced Unionist. In 1849 Monsell was instrumental in bringing the Good Shepherd nuns to Limerick.[180] In 1853 he collaborated with Bishop Ryan in introducing the Redemptorist Order, who at the time of writing have played an enormous role in the spiritual life of Limerick for over 150 years.[181] In 1861, as Chairman of the Limerick Board of Poor Law Guardians, he introduced the Sisters of Mercy to what is now St Camillus Hospital. This was the first time that Catholic religious sisters had been appointed as nurses in a public hospital, and it paved the way for the subsequent and enormous expansion of their role in this area all over Ireland.[182] Monsell was closely associated with the construction of St John's Cathedral (which was built between 1856 and 1861), the architect of which, Philip Charles Hardwicke (1820–90), was a Tractarian and a friend of the third Earl of Dunraven.[183] In 1856 Monsell donated to the cathedral a magnificent white marble statue of the Virgin Mary by the Italian sculptor Giovanni Benzoni (1809–73).[184] Pope Pius IX instituted indulgences for all those who should recite prayers in front of this statue. Monsell also donated the huge statue of St John the Baptist (to whom the cathedral is dedicated), which stands on the façade above the main entrance.

This ostentatious holiness was combined with a strict sense of morality and code of personal conduct. Monsell resembled Gladstone, O'Connell and many other contemporaries in his combination of scrupulous piety and political expediency (not surprisingly they were often accused of being hypocrites). Parry has written that 'Victorian politicians were as ambitious, cunning, vain, self-deluding, and inconstant as the general run of performers on the public stage have been, but none of this debarred them from having religious preconceptions.'[185]

Monsell emerges from contemporary sources as a rather solemn, stern figure, with his cultured English accent, tall imposing frame and formal clothes (he always dressed in the garb of a London gentleman, even when at Tervoe). However, this typical Victorian gentleman was a very warm family man. When his beloved wife Anna Maria died at the seaside resort of St Leonards in Sussex on 7 January 1855, he was devastated. He was now 42 years old, with no wife and no heir. In his grief he erected a Victorian Gothic memorial cross to his wife at Tervoe, the little village which the Monsells had built on their estate. In a typical example of the philanthropy of the times, he arranged that each year on the anniversary of Lady Anna Maria's death, alms to the value of £1 each were to be given to twenty poor widows. A rumour even began to circulate that he was about to enter the religious life.[186] Instead, during one of his frequent visits to France, Monsell was introduced to a young French noblewoman, Marie Louise Ernestine Berthe de Montigny (1835–90). Her father, Philippe Auguste Comte de Montigny-Boulanvilliers (1789–1866), was a noble of the *Ancien Régime* who had served in the *Grand Armee* and was decorated with the *Légion d'honneur*. The Comte was highly impressed by Monsell's gentle and noble character, and gladly consented when he asked for Berthe's hand in marriage. The large age gap between them (Monsell was 44 and Berthe was 22) did not seem to bother any of the parties, and they were married on 23 February 1857 in Madame Swetchine's private chapel.[187]

Monsell's second marriage was as happy as his first had been. Berthe was a pretty young woman, who quickly learnt to speak English. On 5 March 1858 she presented her husband with the long-awaited son and heir, Thomas William Gaston, later the second Lord Emly, who was born in Paris. A little girl, Mary Olivia, quickly followed in 1859, also born in France. Berthe brought renewed joy into her husband's life. She was quite as pious as he was, and introduced the new devotion to our Lady of Lourdes into her Irish home. The apparitions at Lourdes occurred in 1858, and Berthe erected the first Lourdes grotto built in Ireland at Tervoe, where it still stands, a place of local pilgrimage. Following her death in 1890, Monsell erected a memorial cross to her beside her beloved grotto.[188]

Berthe also strengthened and deepened his attachment to France. When the Comte de Montigny died in 1866, his inheritance was shared between his three daughters as he had no son. In this way Monsell came into an estate near the town of Montoire, in the Loire valley, which had been the playground of the kings and nobles of France for centuries. The estate contained the Château de Drouilly, which was to be Monsell's second home for the rest of his life and which remained in the ownership of the Monsell family until the middle of the twentieth century. He spent so much time there that he ceased to be a visitor and came to be a resident. Coincidentally, Monsell's friend and neighbour, Eyre Massey, third Baron Clarina (1798–1872), was married to Susan Elizabeth Barton (1810–86) of the Anglo-French wine-producing dynasty, whose estates were divided between Ireland and France. Nevertheless, intermarriage between the Irish and French élites was uncommon at this time, so Monsell came to have a fairly unusual and intimate relationship with France. Both of his children were born there, he was in France in 1870 during the Franco-Prussian War, and in 1880 he even described himself in the House of Lords as a French landlord.[189] His residence in Montoire also deepened his connections with French Liberal Catholicism, as Bishop Dupanloup lived sixty-five miles away in Orleans, while Falloux's residence in Angers was fifty miles distant. Bishop Pie's diocese of Poitiers also lay nearby, while Berthe's cousin Charles Amable de la Tour d'Auvergne Lauraguais (1826–79) was archbishop of the neighbouring diocese of Bourges (1861–79). Above all, Monsell gained a unique insight into the culture of another land. Montoire is in the department of Loire-et-Cher, and thus he witnessed at first hand the apex and decline of the Second Empire; the battle between clericals and anti-clericals under the Third Republic; and the effects that economic depression in the 1870s and 1880s had on landlord–tenant relations, which curiously paralleled contemporary developments in Ireland, for there was also constant friction between French landowners and their tenants.[190]

No account of Monsell the man would be complete without a brief account of his hobbies. He read a great deal and was reputed to have 'the widest and most profound knowledge of Catholic literature, and even of Catholic theology of any laymen in the United Kingdom'.[191] He could quote extensively and effortlessly from the voluminous works of Newman, while other favourite authors included Shakespeare, Scott, Byron, Dante, Vergil and Horace. His other chief pastimes included the typical gentry habits: he hunted and shot, and was a capital yachtsman, often sailing along the Shannon to visit his friends, the de Veres and the O'Briens. He enjoyed playing whist. He was also a compulsive club-man. He was a member of the Limerick County Club (now the Augustinian Priory) on O'Connell St, Limerick, and served on the committee. From 1854 he was a member of the Athenaeum Club, situated on London's Pall Mall, one of London's principal clubs and the one most frequented by intellectuals and literary figures.[192] In 1884 its membership included 37 bishops, 132 other clergy, 121 Peers and 47 MPs, so Monsell was in congenial company.[193] He also joined the Stafford Club, which was established by Cardinal Wiseman in 1853 as a meeting place for prominent lay Catholics. Its original premises were at 3 Stafford St, London, and it moved to Saville Row in 1862. In 1867 Monsell used the club as a venue to inflict a severe reverse on Archbishop Manning, at the time of the controversy over the establishment of a Catholic Hall at Oxford. After the Stafford ceased to exist in 1875, Cardinal Manning set up St George's Club as a replacement, which Monsell soon joined, but it also closed its doors within a short time.[194]

NOTES

1. Matthew Potter, 'A Roman Catholic Francophile Anglo-Irishman: William Monsell 1812–94', in Colin Graham and Leon Litvack (eds), *Ireland and Europe in the Nineteenth Century* (Dublin: Four Courts Press, 2006), pp.77–88.
2. Hansard, CXCIX, 1023 (1 March 1870).
3. Monsell to Aubrey de Vere, 19 February 1848, quoted in Ward, *Aubrey De Vere,* p.138.
4. Monsell to William Smith O'Brien, 31 October (1847?), Smith O'Brien papers, NLI, MS 440, no. 2160.

5. Hansard, CLXXXIX, 222 (26 July 1867).
6. William Monsell, 'Address of the Rt. Hon. William Monsell M.P. Vice-President at the Annual meeting of the Statistical and Social Enquiry Society of Ireland on 22nd January, 1869', in *Journal of the Statistical and Social Enquiry Society of Ireland*, 5, 36 (1868/1869), pp.53–69.
7. Ibid., *passim.*
8. Ibid., p.68.
9. Ridden, 'Making Good Citizens', pp.222–3.
10. Monsell, 'Address at the Annual Meeting of the Statistical and Social Enquiry Society', p.54.
11. Ridden, 'Making Good Citizens', p.218.
12. This was even more true of Sir Samuel Ferguson; see Denman, *Samuel Ferguson, passim.*
13. Adare to Monsell 22 May 1847, MP, NLI, MS 8318 (10).
14. Moriarty to Gladstone 28 November 1868 in Gladstone Papers, British Library, hereafter referred to as GP, Add. MS 44416.
15. Colley, *Britons,* pp.155–64.
16. Ibid., p.7.
17. Ibid., p.167.
18. Ridden, 'Making Good Citizens', pp.12 and 209.
19. Emly to Duffy, 2 January (1881), Gavan Duffy papers, NLI, MS 8005/23.
20. William Monsell, *A Roman Catholic Liberal Peer on the Irish Home Rule Bill – Speech by Lord Emly,* Vol. 3, no. 95 (Dublin: Irish Unionist Alliance Publications, 1894), p.2.
21. Colley, *Britons*, p.167.
22. Ibid., pp.155–70.
23. D.G. Boyce, 'Edward Carson (1854–1935) and Irish Unionism', in Brady, *Worsted in the Game*, p.149.
24. Ibid.
25. Ibid. pp.150 and 152–3.
26. Ibid. p.147.
27. Hansard, CLXXXIX, 223 (26 July 1867).
28. Ibid., 222–3.
29. Ibid., 223.
30. Ibid., 223.
31. Hansard, CXC, 1689 (16 March 1868).
32. Monsell to Newman, 31 August 1869, NP, NP/VC/VAT/1.
33. Hansard, CXC, 1696 (16 March 1868).
34. Boyce, 'Edward Carson', *passim,* and Ridden, 'Making Good Citizens', pp.214–17. For Spring Rice's use of the term, see Hansard, XXII, 1194 (24 April 1834).
35. Boyce, 'Edward Carson', pp.149–50.
36. Hansard, CXC, 1690 (16 March 1868).
37. Ibid., 1690.
38. Monsell to Newman, 3 March 1873, NP, NP/M/6.
39. Hansard, CCXCVIII, 1368 (8 June 1885).
40. Hansard, CXC, 1690 (16 March 1868).
41. Hansard, CCLIV, 1867 (2 August 1880).
42. Monsell, *A Roman Catholic Liberal Peer on the Irish Home Rule Bill*, p.2.
43. Ibid., p.1.
44. See Ridden, 'Making Good Citizens', pp.213–17 and 220–5.
45. For Monsell's policy statements to the Commons, see Hansard, CLXXXIX, 219–26 (26 July 1867) and Hansard, CXC, 1688–98 (16 March 1868).
46. Jonathan Parry, *The Rise and Fall of Liberal Government in Victorian Britain* (New Haven and London: Yale University Press 1993), p.4.
47. Monsell, *A Roman Catholic Liberal Peer on the Irish Home Rule Bill*, p.1.
48. For Liberalism, see Harry K. Girvetz, *From Wealth to Welfare: The Evolution of Liberalism* (Stanford, CA: Stanford University Press,1963) and W.A. Orton, *The Liberal Tradition. A Study of the Social and Spiritual Conditions of Freedom* (New Haven and London: Yale University Press, 1945).
49. Parry, *Rise and Fall of Liberal Government*. See also his *Democracy and Religion. Gladstone and the Liberal Party 1867–1875* (Cambridge: Cambridge University Press, 1986).

50. Parry, *Rise and Fall of Liberal Government*, p.1.
51. *Limerick Reporter*, 4 June 1847.
52. (William Monsell) 'Catholic Policy', in *The Rambler*, 5, ns 13 (May 1861), p.11.
53. Monsell, *Roman Catholic Liberal Peer on the Irish Home Rule Bill*, p.2.
54. Parry, *Rise and Fall of Liberal Government*, p.4.
55. Ibid.
56. Ibid.
57. Ibid.
58. (Monsell) 'Catholic Policy', p.11.
59. Hansard, CLXXII, 1006 (17 July 1863).
60. Parry, *Rise and Fall of Liberal Government*, p.5.
61. Monsell to Newman, 19 April and 25 April 1856, NP (N/1).
62. Parry, *Rise and Fall of Liberal Government*, p.5.
63. Ibid.
64. (Monsell) 'Catholic Policy', p.1.
65. Parry, *Rise and Fall of Liberal Government*, p.5.
66. K. Theodore Hoppen, 'Tories, Catholics and the General Election of 1859', in *Historical Journal*, 13, 1 (1970), p.60.
67. For the history of the Society, see Mary E. Daly, *The Spirit of Ernest Enquiry, The Statistical and Social Inquiry Society of Ireland 1847–1997* (Dublin: Institute of Public Administration, 1997).
68. For Monsell's involvement in the Society, see R.D. Collinson Black, *The Statistical and Social Enquiry Society of Ireland, Centenary Volume 1847–1947* (Dublin: Eason and Son, 1947), pp.79–80, 112, 147.
69. Parry, *Rise and Fall of Liberal Government*, p.6.
70. (Monsell) 'Catholic Policy', pp.6–7, 10, 11.
71. Parry, *Rise and Fall of Liberal Government*, p.14.
72. William Monsell, *Extract from a lecture delivered to the Young Men's Society of Newcastle on the 8th December, 1861, by W. Monsell. M.P., followed by some remarks by Dr Moriarty, Bishop of Kerry* (Limerick: privately published, 1861).
73. Ibid.
74. Parry, *Democracy and Religion*, p.105.
75. Ibid., p.116.
76. (William Monsell) 'University Education in Ireland', in *Home and Foreign Review*, 2 (January 1863), p.32.
77. Hansard, CCXX, 970 (3 July 1874).
78. Ibid.
79. Ibid.
80. Monsell, *Address to the Statistical and Social Enquiry Society*, p.69.
81. Terence Kenny, *The Political Thought of John Henry Newman* (London: Longmans, Green and Co., 1957).
82. Ibid., p.7.
83. Ibid., p.32.
84. Ibid., pp.127–65.
85. Ibid., p.178.
86. Ibid., pp.35 and 171.
87. Ibid., p.107.
88. Ibid., p.115.
89. Ibid., pp.118–26.
90. Ibid., p.3.
91. Ibid., p.23.
92. Ibid., pp.15 and 53–6.
93. Ibid., pp.14–15.
94. Ibid., p.80.
95. Ibid., p.59.
96. Ibid., pp.66–73.
97. Hoppen, *Elections Politics and Society in Ireland*, p.258.
98. Ibid., p.259.
99. Ibid.

100. George L. Bernstein, 'British Liberal Politics and Irish Liberalism, after O'Connell', in Steward J. Brown and David W. Miller (eds), *Piety and Power in Ireland 1760–1960. Essays in Honour of Emmet Larkin* (Notre Dame, IN: University of Notre Dame Press, 2000), pp.43–64.
101. Ibid., p.45.
102. Ibid., p.49.
103. Ibid., pp.50–1.
104. Ibid., p.44.
105. Ibid., p.273.
106. (Monsell) 'Catholic Policy', p.9.
107. Ibid., p.11.
108. Horgan, 'Irish Catholic Whigs in Parliament', p.9.
109. Andrew Shields, *The Irish Conservative Party, 1852–1868. Land Politics and Religion* (Dublin and Portland, OR: Irish Academic Press, 2007).
110. For the economic revival of the landlords, see W.E. Vaughan, *Landlords and Tenants in Mid-Victorian Ireland* (Oxford: Clarendon Press, 1994), and Dooley, *Decline of the Big House*, pp.30–4. For their political position in this period, see Boyce, *Nineteenth-Century Ireland*, pp.124–53 and Hoppen, *Elections Politics and Society in Ireland*, pp.89–170.
111. The development of this ideology is described in R.F.B. O'Ferrall, 'The Growth of Political Consciousness in Ireland 1823–1847: A Study in O'Connellite Politics and Political Education' (unpublished Ph.D thesis, Trinity College Dublin, 1978), pp.101–57.
112. See D.G. Paz, 'Sir Thomas Wyse (1791–1862)', in *Oxford DNB,* and J.J. Auchmuty, *Sir Thomas Wyse 1791–1862 The Life and Career of an Educator and Diplomat* (London: P.S. King and Sons, 1939).
113. Horgan, 'Irish Catholic Whigs in Parliament', p.21.
114. Ibid., p.22.
115. Ibid., p.43.
116. Ibid., p.95.
117. Monsell to O'Hagan, 16 October 1864, Teeling papers, hereafter referred to as TP, NLI, MS 17871(4.)
118. Among the few modern works that refer to them by name is Boyce, *Nineteenth-Century Ireland,* pp.61, 67-8.
119. For the Liberal Catholics see also Josef Altholz, *The Liberal Catholic Movement in England: The Rambler and its Contributors 1848–62* (London: Burns and Oates, 1962), and Hugh A. MacDougall, *The Acton–Newman Relations: The Dilemma of Christian Liberalism* (New York: Fordham University Press, 1962).
120. Ward, *William George Ward and the Catholic Revival*, pp.101–29.
121. MacDougall, *Acton–Newman Relations,* p.105.
122. Ibid. See also Alec Vidler, *Prophecy and Papacy: A Study of Lamennais, The Church and the Revolution* (London: SCM Press, 1954).
123. The best book in English on Montalambert is James C. Finlay, *The Liberal Who Failed*, (Washington, DC: Corpus Books, 1968).
124. Margaret Oliphant, *Memoirs of Count De Montalambert*, 2 vols (London: W. Blackwood and Sons, 1872).
125. For Montalambert and Ireland see Marc Serge Riviére, 'In Defence of Irish Catholicism: Charles de Montalambert's Aborted History of Ireland and Journal In Time', in Eamon Maher and Grace Neville (eds), *France–Ireland: Anatomy of a Relationship, Studies in History, Literature and Politics* (Frankfurt on Main: Peter Lang, 2004), pp.147–61, and Serge Riviére and Jenny O'Connor, 'The Representation of the Irish Cultural Landscape in the Journals of Montalambert (1830) and Tocqueville (1835)', in Eamon Maher, Eugene O'Brien and Grace Neville (eds), *Reinventing Ireland through a French Prism* (Frankfurt on Main: Peter Lang, 2007), pp.41–60.
126. Alfred Cobban, *History of Modern France*, (3 Vols (Harmondsworth: Penguin, 1961–2), Vol. 2, p.154.
127. Alan Grubb, *The Politics of Pessimism: Albert de Broglie and Conservative Politics in the Early Third Republic* (Newark, DE: University of Delaware Press, 1996).
128. There is no modern biography of Dupanloup in English, but see Margaret O'Gara,

Triumph in Defeat: Infallibility, Vatican I, and the French Minority Bishops (Washington, DC: Catholic University of America Press, 1988).
129. Ward, *William George Ward and the Catholic Revival*, p.127.
130. Ibid.
131. Ibid., pp.130–53. See also Altholz, *Liberal Catholic Movement in England* and MacDougall, *Acton–Newman Relations, passim.*
132. Roantree, 'William Monsell and the Catholic Question', pp.5–6, 169–70.
133. For the anglophilia of the French and German Liberal Catholics, see Matthias Buschkuhl, *Great Britain and the Holy See, 1746–1870* (Dublin: Irish Academic Press, 1982), pp.133–45.
134. Thomas J. Morrissey, 'Some Jesuit Contributions to Irish Education' (unpublished Ph.D. thesis, University College Cork, 1975), p.164.
135. See Kieran O'Shea, 'David Moriarty (1814–77): III Politics', in *Journal of the Kerry Archaeological and Historical Society*, 5 (1972), pp.86–102.
136. J.H. Plumb, *The First Four Georges* (London: Batsford, 1956), p.35.
137. Ibid.
138. See Michael McConville, *Ascendancy to Oblivion. The Story of the Anglo-Irish* (London and New York: Quartet Books, 1986), pp.242–52.
139. Philip Magnus, *King Edward VII* (Harmondsworth: Penguin, 1964), p.97.
140. Jonathan Dewald, *The European Nobility 1400–1800* (Cambridge: Cambridge University Press, 1996), p.3.
141. See Patrice Higonnet, *Paris: Capital of the World* (Cambridge, MA: Harvard University Press, 2002).
142. M.V. Woodgate, *Madame Swetchine (1782–1857)* (Dublin: Browne and Nolan, 1948), p.95. This remains the best work in English on this enigmatic woman. See also Anon., 'Madame Swetchine and her Salon', in *The Month*, 1 (July to December 1864), pp.163–76.
143. 'Madame Swetchine and her Salon', p.166.
144. Monsell to Dunraven, undated, (1857), DP, D3196/F/10, no. 40.
145. Newman, *Letters and Diaries*, Vol. 19, Monsell to Newman, 16 March 1861, pp.483-4. See also Monsell to Dunraven, 22 January (date uncertain), DP, D3196/F/10, no. 43.
146. Matthew Potter, 'Lord Emly and Pope Pius IX', in *Studies*, 92, 368 (winter 2003), pp.396–404.
147. Aubrey De Vere to Robin O'Brien, 26 April 1894, De Vere papers, Trinity College Dublin, hereafter referred to as DVP, MS 5053–4, no. 276.
148. Hansard, CLX, 1479–86 (17 August 1860); CLX, 1583–6 (20 August 1860); CLXI, 1229–31 (1 March 1861); CLXII, 250–2 (22 March 1861).
149. Hansard, CLXX, 1406–10 (24 July 1863).
150. *Munster News*, 21 April 1894.
151. Chris Cook and Brendan Keith, *British Historical Facts 1830–1900* (London: Macmillan, 1975), p.100.
152. See *Thom's Irish Almanac and Official Directory* (Dublin: Thom, 1844–80), 1848 to 1865 inclusive.
153. For the *beau monde* in London, see Leonore Davidoff, *The Best Circles. Society, Etiquette and the Season* (London: Croom Helm, 1973).
154. Cussen, 'Caleb Powell, High Sheriff of County Limerick, 1858, sums up his Grand Jury', p.420.
155. *Munster News*, 21 April 1894.
156. Caroline, Lady Dunraven to Lord Adare (August 1847), DP, D3196/E/7/9, and 'Tenants Votes County Limerick Election, 1859', D3196/F/5/12.
157. See *Thoms' Directory*, 1840 to 1883 inclusive.
158. Duffy, *To and From Ireland*, pp.79–105.
159. *Report on Colonisation. Minutes of Evidence 1847,* pp.197–216 and 231. Also, see Hansard, CIII, 145–8 (2 March 1849); CIV, 573–7 (20 April 1849).
160. Hansard, C, 105–9 (4 July 1848); C, 600–2 (20 July 1848); CIV, 573–7 (20 April 1849).
161. Hansard, CLV, 420 (25 July 1859).
162. *Evidence taken before the commissioners appointed to enquire into the occupation of land in Ireland* PP 1845 (20), hereafter referred to as Devon Commission, p.739, 26 August 1844.
163. *DNB*, Vol. 24, pp.1059–60.

164. *Report from Her Majesty's Commissioners of Enquiry into the Workings of the Landlord and Tenant (Ireland) Act, 1870 and the acts amending same*, PP 1881(18), hereafter referred to as *Bessborough Commission, Minutes of Evidence*, pp.676–7, 26 October 1880.
165. *Munster News*, 21 April 1894.
166. *Bessborough Commission. Minutes of Evidence*, pp.676–7.
167. Ibid., p.677.
168. Hansard, CLXXVI, 72–4 (21 June 1864); CLXXVII, 707 (24 February 1865); CLXXVIII, 617–18 (31 March 1865); CCLIV, 1867 (2 August 1880).
169. Hansard, CCLI, 416–17 (5 March 1880).
170. Hansard, CXC, 1693 (16 March 1868).
171. Hansard, CLXII, 849–50 (19 April 1861).
172. Alexander Somerville, *Letters from Ireland during the Famine of 1847* (edited by D.K.M. Snell) (Dublin: Irish Academic Press, 1994), pp.82–3.
173. Ibid., p.83.
174. Poirteir, *Famine Echoes*, p.199.
175. *Bessborough Commission. Minutes of Evidence*, 26 October 1880.
176. *Munster News*, 21 April 1894.
177. Ibid.
178. Fr Edward P. O'Callaghan, OFM, 'Bishop Edward Thomas O'Dwyer and the Course of Irish Politics 1870–1917' (unpublished MA thesis, University College Galway, 1976), pp.20–1, 171–2, and 199–202.
179. See Roantree 'William Monsell and the Catholic Question', p.271.
180. See *Munster News*, 21 April 1894, and Hanley, 'Past Glories of Tervoe'.
181. Anonymous, *Fifty Years at Mount Saint Alphonsus, Limerick, 1853–1903* (Limerick: O'Connor and Co., 1903), pp.2–3.
182. Maria Luddy, 'Angels of Mercy: Nuns as Workhouse Nurses, 1861–1898', in Greta Jones, and Elizabeth Malcolm (eds), *Medicine, Disease and the State in Ireland, 1650–1940* (Cork: Cork University Press, 1999), pp.102–17, and Damien Jude Moane, 'The Limerick Workhouse: 1841–1861' (unpublished MA thesis, Mary Immaculate College, University of Limerick, 2002), pp.140–7.
183. John Fleming, *St John's Cathedral, Limerick* (Dublin: Four Courts Press, 1987), p.45.
184. Ibid., pp.57–8.
185. Parry, *Democracy and Religion*, p.5.
186. Newman, *Letters and Diaries*, Vol. 16, p.382, Newman to Flanagan, 16 February 1855.
187. For Monsell's second marriage, see Hanley 'Past Glories of Tervoe'.
188. Potter, *Catholic Unionist*, p.45.
189. Hansard, CCLIV, 1866 (3 August 1880).
190. Roger Magraw, *France 1815–1914: The Bourgeois Century* (London: Fontana, 1983), pp.174–8, 257–9, 323–6 and 332–4.
191. *Munster News*, 21 April 1894.
192. For the Athenaeum Club, see Henry R. Tedder, *The Athenaeum 1824–1924. A Centenary Record* (London: Reprinted from the Times, 1924); Humphrey Ward, *History of the Athenaeum 1824–1925* (London: Athenaeum Club, 1926); and Frank Richard Cowell, *The Athenaeum: Club and Social Life in London, 1824–1974* (London: Heinemann, 1975).
193. See Ward, *History of the Athenaeum*, p.87.
194. For the Stafford and St George's clubs, see Newman, *Letters and Diaries*, Vol. 18, pp.548–9.

CHAPTER FIVE

Waging the Crimean War

Monsell's conversion coincided with a major political and religious crisis in Britain and Ireland. Pope Pius IX had decided to restore the Catholic hierarchy in England and Wales, and in 1850 he appointed Nicholas Wiseman (1803–65) Cardinal and Archbishop of Westminster.[1] Wiseman then returned to England as head of the newly established hierarchy. England and Wales were divided into thirteen dioceses in place of the eight vicariates-apostolic which had been the previous administrative divisions of the Church there. The necessity for this measure seemed obvious to the Pope and his advisors, for the Catholic population in England and Wales had increased from 75,000 in 1770 to 750,000 in 1851 (largely due to the huge influx of immigrants from Ireland, especially in the 1840s), but they also inadvertently triggered off the greatest anti-Catholic agitation in Britain and Ireland of the entire nineteenth century.[2]

There were a number of reasons for this. One was growing fears in Britain that Catholicism was becoming a serious menace to the civil and religious establishments. The association of Catholicism with despotism and treasonous plotting had entered the English folk memory at the time of the Reformation, and remained firmly embedded there, even into the Victorian age, a period of increasing religious toleration and liberalism. Many worried English Protestants discerned a Catholic threat everywhere – from the huge influx of papist Catholics from Ireland, the growth of Tractarianism in the Church of England, the stream of conversions from amongst adherents of the Oxford Movement, the rise of Ultramontanism in the Roman Church, the Catholic revival on the continent of Europe. Seen in this light, Pius IX's actions seemed to be part of a great and insidious tendency, a world-wide resurgence of the age-old ecclesiastical tyranny of the Roman Church.[3]

Lord John Russell, a promoter of religious toleration but personally strongly anti-Catholic, was one of the chief players in the drama that followed. On 14 October 1850 the *Times* published Cardinal Wiseman's tactless and triumphalist pastoral letter to the English Catholics, announcing the restoration of the hierarchy.[4] It was a public-relations disaster of the highest order and provoked a series of furious public attacks. Lord John Russell now hastened to put himself at the head of the ferocious anti-Catholic campaign. On the 4 November 1850, happily falling the day before Guy Fawkes' Day, he addressed an open letter to Edward Maltby, the Anglican Bishop of Durham, in which he condemned the Pope's 'pretension to supremacy over the realm of England' and the 'mummeries of superstition' of the Papist Church.[5] This outburst literally as well as metaphorically fanned the flames of hatred, as the Pope and Wiseman joined Guy Fawkes in being burnt in effigy throughout the length and breadth of the country the following day. Catholic churches were desecrated, protest meetings held, and a shower of anti-Catholic pamphlets descended on the public. In these circumstances, Monsell's decision to become a Catholic on 12 December was a courageous one indeed.

Early in 1851 Lord John Russell introduced the Ecclesiastical Titles Bill before Parliament, which made it illegal for a Catholic prelate to assume a title taken from a British place-name (e.g. Archbishop of Westminster).[6] To Catholics in both Britain and Ireland, Russell's action seemed to herald a return to the Penal Laws. The Irish Liberals were split over the issue. Many of them were Catholics, so it was inevitable that most of them should oppose the bill.[7] On the first reading thirty-nine Irish Liberals opposed the bill, thirteen of them Protestants; only six, all Protestants, voted for it. On the second reading the opposition was even more marked, for forty-eight Irish Liberals, including seventeen Protestants, voted against it, while only eight, again all Protestants, supported it.[8] Despite this, the bill passed by huge majorities, for the Conservatives as well as the main body of the Liberal party voted in favour. It became law, but although remaining on the statute book for twenty years, it proved to be a dead letter and no prosecution was ever brought under its provisions.

While Russell's 'Penal Law' proved to be a mountain that brought forth a mouse, it had considerable political effects. The Irish Liberals (around twenty-five in number) who had opposed it formed themselves into a separate body and christened themselves 'The Irish Brigade', although their enemies sometimes called them 'The Pope's Brass Band'. In the summer of 1852 the Irish Brigade formed an alliance with the Tenant League, which had been set up in 1850 to fight for the rights of tenant farmers who had suffered grievously at the hands of the landlords during and after the Great Famine. Following the general election of

1852 (in which Monsell was returned, unopposed, for County Limerick) some forty-eight MPs were elected, pledged to the policy of independent opposition.[9] They formed a distinct Irish party in Parliament and pledged themselves to act together and to remain aloof from the British parties, unless their policy demands were met. These consisted of the repeal of the Ecclesiastical Titles Act, the disestablishment of the Church of Ireland, lower rents and protection of tenant right. The pledge taken by party members included a promise not to take office in any British administration that did not concede these demands.[10]

Monsell, who had been a staunch supporter of the Russell administration in 1848 and 1849, deplored the Ecclesiastical Titles Bill, but as a recent convert to Catholicism played a minor role in the debates during its stormy passage through the Commons and spoke only briefly on 23 May, 6 June and 20 June 1851.[11] Despite this, he had become estranged from the British Liberals, and in the Commons sessions of 1851 and 1852 he ceased to be a supporter of Russell. By one reckoning, Monsell's voting pattern at this time would classify him as a member of the Irish Brigade, although, significantly, he did not attend party meetings of the Brigade.[12] There is other evidence to support this contention.[13] The period 1852–3 saw Monsell's political pendulum finally coming to rest. On 20 February 1852 Russell was finally forced to resign. His administration had been disastrous from both the Irish and Catholic point of view, for he had presided over the worst years of the famine, the terrible landlord–tenant crisis that followed, and the deplorable 'Papal Aggression' campaign of 1850–1. Even the Conservative administration led by Lord Derby (who became Prime Minister) and Disraeli (as leader of the House of Commons) which took office in his place seemed a distinct improvement. The general election that followed was a triumph for the Independent Opposition party, and the Liberals in Ireland were reduced to a small rump. Nevertheless, Monsell was a firm adherent once more. An analysis of the Irish Liberal MPs elected between 1852 and 1857 demonstrates that Monsell fulfilled none of the criteria used to classify members of the Independent Opposition party.[14] He did not pledge himself to this policy in his election address, nor at his adoption meeting, and did not attend either the tenant league conference of September or the religious equality conference of October 1852 at which MPs had accepted resolutions on independent opposition. Although his voting records in 1851–2 would seem to indicate that he was a Brigadier, his own political philosophy and his voting pattern before and after the Papal Aggression crisis clearly point to his never having really belonged in their ranks.

In the crisis of 1850–2, as at the time of his election in 1847, Monsell had avoided fettering himself with any awkward promises or pledges that might hamper his freedom of action in the future. His behaviour on both occasions was both principled and politically astute. Monsell took oaths very seriously indeed, as is demonstrated in the letter which he wrote to Newman on 12 February 1851 agonising over the oath that he had to take, as a Catholic MP.[15] In 1864 it was similar scruples that was to prevent him from becoming involved in the National Association.[16] Thus, it would be quite wrong to describe Monsell as a cynical political opportunist, but it would be equally naïve to overlook the very supple and subtle way in which he was able to retain his freedom of manoeuvre in both 1847 and 1850–2.

The culmination of the political crisis of 1851–53 came in December 1852, when Derby's Conservative administration was defeated. The new Prime Minister was the Peelite fourth Earl of Aberdeen (1784–1860), whose administration was a coalition of the Liberals and the Peelites, the only coalition government to rule Britain in the period 1783 to 1915.[17]As well as the Prime Minister, the Chancellor of the Exchequer (Gladstone), the First Lord of the Admiralty (Sir James Graham) and the Secretary for War and the Colonies (Duke of Newcastle) were among the most prominent Peelite ministers. The Peelites had always been interested in securing Irish support, and as strenuous opponents of the Ecclesiastical Titles Bill, were highly thought of in Ireland. Consequently, Aberdeen offered positions in his administration to John Sadlier (1815–56) and William Keogh (1817–78), two of the leaders of Independent Opposition. The former became a Lord of the Treasury and the latter Attorney-General for Ireland. In addition, both the chief posts in the Irish administration, Lord-Lieutenant and Chief Secretary, were given to Peelites. These attempts at conciliating Irish opinion sadly backfired, however. Sadlier and Keogh's acceptance of office triggered off a ferocious controversy in Ireland, and they were denounced as traitors and pledge-breakers.

Monsell was also offered and accepted a position in the new administration. Aberdeen appointed him Clerk of the Ordnance, and he took office on 13 January 1853. He escaped most of the opprobrium heaped on Sadlier and Keogh, for, as the *Nation* newspaper stated, he 'has broken no pledge, belied no antecedents, forfeited no principles', but he was still criticised in many quarters for taking office in an administration that included the Catholic *bête noire*, Lord John Russell.[18] Monsell himself was reassured by the predominance of the Peelites in the Cabinet, and was bound to Gladstone by strong ties of personal friendship. After all, he himself was a former Peelite of sorts, and their outlook on life and general political philosophy was congenial to him.

However, the beginning of his official career in 1853 was to be as dogged by controversy as its conclusion twenty years later was to be clouded by scandal. Russell, not content with the harm which he had already caused with his Ecclesiastical Titles Act, now proceeded to stir anew the hornets' nest of Catholic religious sensibilities. On 31 May 1853, during a debate in the Commons on the ecclesiastical revenues of Ireland, he roundly attacked the Catholic Church, stating that 'it has been but too evident of late years, that the Roman Catholic Church has aimed at political power, and having aimed at political power, it appears to me to be at variance with a due attachment to the Crown of this country – with a due attachment to the duties that a subject of the state should perform towards the state'.[19] As Whyte puts it, 'this was tantamount to saying that no devout Catholic could be a loyal subject'.[20] On 2 June the three Catholic office-holders, Sadlier, Keogh and Monsell, resigned. Russell, clearly taken aback, wrote to Aberdeen stating that 'I feel so much the disadvantage to you of the loss of Mr Monsell and other Roman Catholic members of your government that I think you had better, as an alternative, allow me to retire, and retain their services.'[21] Aberdeen sent Newcastle to see Monsell, to find out on what terms, if any, they could remain in the administration. Roantree has pointed out that throughout the crisis it was Monsell who was regarded as the most prominent of the three Catholic office-holders, thus demonstrating how senior was his status as a Catholic Whig MP already.[22] The Prime Minister himself then wrote to Monsell on the issue, stating that Lord John's sentiments were 'not shared by me nor by many of my colleagues'.[23] The following day, the three office-holders withdrew their resignations while the disclaimer by Aberdeen appeared even stronger when published by the *Times* on 6 June, for by a misprint, the phrase 'many of my colleagues' appeared as 'any of my colleagues'.[24]

This crisis, and its implications for Monsell, has been variously interpreted by commentators. Whyte describes it as a great victory for Monsell and his two colleagues and claims that they were only able to humiliate Russell because they were office-holders.[25] John Biggs-Davison and George Chowdharay-Best, authors of a rare work on Catholic Unionism, write that the affair shows that Monsell and his two colleagues were 'no place-seeking ciphers', and 'that Catholics in office were influential'.[26] On the other hand, Roantree maintains that 'the office-holders' demonstration of their effectiveness was blunted by the rapidity with which they returned to office, and by the obsequiousness mainly of Monsell's second letter to Aberdeen'.[27] This letter read in part: 'henceforth unless I shall learn from your Lordship's own lips, or from formal acts, that the policy of the government is changed, I shall accept every fresh difficulty which attends its course, as a fresh reason for offering to your Lordship, a continuance of the services, humble as they are, which

I am capable of rendering'.[28] The accidental publication of the letter was an embarrassment, and somewhat dulled the lustre of the victory over Russell. Frederick Lucas (1813–55), one of the leaders of the Independent Opposition party and editor of the Catholic newspaper the *Tablet*, wrote that 'even Mr Monsell, to speak it most mildly, has not raised himself by the transaction'.[29]

Two points should be borne in mind. Firstly, Monsell had acted throughout according to his principles. He had taken no pledge to abstain from office, as even Lucas conceded, and thus 'almost escaped condemnation' on that score.[30] Indeed, the episode can be taken as an example of the wisdom of taking office, as Whyte has claimed, and is perfectly consistent with Monsell's belief that it was only by being part of the administration that a Catholic could effect change. Secondly, while Russell hadn't been forced to resign, and indeed remained part of the administration, his defeat was a real one. The Catholic Liberals were a small minority in the administration, and an even more insignificant element in the overwhelmingly Protestant Imperial Parliament, and it would have been unrealistic to expect them to be able to wring any further concessions from an essentially well-disposed Prime Minister. Monsell's 'remarkably servile' letter, while reminiscent of the manner in which Mr Collins addressed Lady Catherine de Bourgh, had not been intended for publication, and such language was regularly used by contemporaries when addressing their political patrons. Indeed, it can be argued, particularly in view of the ultimate melancholy fate of the Independent Opposition party, that Monsell had a more realistic grasp of the possibilities open to Catholic politicians at this period than had the Independents, and had again demonstrated his acute political instinct for survival. At any rate, the chief result of the events of 1851–3 was that Monsell was now firmly anchored to the Liberal party, which was to be his political home for the next thirty years.

The dominant figure in the Irish Catholic Church of the nineteenth century is Paul Cullen (1803–78), successively Archbishop of Armagh (1849–52), Archbishop of Dublin (1852–78) and Ireland's first Cardinal (from 1866).[31] His position inevitably made him as much a political as a religious figure. Cullen was an Ultramontane, but that did not prevent him from becoming close friends with Monsell (as with Monsell's relations with Cardinal Pie and Pope Pius IX himself). They collaborated closely throughout the 1850s, as the fundamental incompatibility of their ideologies did not create major difficulties until the following decade. Both were pragmatists, and this helped their mutual relations to flourish. It was at this time that Monsell emerged as the spokesman for the Catholic hierarchy in Parliament, and the point of contact between them and successive British governments. Throughout this period he campaigned in support of his two lifelong interests; educational reform and civil and religious equality.

In the 1850s the Catholic University occupied a great deal of Monsell's time and efforts.[32] In 1850 the Queen's Colleges (now known collectively as the Queen's University) had been condemned by the Synod of Thurles, and the Bishops announced their intention of setting up a Catholic University in Ireland. Monsell's closest friend, Newman, was appointed Rector of the new institution in 1851. Cullen was the instigator of all of these developments, and indeed, Monsell had been among those who had encouraged him to appoint Newman.[33] The latter made several visits to Ireland before the university actually came into existence in 1854. He visited Limerick twice in his entire life, in 1852 and 1854. His first visit was in August 1852, when he preached a sermon in St Michael's Church to raise funds for the new orphanage for girls in Mount St Vincent (now the Scoil Carmel Secondary School).[34] Monsell was away from Limerick at the time, but he gave Newman the use of Tervoe House, where he stayed from 3 to 9 August 1852, his only visit there. He had the house to himself for the week, and completed Discourses seven and eight of what became *The Idea of a University*.[35] The latter is made up of two volumes, originally published independently. Volume two, entitled *Lectures and Essays on University Subjects*, was dedicated to Monsell (November 1858). This dedication was retained when *The Idea of a University* was published in 1873. In this work Newman sets out his philosophy of university education, and his dedication demonstrates both his high esteem for Monsell and his perception of him as a major figure in Irish education.

Monsell was an enthusiastic supporter of the Catholic University, and assisted Newman in raising funds, recruiting students and rallying support. However, in February 1853 he approached Newman with a proposal that the Catholic Church should withdraw its censure of the Queen's Colleges. Newman rejected this idea out of hand, and no more was heard of it until 1856.[36] It seems that Monsell was attempting to square the circle, by having the Government and Catholic institutions operating together. Monsell's enthusiasm for the Catholic University became stronger when it had actually commenced operations. Early in 1857 he wrote to Newman that 'I can conceive no greater blessing than its success, and no more lamentable misfortune than its failure.'[37] His opinion was not widely shared in Ireland, however, and it failed to prosper. Funds were low, the Catholic gentry and middle classes were apathetic, and even Monsell's fellow Catholic Whigs refused their support. On 13 July 1854 he wrote to Newman: 'I applied to Lords Kenmare,

Castleross and Fingal to give their names to the university, and was surprised to find that they objected to do so.'[38]

Two major problems, however, were the lack of official recognition and the growing rift between Newman and Cullen. On 28 June 1854 Newman wrote to Monsell enquiring 'whether the new university here wished a charter from the government, or what its views were'. He himself was doubtful: 'I cannot fancy the government giving one in the present state of proceedings.'[39] As usual, Monsell urged caution: 'I think it would be unwise now to moot in any way the question of a charter. Until the university exists, it will not be recognised. To recognise it at any time will be unpopular, and therefore its recognition will be avoided even by our friends as long as it can be with decency.'[40] By 1856 Newman was prepared to contemplate affiliation with the Queen's University, and had thus implicitly accepted Monsell's proposal of 1853. Monsell regarded this as a 'makeshift, but it would by increasing your numbers hasten the time when you could command a regular charter'.[41] The subject was not to be broached with any administration until 1858, and this lack of official recognition for its degrees, and consequent lack of financial backing and of prestige, was a fatal shortcoming.

The breach between Cullen and Newman was the second major handicap.[42] There was an obvious temperamental difference between the authoritarian and Ultramontane Cullen, who had lived in Rome for thirty years, and the Oxonian convert Newman, who was a leading Liberal Catholic, so their visions of the Catholic University were correspondingly poles apart. Cullen wanted a specifically Irish institution, catering for Irish students and with the particular aim of counteracting the hated Queen's Colleges.[43] Newman, on the other hand, envisaged his university as being for English-speaking Catholics from all over the world.[44] Cullen and Newman did not enjoy a cordial relationship, and the latter complained bitterly to Monsell of the archbishop's 'rudeness' in not replying to his correspondence. Monsell accounted for this in a singular fashion. He wrote to Newman on 7 September 1855: 'I cannot account for Dr Cullen's conduct except in one way – in Ireland, one often meets with people of his class, kind and considerate after their fashion, but moving in a sphere completely different from ours, and therefore acting in a manner in which if we acted, we should shew [*sic*] a want of consideration and respect for others ... I cannot conceive that there can be intentionally any want of [respect] towards you.'[45] Eventually, the accumulation of problems brought about Newman's resignation as Rector in 1858. Monsell feared that Newman's departure would ruin the university and tried to dissuade him from going, but to no avail.[46]

Cullen and Monsell collaborated more successfully in other matters.

When Aberdeen's government found itself under pressure to set up an enquiry into St Patrick's College, Maynooth, Cullen was alarmed, as one of the instigators of this measure, Richard Spooner MP for North Warwickshire was a notorious anti-Catholic. Monsell advised both Aberdeen and Cullen that a Royal Commission would be a safer way of carrying out the investigation than a committee of either the Lords or the Commons. Aberdeen complied with this advice, while Cullen fully approved. This is one of the best examples of Monsell successfully acting as an intermediary between the Government and the hierarchy.[47]

At a later stage the Independent Opposition party came into conflict with Cullen, who suspected that it was tinged with anti-clericalism and revolutionary doctrines. His terrible experiences of revolution in Rome in 1848–9 had made him morbidly suspicious of any such developments and he equated Charles Gavan Duffy (1816–1903), one of the leaders of Independent Opposition, with the fiery Italian anti-clerical nationalist Guiseppi Mazzini.[48] In 1853 and 1854 Cullen introduced regulations curtailing the role of priests in politics.[49] The Catholic clergy had played a major role in the Independent Opposition party from the start, so that Cullen's measures represented a major threat to its existence. Frederick Lucas took the extreme step of appealing Cullen's decision to the Pope.[50] He travelled to Rome at the end of 1854, where the Pope asked him to submit a written statement of his case. Lucas returned to England, having begun work on this document, but died soon after, and his appeal was presented to the Pope posthumously.[51] In it, Lucas denounced the Catholic Whigs by name, and while he conceded that Monsell was 'an honest friend of Catholic rights and is sincerely anxious to obtain redress', he described his 'dependent and place-taking party' as existing 'first of all to serve itself, to serve the interests and private purposes of its members'.[52] He went on to say that 'Dr Cullen, in the person of Mr Monsell, has enlisted the Catholic members under the flag of Lord Palmerston', and described this as a mistaken policy.[53]

Monsell played a major role in the affair, for he wrote a letter strongly attacking Independent Opposition, and Cullen made good use of this document in Rome. Cullen wrote to Monsell on 10 March 1855 from Rome: 'I showed your letter to His Holiness, who seemed much pleased with it. I showed it also to Cardinal Antonelli, Secretary of State [in effect Prime Minister] who highly approves of your views, and remarked that the system of so-called independent opposition would be likely to produce the evils occasioned in Italy by Mazzini's principles. Your statement of the case will have the effect of exploding the pretended appeal to Rome.'[54] Lucas's death brought about the end of the business, for no official reply was ever given to his memorial. Duffy emigrated to Australia soon after and the Independent Opposition party maintained but a feeble existence until its final demise as an organised party in 1859, although it lingered on as a group of individuals until 1866. This affair marked Monsell's first intervention at the Vatican, where he was to be an influential figure until his death. He became a close friend of Pius IX, and was thus assured of a hearing in the highest circles of the Church.[55]

During this entire period, however, Monsell's chief preoccupation was with his office of Clerk of the Ordnance, to which he was appointed on 13 January 1853.[56] In Britain the army and navy had separate administrations until the Ministry of Defence was established in 1964. The navy was headed by a Cabinet minister known as the First Lord of the Admiralty, who was assisted by the Board of the Admiralty, but in the 1850s the administration of the army was far more complex. The chief minister was the Secretary of State for War and the Colonies, who was responsible for directing policy but was mainly preoccupied with the Colonial Department, where he was based, and exercised only a general nominal superintendence over the War Office. Under him was a bewildering series of separate departments, with overlapping and sometimes conflicting functions. The Secretary-at-War was responsible for the financial affairs of the army, while the Commander-in-Chief held supreme command of the army under the Sovereign. There was considerable scope for confusion and conflict between these two high officials, who were both based in the Horse Guards.

The most important of the other authorities was the Board of Ordnance, which ranked as one of the great departments of state. Founded in 1414, it was reconstituted in 1683 into the form which it was to preserve, largely unaltered, into the nineteenth century. It supplied the army and navy with arms and ammunition, and built and equipped barracks and fortifications. It was concerned with the invention and development of weapons, arranged for their manufacture in its own manufacturing departments, or purchased them from civilian contractors. It stored arms and ammunition, and provided tents and other camp equipment for the army. The Ordnance Office established its own training school for cadets, the Royal Military Academy, Woolwich, and a school for specialist training in engineering, the School of Military Engineering at Chatham. The manufacturing departments of the Ordnance Office consisted of the Royal Arsenal at Woolwich, where guns and artillery were made and which included the Royal Laboratory; the Royal Gunpowder Factory at Waltham Abbey; and the Royal Small Arms Factory at Enfield.[57] Thus, the Board was a highly significant department responsible for thousands of officers and men, barracks and depots scattered throughout the world.

The head of the department was the Master-General of the Ordnance, who was president of the Board and Commander-in-Chief of Ordnance troops grouped into two regiments – the Royal Artillery and the Royal Engineers. Except on the battlefield, these two regiments were independent, and not subject to the War Office or the Commander-in-Chief of the Army. The Master-General always had a seat in the Cabinet until 1828, but never after that date. He was assisted by the Board of Ordnance, which in 1852 consisted of three officials: the Surveyor-General was the technical officer responsible for the quality of the stores; the Controller and Principal Storekeeper was responsible for the quantity of the stores; and the Clerk of the Ordnance prepared the budget, dealt with money accounts, drew up contracts and bargains and kept a record of each stock transaction, from which he was to compile an annual ledger.[58] This latter was the post to which Monsell was appointed in 1853.[59]

However, when Monsell arrived at the Office of the Board (which was situated on London's Pall Mall) early in 1853, he found a department that had seen better days. The decline in the position of the Master-General was shown by his exclusion from the Cabinet since 1828. From 1827 the Master-General virtually ceased to be President of the Board, took very little part in the business of the department and seldom attended a board meeting. There were supposed to be three per week, but they were merely occasions on which members signed prepared documents without discussion and one member could transact all the business.[60] Real power was concentrated in the hands of the permanent civil servants, largely due to the lack of administrative experience of the board members, including Monsell himself. Even more ominously, the Ordnance Department, in common with the rest of the armed forces establishments, had been subject to sharp reductions in both numbers and expenditure following the end of the Napoleonic Wars in 1815. The prevailing liberal and utilitarian philosophies placed more emphasis on social reform, pacifism and material progress than on old-fashioned military and naval expenditure, while the administrative structures of the army and navy were notoriously inefficient and riddled with corruption and graft. The lack of any serious threat from a foreign enemy since the defeat of Napoleon meant that by 1853 Britain was less prepared for war than at any other time in the nineteenth century.[61]

Monsell's position at the Board of Ordnance was a subordinate one. His chief was the Master-General, Lord Fitzroy Somerset, first Baron Raglan (1788–1855), who had been appointed in 1852. Indeed, it is doubtful if Monsell would have been able to make much of an impact there, but for the outbreak of the Crimean War, in March 1854.[62] After the defeat of Napoleon in 1815, Britain and Russia had emerged as the two most formidable powers in the world.[63] Russia's image in Western

Europe between 1815 and 1854 was not unlike that of the Soviet Union between 1945 and 1989, as she appeared to be a vast autocratic, expanding empire that posed a serious threat to liberty everywhere. The British were particularly apprehensive of Russian imperialism, which appeared to threaten their vital interests in Asia, particularly in India. When Russia and the decadent Ottoman Empire went to war, on 4 October 1853, Britain and France, fearing that the Tsar would become dominant in the Balkans and perhaps the Middle East, came to the aid of the Sultan. The two western powers declared war on Russia and set about invading the Crimean peninsula and capturing Russia's great naval base on the Black Sea, Sebastopol. In the first half of 1854 an army of British and French troops landed in the Crimea to achieve this objective.

Public opinion at the time believed that this war, involving the three greatest powers in the world, was going to be a great struggle like the Napoleonic Wars.[64] In fact, the Crimean War proved to be curiously indecisive, and the British people were to be sadly disappointed at 'the war that would not boil'.[65] In the military and administrative history of the United Kingdom, it is notorious for the sheer incompetence with which it was conducted. Lord Raglan, who had seen no active service since 1815, was appointed Commander-in-Chief of the British forces in the Crimea and departed in mid-April 1854, leaving the Board of Ordnance without an effective head. The office of Lieutenant-General of the Ordnance (deputy to the Master-General), which had been abolished in 1828, was now revived, and Sir Hew Ross (1779–1868) was appointed to the post to take charge in Raglan's absence, but in practice he did not exercise his authority, thinking that his duties did not extend beyond the purely military sphere. The Surveyor-General (who was the principal civil officer) went to the Crimea with Raglan. Thus, only two board members were left to conduct its affairs – Sir Thomas Hastings (1790–1870), who was Controller and Principal Store-Keeper, and Monsell himself, who represented the Board in Parliament. The Ordnance Office had a very important role to play in the war effort against Russia, but Monsell and Hastings became bitter rivals within a short time, and their quarrels and intrigues bedevilled the whole running of the department. Sir Thomas was an elderly and pompous gentleman, who had been appointed to the Ordnance in 1845, after some forty years service in the navy. He resented Monsell's determination to push ahead with decisions with or without his consent.[66]

The disputes between them largely centred on the best method of supplying arms and armaments for the troops in the Crimea. During the nineteenth century the Royal armaments factories tended to be expanded in wartime, but the private armaments industry was favoured during periods of peace.[67] When the Crimean War broke out, Monsell found that the Ordnance stores were severely deficient in most of the materials of war, especially shells and guns. In particular, there was a severe shell shortage in the Crimea itself (similar scares were to occur during the First and Second World Wars). Monsell doubted the ability of the private arms manufacturers in London, Birmingham and Coventry to supply the necessary arms, believing them to be expensive, inefficient and slow to adapt to technical changes.[68] This led him to place much greater emphasis on the Government's own manufacturing establishments. Here, Monsell showed his pragmatism and completely non-ideological approach to increasing government involvement in an area where the private sector was performing inadequately. The implementation of this policy brought him into conflict in the Commons with MPs representing constituencies where the private armaments manufacturers were concentrated, particularly Charles Newdigate (1816–87) MP for North Warwickshire from 1843 to 1885. Their lifelong antipathy was largely caused by Newdigate's strong anti-Catholic views and prejudices, but he also championed the munitions firms in his constituency against what he considered to be Monsell's attacks on their shortcomings. Within the Ordnance Department itself, Hastings also took the part of the private arms manufacturers, so Monsell found himself fighting his own private war on two fronts, which, if devoid of the bloodshed of the Crimean conflict, was its equal in bitterness and confusion.

Monsell was eventually able to carry the day because he enlisted the aid of a powerful ally. At the outbreak of hostilities, the Duke of Newcastle was Secretary of State for War and the Colonies, but in June 1854 responsibility for the latter was transferred from him and given to a separate Secretary of State. This was done at the instigation of Lord John Russell, who wanted to consolidate the various military departments under one minister.[69] Newcastle was now able to concentrate on the war effort, but though very industrious, and full of self confidence, he was of only average ability and had poor management skills.[70] Nevertheless, Monsell formed a close alliance with him (after all, they were old friends and disciples of Robert Peel) and used this connection as a powerful weapon in his battles at the Board of Ordnance. Newcastle himself believed that his power over the Ordnance Department was complete.[71] He soon formed the habit of issuing instructions to the Ordnance Office through verbal communication with Monsell, which was contrary to official procedure.[72] Hastings was most annoyed by this, and complained that the practice of the Ordnance Office had changed totally from the time of Newcastle's surrender of the Colonial ministry in June 1854. Hitherto, the Secretary of State had not involved himself in the running of the office, and the Board made decisions at regularly constituted meetings. From June 1854, Hastings claimed, the official procedures were disregarded after Raglan had gone to the Crimea, Newcastle became *de facto* head of the Ordnance Office and began issuing orders verbally to Monsell. The latter then executed these instructions without reference to the Board, which was effectively marginalised, a development symbolised by Monsell's practice of conducting departmental business in his own office, rather than in the boardroom.[73] Hastings, elderly, pompous, bumbling, was clearly no match for Monsell, a younger and abler man who had a clear agenda and acted on it.

In the meantime, Monsell had turned to reforming the Government's arms factories. In May 1854 he related: 'I found that the state of our supply of shells was most lamentable, and in point of fact, if any general action had taken place at this time, we should have been in the worst possible position.'[74] He appointed Captain Edward Boxer to implement his policy. Colonel Wilson was Director of the Royal Laboratory at Woolwich, and Captain Boxer was his second-in-command, with the title of Firemaster. However, Monsell had unlimited confidence in Boxer's abilities (as indeed did Boxer himself) and authorised him to do whatever was necessary to increase productivity. He authorised Boxer to spend £7,000 on installing machinery to process unfinished shells acquired from the private manufacturers. This enterprise was a great success, but the private sector could not provide the shells fast enough, so Monsell and Boxer set up a government factory in March 1855 to manufacture the shells themselves. The sum of £10,000 was expended on this establishment, which was also a great success, although Monsell arranged for it to be much larger than had been agreed by Hastings. Although the shortage of shells was ended, both Colonel Wilson and Hastings were much put out by these developments. Wilson believed that he was being bypassed in favour of his subordinate, Boxer, while Hastings felt that he was being deceived.

Monsell was delighted with this success and turned to the manufacture of small arms. On 27 February 1854 he brought forward a proposal to close the two existing government gun factories, at Enfield and Birmingham, and replace them with a large new factory at Woolwich. This was because the private manufacturers were unable to supply the needs of the Ordnance Department; they were too expensive and would not be able to adjust quickly to technological change.[75] This proposal was referred to a Small Arms Committee, which recommended instead that 'a manufactory should be tried on a limited scale, which would serve as an experiment'.[76] In fact, the 'limited' factory erected in Enfield rapidly expanded into a huge establishment and the number of its employees grew from 60 or 70 in 1855, to between 1,200 and 1,500 in 1864.[77] One of Monsell's least successful innovations was the establishment of a gun foundry at Woolwich for the manufacture of cannon. However, after £200,000 had been expended on manufacturing one hundred useless pieces of artillery (for the wrong iron had been used in their manufacture), the establishment was closed down.[78]

Hastings opposed Monsell's policy and championed the private manufacturers at every turn. He became estranged from both Monsell and Newcastle, and his authority diminished more and more. On the other hand, Monsell grew more and more confident and pursued his agenda with increasing vigour. He soon came into conflict with Ross as well as with Hastings as a result of Captain Boxer's arrogance and lack of tact.[79] Following a huge row with Colonel Wilson, Boxer received 'a most severe reprimand' from the Lieutenant-General and Board on 24 January 1855, in the presence of four military officers. Monsell had been away while these events were occurring, his wife having just died, but on his return he forced Ross and Hastings to withdraw the original minute of censure, which he thought 'insulting' and injurious to the feelings of Boxer, 'a gentleman and a man of honour', and to substitute in its place a more mildly worded one.[80] Not surprisingly, Ross and Hastings were furious at this high-handed action, and were particularly incensed that Monsell had threatened to report the matter to Newcastle unless his wishes were complied with.

This was a time of great strain for Monsell. His wife was dying for several months towards the end of 1854, and he was obliged to be absent from the Board a great deal. At the same time, the Government was falling apart. The British Army had borne the brunt of the fighting in the Crimea in the autumn of 1854, winning victories at the Alma (20 September), Balaclava (25 October) and Inkerman (5 November).[81] However, Sebastopol had not been captured, and the allied armies were obliged to spend the winter of 1854/5 in the Crimea. Conditions in the British quarters were dreadful, with shortages of supplies, inadequate shelter, and poor medical services. The army was decimated by cholera, dysentery and malaria and the medical facilities were appalling until Florence Nightingale travelled to the East. In Britain, the patriotic fervour that had reached its peak at the time of the three great victories quickly turned to gloom when 'just before Christmas 1854, the *Times* began its famous revelations about the state of the troops then settling down to besiege Sebastopol'.[82] British public opinion was outraged, and a mood of anger, sorrow, shame and self-searching descended on the nation for the first six months of 1855.

Meanwhile, Aberdeen was unable to keep his bickering Cabinet in order. In January 1855 John Arthur Roebuck, a truculent radical MP whose nickname was 'Tear 'em Roebuck', brought a motion before the Commons calling for a select committee to be established to enquire into the state of the army before Sebastopol. The Government opposed this motion, making it a matter of confidence, but was defeated by 305 votes to 148, 'a defeat frequently described as one of the most shameful ever inflicted upon a British government'.[83] The Aberdeen coalition collapsed and after a week of inglorious confusion and intrigue a Liberal government took office on 6 February 1855.[84] It was led by Henry John Temple, third Viscount Palmerston (1784–1865), who had very great experience but who was unscrupulous, forceful and dedicated to maintaining British prestige throughout the world. He was anathema to Monsell, who detested the new Prime Minister's indifference to Irish affairs, as well as his hostility to the Catholic Church. Monsell had offered his resignation on a number of occasions to Aberdeen in the winter of 1854/5, due to his enforced absences from the Ordnance Office caused by his wife's mortal illness, and now contemplated resigning again. He wrote to Father Flanagan to say that he had resigned, because he did not think it 'decent or proper to hold office under the premiership of such a man as Lord P[almerston]'.[85] Palmerston, taking the hint, offered his position to Sir Robert Peel, son of the late Prime Minister, but Monsell then intimated that he wanted to stay after all, and was reappointed.

From the point of view of the Ordnance Office, Palmerston's most significant appointment was that of Fox Maule, second Baron Panmure (later eleventh Earl of Dalhousie) (1801–74), as Secretary of State for War.[86] Nicknamed 'The Bison', Lord Panmure was dogged, stolid and self-confident, but was obstinate and of only average ability.[87] Nevertheless, he was determined to sort out the hopeless confusion of the administration of the army in general and of the Ordnance department in particular.[88] Monsell benefited enormously by this appointment, as Lord Panmure made him his confidante and sided openly with him against Ross and Hastings, whose influence was reduced to a nullity. Panmure flatly refused to see Hastings when he called to his office and on 4 May 1855, Hastings dolefully complained to the Roebuck committee that he had not received any communication from nor even seen Lord Panmure since the latter had taken office three months previously.[89]

In the meantime, Roebuck's select committee was appointed and interviewed a large number of witnesses, including Newcastle, Ross, Hastings and Monsell. In the continuing dispute between the last two, which they both carried into their evidence to the committee, Hastings had the advantage of appearing first, on 2, 3, 4 , 7 and 8 May 1855.[90] He was able to deal Monsell a number of blows, accusing him of violating official procedures and of high-handed behaviour in several instances. When Monsell appeared before the committee on 7 and 8 May, he found himself having to rebut Hastings's allegations for much of the time.[91] Nevertheless, he was more precise and organised in his presentation of evidence, and marshalled documentation to support his arguments. His chief justification for his often irregular behaviour was the exigencies created by the war effort.

The final report of the committee appeared on 18 June 1855 and found that the departure of Raglan to the East had left the Ordnance Board without an effective head, leading it to fall into an 'inadequate and disordered state'.[92] The evidence of Hastings and Monsell was cited as ample proof 'of the unsatisfactory state of this department', while Ross was accused of being 'imperfectly acquainted with the constitution of the Board of which he was a member'.[93] However, 'the conflict of authority' between Hastings and Monsell came in for sharp criticism. 'At a time when urgent business required their attention, they were engaged in disputes, in preparing statements and in making appeals to the Secretary of State for War', the report tartly observed. Monsell 'when he differed from the other members of his Board, applied to the Secretary of State, who, by lending his sanction to the Clerk of the Ordnance, enabled him to overrule both his colleagues, and this interfered in a matter involving questions of military discipline as well as of departmental subordination'. Thus Monsell was deemed to be more culpable than Hastings. The final judgement on these squabbles took the form of a sharp rebuke: 'in noticing the unseemly conduct of this Board, and the differences which were brought prominently forward in the evidence, your committee observe with regret, that the public service has suffered from the want of judgement and temper on the part of officers who were entrusted during a critical period with important public duties'.[94]

On the face of it, this seemed a major setback to Monsell, but two factors nullified its effect. Firstly, the report itself was a dead letter, and the whole committee and its proceedings regarded as ineffective and anti-climactic. Secondly, Panmure had already carried out his consolidation of the war departments. On 8 February 1855 the office of Secretary-at-War was merged with that of Secretary of State for War. On 25 May the *London Gazette* published the royal decree 'revoking the letters patent of the Master-General, Lieutenant-General and Principal Storekeeper of the Ordnance' and 'vesting the civil administration of the army and Ordnance in the hands of Fox, Baron Panmure'.[95] While Ross and Hastings lost their posts, Monsell not only survived, but emerged greatly strengthened. The post of Clerk of the Ordnance was retained and granted a status second only to the Secretary of State himself. Monsell's salary was increased from £1,500 to £2,000 per annum and his duties were defined as 'Chief of the Civil Staff of the War Department, and the Executive Officer of the Minister of War, directing all the business of the subordinate departments'.[96] Panmure retained Monsell in this capacity in order to oversee the merger of the two departments.

Monsell enjoyed great authority as Panmure's deputy over the next eighteen months, and his reputation was very high at this period. When Palmerston had been inclined to accept his resignation in February of 1855, two of the most distinguished figures of the century intervened on behalf of Monsell. On 15 February Gladstone wrote to Panmure that

> I should state to you my strong impression that from temper, moderation, firmness, decision and judgement, he [Monsell] is a public servant whom, in relation to the departments with which he has been conversant you will find it most difficult to replace, and I entreat you not part with him if you can help it, since good workmen in these affairs are scarce and work on the other hand being abundant.[97]

On 23 February Queen Victoria wrote to Palmerston that 'she was not aware that Mr Monsell had resigned and she would consider as a great loss as she has heard nothing but praise of the manner in which he conducted the duties of the Ordnance, which was otherwise very weak'.[98]

No doubt these representations induced Palmerston to reappoint Monsell, but there were other testaments to his abilities at this period. Lord Panmure told Palmerston on 22 September 1855 that 'I am glad you were pleased with Woolwich. Let us give credit where it is really due and place on Monsell what you give to me.' Monsell was the real author of the improvements there, he wrote, 'All I have done is to criticise his suggestions and lend the weight of authority to carry them out. Had the activity you saw not been called into life, Sebastopol would not have been evacuated.'[99] Again, on 1 April 1859 Panmure told the Select Committee on Military Organisation that he had retained Monsell after the abolition of the Ordnance Board, 'because I deemed it advisable in making these changes to have the benefit of an experienced officer ... who would contribute by his advice and assistance to bring the new system into a better working order'.[100] By so doing, he had 'all the advantage of Mr Monsell's advice and assistance, which was of the greatest benefit to the Secretary of State, as I can testify from personal experience'.[101] Monsell was further honoured by being sworn in as a member of the British Privy Council on 13 August 1855. He had objected to taking the anti-Catholic oath that a Privy Councillor was obliged to swear, so the matter was referred to the Queen and Prince Albert. Eventually, it

1. 'The Right Hon. William Monsell, the painstaking Irishman' by 'Ape' (Carlo Pellegrini) from *Vanity Fair*, No. 119, 11 February, 1871.

2. William Monsell as a young man, photograph by Michael Martin (The Earl of Dunraven)

3. William Monsell in middle age (Daniel McSweeney)

4. Lady Anna Maria Monsell, first wife of William Monsell, photograph by Michael Martin (The Earl of Dunraven)

5. Berthe Monsell, second wife of William Monsell, (Daniel McSweeney)

6. Tervoe House, Monsell's country seat (Author's private collection)

7. Monsell's son and successor Gaston, second Lord Emly (Author's private collection)

8. Monsell's daughter Mrs Mary de la Poer (Nigel de la Poer)

9. Edwin Richard Wyndham-Quin, third Earl of Dunraven, photograph by Michael Martin (The Knight of Glin)

10. David Moriarty, Bishop of Kerry (Daniel McSweeney)

11. Pope Pius IX (Daniel McSweeney)

12. Thomas O'Hagan, 1st Baron O'Hagan (Daniel McSweeney)

13. John Henry Newman by Thomas Oldham Barlow, after Sir John Everett Millais, 1st Bt (National Portrait Gallery, London)

14. John Acton, 1st Baron Acton by Franz Seraph von Lenbach (National Portrait Gallery, London)

15. William Ewart Gladstone by Sir John Everett Millais, 1st Bt (National Portrait Gallery, London)

16. Paul, Cardinal Cullen photograph by Fratelli D'Alessandri (National Portrait Gallery, London)

17. Bolton Meredith Eyres-Monsell, 1st Viscount Monsell photograph by Bassano (National Portrait Gallery, London)

was altered to meet his objections, and he was sworn in.[102]

Monsell used his enhanced position to further his aims. He continued the expansion of the Royal arms factories with dramatic results. The acreage of the Royal Arsenal increased from 266 in 1853 to 649 in 1861 and the numbers employed increased from 2,500 in 1854 to 10,238 in 1861.[103] Thus he played a decisive role in making the Royal Arsenal the largest military-industrial complex in Europe. However, his greatest achievement was the bringing about of a major Liberal reform. In May 1855 he introduced the principle of recruitment by competitive examination into the Royal Military Academy at Woolwich, which educated cadets who then became officers in the two Ordnance Corps regiments.[104] Prior to this, they had been recruited by patronage. Monsell won Panmure's support for this reform measure and together they implemented it, against the protests of conservative elements in the War Department and in the Woolwich Academy itself. In announcing this innovation to the Commons on 25 May 1855, Monsell referred to the examination system as being designed to 'procure a large number of well-educated and efficient officers for her Majesty's service'.[105] On 22 February 1856 he was able to inform Parliament that 'the result had proved most satisfactory' and the cadets so recruited were possessed not only of 'intelligence, but of military bearing'.[106] This was the first occasion that such a method of recruitment was used in any branch of the British armed forces.[107]

Monsell was to be highly acclaimed for this achievement. Sir Charles Trevelyan, one of the authors of the Northcote–Trevelyan report, later told him that he had conferred a great benefit on the public service by this action, writing that 'I shall never forget the prompt and decisive and permanent public benefit derived from your action, in the application of the open competition system of appointment to the Artillery and Engineers.'[108] This compliment, coming from such a formidable and forbidding figure, was a rare honour indeed! Other tributes were more extravagant, though less accurate. Maurice Lenihan, referring to his period as Clerk of the Ordnance, wrote of it as the time 'when he reorganised the war office in conjunction with Lord Panmure' (as if the latter was only his assistant), while his obituary in the *Munster News* was to usurp on Monsell's behalf the contribution of all other civil service reformers and to state flatly that 'he initiated and carried through the reform which made competitive examinations the road to appointments in the civil service'.[109] Ironically, Monsell's decisive role in the Crimean war effort has never been acknowledged in any of the standard works on the conflict.[110]

The Crimean War was brought to a successful conclusion when Sebastopol was taken by the allies on 16 September 1855 and the Treaty of Paris, which concluded the hostilities, was signed on 30 March 1856.[111]

The most exciting and productive period of Monsell's period as Clerk of the Ordnance was now at an end. His influence had been very great, and he had brought about two major changes of policy – a vast increase in the government manufacturing establishments, and the recruitment of cadets by competitive examination. He was very proud of his achievements, but they were both controversial, and he was obliged to defend them against fierce attacks in later years, most notably in 1858 and 1864. In April 1858 the Conservative government of Lord Derby wanted to dilute the competitive element in the recruitment of cadets to Woolwich by insisting that future cadets would be obliged to first spend a period at the Royal Military College at Sandhurst. In effect, only students of Sandhurst would have the right of entry to Woolwich. Monsell led the defence of his system of recruitment, and was supported by Sidney Herbert, former Secretary of State for War. Monsell brought forward a motion to retain his system on 26 April, and eventually carried the day by 217 votes to 177. This was a major defeat for the Derby government.[112] On 22 July 1864 Richard Cobden (1804–65), one of the great figures of the Victorian age, apostle of free trade and a leader of the Manchester School, attacked the whole concept of government manufacturing establishments, in a very long speech to the Commons.[113] He stated that, 'I am afraid that I must charge him [i.e. Monsell] with having deposited the nest egg which has produced the pernicious brood of which I am complaining.'[114] In a fairly ideologically motivated speech, he flatly denied that the Government should ever undertake to be producers and manufacturers. He maintained that government manufacturing establishments were always bound to be inefficient, expensive and unnecessary and concluded by calling on the Government 'in future to place yourselves entirely in dependence upon the private manufacturing resources of the country'.[115] In his reply, Monsell struck a typically pragmatic note. While Cobden had 'passed an indiscriminate censure upon all government manufacturing establishments', Monsell was prepared to examine each on its merits and maintained that the two chief reasons for the success of the government factories were that they provided the necessities of war which the private sector had failed to do, in the crisis of the Crimean War, and that they did so much less expensively than their commercial rivals. The debate that followed saw a fierce attack on Monsell by Newdigate, but the parliamentary session ended before the motion brought forward by Cobden could be debated further. The latter died before the following session commenced, so the matter was dropped.[116]

Monsell's work of consolidation and reorganisation at the War Department was completed by the beginning of 1857. On 9 February the office of Clerk of the Ordnance was abolished and Monsell was appointed

President of the Board of Health, with the same salary and status as his old post. The General Board of Health, which had been established in 1848, was the forerunner of the modern Department of Health, and its main function was to co-ordinate the work of the various local health authorities in Britain.[117] The President controlled policy, and, as political head, was responsible to Parliament for his department. Unfortunately for Monsell, the Board was in a very weak position by the time he was appointed its head. It was fiercely opposed by many interest groups, both inside and outside Parliament, who regarded it as a useless, corrupt and expensive body (although it had only a staff of eight), and Palmerston's government had very little interest in social reform in general, and the Board of Health in particular. Monsell was aware that his position was neither a comfortable nor a prestigious one, and that the Government had already resolved to get rid of the Board.[118]

In April 1857 there was a general election in Britain and Ireland. The Independent Opposition party, by now on its last legs, contemplated running John George Adair (later the notorious landlord who carried out the Glenveagh evictions in County Donegal in 1861) as a candidate in an attempt to unseat Monsell in County Limerick. Nothing came of this and both Monsell and his friend Stephen de Vere (who had been elected to Parliament in a by-election in 1854) were returned unopposed as the two MPs for County Limerick.[119] The Government had decided to abolish the Board of Health and to transfer its functions to a committee of the Privy Council, and by 9 August Newman could write that Monsell 'is not on good terms with government – and in consequence of the Divorce Bill, will soon, they say, have nothing to do with them'.[120]

Monsell had no longer any interest in being part of the administration, as the Prime Minister clearly did not desire to retain his services. This was recognised by Archbishop Cullen, who wrote to Tobias Kirby, Rector of the Irish College in Rome on 28 May 1857 that 'Mr Monsell loses his place under the Government ... there is now no Catholic in place. Lord Palmerston is so strong he can do without them.'[121] Palmerston's divorce bill was merely the straw that broke the camel's back. This legislation, which did not apply to Ireland, provided for the creation of a special court to handle divorce petitions, put divorce on the same footing as other civil actions, and allowed the remarriage of divorced persons. The Catholic Church was of course implacably opposed, and Monsell wrote to Palmerston announcing his intention to resign. He described holding office under the present circumstances as 'unpleasant', but he had remained on out of a sense of duty. 'I feel myself bound on public grounds,' he wrote, 'to vote against the Divorce Bill, and do not think it right to do so without tendering my resignation to you.'[122] The bill was passed with large majorities and became law, while Monsell's resignation from office took effect from 24 September 1857. He did not make public his reasons for resigning, the newspapers scarcely noticed it, nor was his opposition to the divorce bill mentioned in connection with it.[123] The *Tablet* carried a report on 12 September mentioning his resignation and stating that he was offered the position of Under-Secretary for the Colonies, but that he had declined.[124] This report is not borne out by any correspondence in Monsell's papers. Instead, it would appear that he was happy to end his increasingly untenable and uncomfortable connection with the Palmerston administration. For his part, Palmerston was also content to see Monsell's departure.

Thus ended Monsell's first period as an office-holder. He had been successful in obtaining and retaining office, had played the games of both parliamentary and office politics with skill, and had shown himself to be a successful and innovative administrator. It might have been expected that he would have been on the threshold of a more senior ministerial position, but it was not to be. He was to be out of office, with only one short interval, for the next eleven years.

NOTES

1. For a good account of Wiseman, see Richard J. Schiefen, *Nicholas Wiseman and the Transformation of English Catholicism* (Shepherdstown, VA: Patmos Press, 1984).
2. See Buschkuhl, *Great Britain and the Holy See*, pp.88–92; Denis Gwynn, *Cardinal Wiseman* (Dublin: Browne and Nolan, 1950) pp.110–34; Newsome, *Convert Cardinals*, pp.192–5.
3. See E.R. Norman, *Anti-Catholicism in Victorian England* (London: George Allen and Unwin, 1968).
4. *The Times*, 14 October 1850.
5. Russell to Maltby, 4 November, 1850 quoted in Gwynn, *Cardinal Wiseman*, pp.117–18.
6. Ibid., p.134. See also Newsome, *Convert Cardinals*, pp.193–4 and G.I.T. Machin, 'Lord John Russell and the Prelude to the Ecclesiastical Titles Bill, 1846–51' in *Journal of Ecclesiastical History*, 25, 3 (July 1974), pp.277–95.
7. J.H. Whyte, *The Independent Irish Party 1850–9* (Oxford: Oxford University Press, 1958), p.20.
8. Ibid., p.21.
9. Ibid., pp.89–90.
10. Ibid., pp.86–90.
11. Hansard, CXVII, 1010–17 (20 June 1851); CXV, 1362–4 and 1383 (23 May 1851) and CXVII, 588–90 (6 June 1851).
12. Whyte, *Independent Irish Party*, pp.178–9.
13. Horgan, 'Irish Catholic Whigs in Parliament', pp.129–30.
14. Whyte, *Independent Irish Party*, pp.180–3.
15. Monsell to Newman 12 February (1851), NP (N/P/M2).
16. Edward Norman, *The Catholic Church and Ireland in the Age of Rebellion 1859–1873* (London: Longmans, 1965), p.293.
17. The standard account of Aberdeen's administration is J.B. Conacher, *The Aberdeen Coalition 1852–55: A Study in Mid-Nineteenth Century Party Politics* (Cambridge: Cambridge University Press, 1968).
18. Charles Gavan Duffy, *The League of North and South: an Episode in Irish History 1850–1854* (London: Chapman and Hall, 1886), p.239.

19. Hansard, CXXVII, 945 (31 May 1853).
20. Whyte, *Independent Irish Party*, p.99.
21. Russell to Aberdeen, 2 June 1853, Aberdeen papers in the British Library (hereafter referred to as AP Add. MS 43067, ff. 33–6.
22. Roantree, 'William Monsell and the Catholic Question', p.14.
23. Aberdeen to Monsell 3rd June, 1853, AP Add. MS 43250, f.141.
24. *The Times*, 6 June 1853.
25. Whyte, *Independent Irish Party*, p.100.
26. John Biggs-Davison, and George Chowdharay-Best, *The Cross of St Patrick: The Catholic Unionist Tradition in Ireland* (Abbotsbrook, Bucks: Kensal Press, 1984), p.181.
27. Roantree, 'William Monsell and the Catholic Question', p.149.
28. Monsell to Aberdeen, 4 June 1853, AP Add. MS 43250, ff.147–9.
29. *The Tablet*, 11 June 1853.
30. Whyte, *Independent Irish Party*, p.100.
31. A good introduction to Cullen is Emmet Larkin, 'Paul Cullen (1803–1878)', in *Oxford DNB*. The best biography is Desmond Bowen, *Paul Cardinal Cullen and the Shaping of Modern Irish Catholicism* (Dublin: Gill and Macmillan; Waterloo, Ont.: Wilfrid Laurier University Press, 1983). A major work, though one to be used with caution, is Peadar MacSuibhne, *Paul Cullen and his Contemporaries with their Letters from 1820–1902*, 5 vols. (Naas: Leinster Leader, 1961–77). Cullen features prominently in several volumes of Emmet Larkin's monumental history of the Catholic Church in Ireland in the nineteenth century: *The Making of the Roman Catholic Church in Ireland, 1850–1860* (Chapel Hill: University of North Carolina Press, 1980); *The Consolidation of the Roman Catholic Church in Ireland, 1860–1870* (Chapel Hill: University of North Carolina Press, 1987); *The Roman Catholic Church and the Home Rule Movement in Ireland, 1870–1874* (Chapel Hill: University of North Carolina Press 1990); *The Roman Catholic Church and the Emergence of the Modern Irish Political System, 1874–1878* (Washington, DC and Dublin: Four Courts Press, 1996).
32. An excellent modern account is Colin Barr, *Paul Cullen, John Henry Newman, and the Catholic University of Ireland, 1845–1865* (Notre Dame, IL: University of Notre Dame Press, 2004).
33. Roantree, 'William Monsell and the Catholic Question', p.130.
34. Newman, *Letters and Diaries*, Vol. 15, pp.139–42. See also *Limerick Reporter*, 3 August 1852.
35. Newman, *Letters and Diaries*, Vol. 15, p.141.
36. Ibid., pp.283–4.
37. Ibid., Vol. 17, p.503, Monsell to Newman, 20 January 1857.
38. Ibid., Vol. 16, p.169.
39. Ibid., Vol. 16, pp.179–80, Newman to Monsell, 28 June 1854.
40. Ibid., p.179, Monsell to Newman, 30 June 30 1854.
41. Ibid., Vol.17, p.459, Monsell to Newman, 22 November 1856.
42. Barr, *Cullen, Newman, and the Catholic University of Ireland, passim.*
43. Newsome, *Convert Cardinals*, p.217.
44. Ibid., p.216.
45. Newman, *Letters and Diaries*, Vol. 16, p.538, Monsell to Newman, 7 September 1855.
46. Ibid., Vol. 17, p.503, Monsell to Newman, 20 January 1857.
47. See Roantree, 'William Monsell and the Catholic Question', pp.154–6.
48. Duffy, *League of North and South*, p.174. For Gavan Duffy, see R.B. O'Brien, revised Brigette Anton, 'Sir Charles Gavan Duffy (1816–1903)', in *Oxford DNB*, and Cyril Pearl, *The Three Lives of Gavan Duffy* (Dublin: O'Brien Press, 1979).
49. Whyte, *Independent Irish Party*, pp. 114–15.
50. For Lucas, see Thompson Cooper, revised Josef L. Altholz, 'Frederick Lucas (1812–1855)', in *Oxford DNB*.
51. Whyte, *Independent Irish Party*, p.119.
52. Edward Lucas, *The Life of Frederick Lucas, MP by his Brother*, 2 vols (London: Burns and Oates, 1886), Vol. 2, pp.300, 302 and 314.
53. Ibid., pp.327–8.
54. Cullen to Monsell, 10 May 1855 MP, NLI, 8317(3).

55. Aubrey de Vere to Florence, 27 June 1894, DVP, Trinity College, 5053, no. 278.
56. For the Board of Ordnance, see Major General A. Forbes, *A History of the Army Ordnance Services*, 2 vols (London: Medici Society, 1929), and Norman Skentelbery, *Arrows to Atom Bombs: A History of the Ordnance Board* (London: Ordnance Board, 1975).
57. For the state-run armaments factories, see Brigadier O.F.G.Hogg, *The Royal Arsenal, its Background, Origin and Subsequent History*, 2 vols (London, New York and Toronto: Oxford University Press, 1963), and William Hornby, *Factories and Plant*, History of the Second World War. United Kingdom Civil Series (London: HMSO and Longmans, 1958).
58. Forbes, *History of the Army Ordnance Services*, Vol.1, p.98.
59. For Monsell's activities at the Board of Ordnance see *Reports from the Select committee on the army before Sebastopol with minutes of evidence and appendix*, P.P. 1854–5(9), nos. 4 and 5.
60. Ibid., p.194.
61. For an account of the general decrepitude and confusion of the administration of the British military establishment at this time, see Forbes, *History of the Army Ordnance Services*, Vol.1, pp.193–207 and 257–62.
62. There are many works on the Crimean War. The military aspects of it are dealt with by Lieutenant-General Sir George McMunn, *The Crimea in Perspective* (London: G. Bell and Sons, 1935) and A.J. Barker, *The Vainglorious War 1854–56* (London: Weidenfeld and Nicolson, 1970). A good account of the war's impact on British politics is Olive Anderson, *A Liberal State at War* (New York: Weidenfeld and Nicolson, 1967). For Ireland, see David Murphy, *Ireland and the Crimean War* (Dublin: Four Courts Press, 2002).
63. For the international background, and especially the Anglo-Russian rivalry of the nineteenth century, see David Gillard, *The Struggle for Asia, 1828–1914. A Study in British and Russian Imperialism* (London: Metheun, 1977) and M.S Anderson, *The Ascendancy of Europe. Aspects of European History, 1815–1914* (London: Longmans, 1972), pp.1–70.
64. Anderson, *Liberal State at War*, pp.1–7.
65. A.J.P. Taylor's derisive term for it. See A.J.P. Taylor, *Europe: Grandeur and Decline* (Harmondsworth: Penguin, 1967), p.67.
66. For Ross and Hastings, see respective articles in *DNB*: Vol. 17, pp.261–4 and Vol. 9, p.136.
67. Hornby, *Factories and Plant*, p.6.
68. Hansard, CXXX, 1399–1406 (27 February 1854).
69. Anderson, *Liberal State at War*, pp.54–6.
70. Ibid., p.34.
71. *Third report from the Select Committee on the Army before Sebastopol; Minutes of evidence*, p.144.
72. *Fourth report from the Select Committee on the Army before Sebastopol; Minutes of Evidence*, pp.77–8.
73. For this controversy, see *Fourth report on the Army before Sebastopol*, p.113. For the evidence of Hastings and Monsell on the same matter, see pp.30–40 and pp.110–13 respectively.
74. Ibid., p.117. For Monsell's account of this episode, see pp.113–38.
75. Hansard, CXXX, 1399–1406 (27 February 1854).
76. Hansard, CXXXVII, 115 (5 March 1855).
77. Hansard, CLXXVII, 1917 (22 July 1864).
78. Hansard, CLXXVII, 1910 (22 July 1864).
79. *Fourth Report on the Army before Sebastopol*, pp.125–32 and 138–42.
80. Ibid., p.140.
81. McMunn, *Crimea in Perspective*, pp.56–142.
82. Anderson, *Liberal State at War*, p.27.
83. Ibid., p.43.
84. For the collapse of the administration see Anderson, *Liberal State at War*, pp.37–47 and Conacher, *Aberdeen Coalition*, pp.492–548.
85. Newman, *Letters and Diaries*, Vol. 16, p.382, Monsell to Flanagan February 1855. See also Palmerston to Queen Victoria, 23 February 1855 in Royal Archives Windsor Castle, RA A24/6, for the new prime minister's intention of appointing Peel to Monsell's position.
86. John Sweetman, 'Fox Maule, second Baron Panmure and eleventh Earl of Dalhouisie (1801–1874)', in *Oxford DNB*.
87. Anderson, *Liberal State at War*, pp.62–6.
88. Ibid., p.62. For a discussion of this topic see pp.50–69.

89. *Fourth report on the Army before Sebastopol*, p.78.
90. Ibid., pp.29–110 and 132–4.
91. Ibid., pp.110–32 and 134–55.
92. *Fifth report from the select committee on the army before Sebastopol with the proceedings of the committee and an appendix*, 1855, p.8.
93. Ibid., pp.8–9.
94. Ibid., p.9.
95. *London Gazette*, 25 May 1855.
96. *Army Civil Departments. Copy of an order of the Queen's most Excellent Majesty in Council (passed on the 6th day of June, 1855) regulating the establishments of the civil departments of the Army*, PP 1854–5 (32) , p.2.
97. Gladstone to Panmure, 15 February 1855, The Dalhousie Muniments (GD45), in The National Archives of Scotland, Edinburgh, GD 45/8/186.
98. Queen Victoria to Palmerston, 23 February 1855, Palmerston Papers, Broadland Archives, University of Southampton, RC/F/564.
99. Panmure to Palmerston, 22 September 1855, Palmerston Papers, GC/PA/119/1.
100. *Report from the Select Committee on Military Organisation, together with the proceedings of the Committee Minutes of Evidence and Appendix*, PP 1860(7), p.14.
101. Ibid.
102. Charles C.F. Greville, *A Journal of the Reigns of King George IV, King William IV, and Queen Victoria,* edited by Henry Reeve, 8 vols (London: Longmans, Green and Co., 1874–87), Vol. 7, pp.259 and 285.
103. Hogg, *The Royal Arsenal*, Vol. 2, pp.1289–91.
104. Hansard, CXXXVII, 1191 (25 May 1855).
105. Ibid.
106. Hansard, CXL, 126809 (22 February 1856).
107. For a discussion of this issue, see B.D. Malcolm, 'Educational Reform at the Royal Military Academy Woolwich and the Royal Military College Sandhurst, 1854–1874' (unpublished M.Phil. thesis, Kings College, University of London, 1985).
108. Charles Trevelyan to Monsell 25 July 1876, Monsell of Tervoe Papers, in NLI, hereafter referred to as MTP, MS 20679.
109. Lenihan, *History of Limerick*, p.474 and *Munster News*, 21 April 1894.
110. Forbes, Hogg and Skentelbery have all overlooked his contribution.
111. Anderson, *Liberal State at War*, pp.27, 275 and 281–2.
112. Hansard, CLXIX, 1724–43 (26 April 1858).
113. Hansard CLXXVII 1907–32 (22 July 1864).
114. Ibid., 1909.
115. Ibid., 1931–2.
116. Ibid., *passim.*
117. See Royston Lambert, *Sir John Simon 1816–1904 and English Social Administration* (London: Macgibbon and Kee, 1963), pp.221–60.
118. Hansard, CXLVII, 311–12 (23 July 1857).
119. For Adair's candidacy, see Dunraven to his mother 29 March 1857, DP, D 3196/e/8/ 17, and DVP, Trinity College, MS 5056.
120. Newman, *Letters and Diaries*, Vol. 18, p.117, Newman to William Kirby Sullivan, 9 August 1857.
121. Quoted in Larkin, *Making of the Roman Catholic Church in Ireland*, p.383.
122. Monsell to Palmerston 24 July1857, Palmerston Papers. GC/GR2494.
123. See *The Tablet, Limerick Reporter, Limerick Chronicle, Freemans Journal* and *Munster News* for August, September and October 1857.
124. *The Tablet*, 12 September 1857.

CHAPTER SIX

In the Wilderness

From 1857 to 1868 Monsell's career was in eclipse. However, he was in no sense idle during these years, either in respect of the ebb and flow of parliamentary politics and advantage, or in respect of the broad range of causes to which he was committed and in which he exerted himself. Accordingly, his public life and pronouncements during this time are especially revealing, during these years in the wilderness. His departure from office signalled a permanent breach with Palmerston, which was most unfortunate as the latter remained Prime Minister until his death in 1865 (except for a brief Conservative interlude in 1858–9).[1] In addition, Palmerston was almost entirely indifferent to Irish affairs and made no attempt either to conciliate the Catholic Whigs or to remedy Irish grievances.[2] His Irish policy reached its nadir when he appointed the absurd, highly incompetent and fervently anti-Catholic Sir Robert Peel (1825–95) as Chief Secretary in 1861. This disastrous man continued in office until 1865, making a host of enemies in the process.

In these circumstances, many Catholics began to look to the Tories with a new-found interest and Disraeli saw the opportunity to woo Catholic voters in both Britain and Ireland. When Lord Palmerston unexpectedly fell from power in February 1858, Lord Derby again became Prime Minister, with Disraeli as Chancellor of the Exchequer. At this stage the 105 Irish MPs were divided into 48 Tories (all Protestants), 42 Liberals (23 Protestants and 19 Catholics) and 15 Independents (3 Protestants and 12 Catholics).[3] Since the 1857 general election the Irish Independents had, at least partially, given general support to the Tories. One of their leaders, John Francis Maguire (1815–72), who sat successively for Dungarvan (1852–65) and Cork (1865–72), was particularly anxious to extend this fledgling Tory–Catholic alliance.[4] Other factors favouring such an *entente* included the pro-Tory views of Cardinal Wiseman, who followed up his triumphant visit to Ireland in 1858 with increasing involvement in Irish politics, and the apparently more favourable policy of the Conservatives towards the Papacy in the looming crisis in Italy. England, unlike Ireland, had a large number of Catholic Tories who bitterly opposed the Catholic Whigs, while Lord Derby himself thought that Catholics and Tories were 'natural allies'.[5]

In the meantime, the quest for a government charter for the Catholic University commenced. On 8 May 1858 Cullen wrote to Monsell, asking him 'to apply for a charter for the Catholic University to Lord Derby'.[6] On 6 June Monsell wrote to Newman: 'I have seen Disraeli about the charter. He entered into the question with interest, was extremely civil and agreeable, but of course did no more than promise to take the matter into consideration.'[7] The Independent Oppositionists were determined that the Catholic Whigs should not steal their thunder, and on 24 August one of their leaders, George Bowyer, MP for Dundalk, wrote to Newman: 'I wish I had known what was going on for Monsell and de Vere are names likely to indispose the government as they are *incurable* Palmerstonians ... you may depend upon it that Disraeli will pay very little attention to their representations – though the name of Maguire will have weight.'[8] In March 1859 a deputation led by Maguire and Bowyer called on Disraeli, requesting the charter, and he was pleasant but non-committal.

The ensuing general election of 1859 was one of the hardest-fought of the entire century. In Ireland the Conservatives mounted a highly effective campaign organised by their energetic and efficient Chief Secretary, Lord Naas, who established a national fighting fund of £7,800, which he used to subsidise Tory and Tory-backed candidates throughout the country. In contrast, the Liberals were organised (insofar as they were organised at all) on a local basis.[9] The election in County Limerick was one of the most vicious campaigns in Ireland, and Monsell had to fight for his seat for the only time in the period 1847 to 1874. In the nineteenth century many parliamentary seats were uncontested, and members were often returned unopposed, as happened to Monsell at the general elections of 1852, 1857, 1865 and 1868, and on the occasions of his appointment to government office in 1853, 1857, 1866 and 1871. From 1706 to 1919 when an MP was appointed to government office, he had to stand again for election.[10] It was Monsell's constant boast that he was always returned to Parliament with all-party support, but in 1859 the vigour of Naas's campaign put him on the defensive. It was not anticipated that Monsell's seat would be in any danger, but the second seat was the real bone of contention, as Stephen de Vere did not stand again.

The other two candidates were Samuel Dickson, a Protestant, nominally a Liberal but really a Tory who was in receipt of both the support of the local Tory landlords and a subsidy of £600 from Lord Naas, and

Edward John Synan, a Catholic and a Liberal who received the support of the Catholic clergy, including Bishop Ryan. Polling in County Limerick occurred on 16 May, and the result was a resounding personal victory for Monsell. The electorate numbered 6,481, and Monsell polled 4,020 votes. A personal vote consisting of 62 per cent of the electorate was impressive, even under the restricted franchise of the time. However, Dickson was also returned with 2,626 votes, while Synan polled 2,369 votes and was defeated. Clearly, many of the electors must have plumped for Monsell, and some of those supporting Monsell had split their vote between him and Dickson.[11] The landlords had defeated the clergy in the battle for the second seat, which was in line with the national trend, for Ireland returned 58 Tories at this election, their highest ever post-1829 figure. In addition seven Catholic Independents were returned, who were inclined to support the Tories for the lifetime of the next parliament (which lasted until 1865).[12] Nevertheless, in the United Kingdom as a whole the Liberals were victorious and Palmerston again became Prime Minister, which meant that Monsell, despite his impressive electoral performance, was not appointed to any post.

The rift between the British and Irish Liberals, never fully healed since the Ecclesiastical Titles Act, was greatly widened by the Italian Crisis of 1859–61. The Risorgimento, the movement for Italian unification, came into direct conflict with the Catholic Church and its now implacably conservative head, Pope Pius IX, as the overthrow of the Papal States (one of Italy's largest political divisions with a population of 3.5 million) was a necessary prerequisite for the attainment of a united Italy.[13] Nearly all of the Pope's dominions were absorbed into the new state in 1860, leaving Rome and a small area around it under Papal rule and French protection until 1870. In many respects the Italian Crisis resembled the Spanish Civil War eighty years later, both in its crystallisation of the ideological struggles of the time and its effect on Ireland, where Catholic opinion was overwhelmingly in favour of the Pope.[14] The most spectacular manifestation of this loyalty was the extraordinary Irish Brigade of St Patrick, an army of Irish recruits who fought in the Papal Forces in the campaign of 1860 and who though defeated, were acclaimed as heroes in Ireland on their return.[15] In Britain, on the other hand, there was strong support for the Risorgimento and it was pro-Italian sentiment which acted as a major catalyst in bringing about the alliance between the Whigs, the Peelites and the Liberals and the reconciliation between the two previously antagonistic Liberal leaders, Russell and Palmerston, thus giving birth to the modern Liberal party in 1859. Both Prince Albert and Palmerston believed that Pius IX would be the last Pope, and the British government, while pursuing a policy of studied neutrality, threw its moral weight behind the Italians to the fury of the Irish Liberals.

Monsell publically championed the Pope and on 1 December 1859 delivered 'a Lecture on the Roman Question' in Limerick city, which was published the following year.[16] Typically, Monsell defended the Pope's sovereignty on pragmatic grounds, namely 'that we do not wish him to be a subject, because if he were a subject, he could not exercise independently his spiritual office'.[17] If a great European war were to break out, involving Britain and another great power, 'could it be in the interest of our government that the Pope should be a subject of that hostile power, issuing his bulls from Paris or Vienna, instead of being in possession of that independence which Pius VII asserted when he refused at the price, even of his liberty, to take part in the war which the first Napoleon waged against England?'[18] He squarely faced critics of the Pope's regime by arguing that while not devoid of blemishes, it was in fact a benevolent and reforming government.[19] Monsell's address was warmly applauded in some quarters. Cullen wrote on 7 December: 'I have sent a copy of your excellent address to Rome.' The Pope himself, having read it, expressed his gratitude to its author.[20] Among the Liberal Catholics, however, there was less enthusiasm. Ironically, most of Monsell's closest friends disagreed with his thesis. Newman used the *Rambler* (the periodical of which he was then editor) to anonymously cast doubts on the usefulness of the temporal power.[21] Lord Dunraven told Monsell that he found the *Rambler's* opinions much more to his liking than 'the Manning–Faber view'.[22] Stephen de Vere wrote to Monsell on 6 December: 'I have no sympathy with the Pope as a misgoverning temporal prince. I have all sympathy with a noble people who after long years of patient suffering have dared to claim their liberty.'[23] With the passage of time, Monsell's own position shifted considerably. On 16 March 1861 he wrote to Newman: 'the Temporal Power in its present form could not be preserved, because it is not in harmony with the spirit of the age'. He still could see the dangers posed if the Pope were to be subject to a king of Italy allied with France in a war against Britain and Austria. His solution was, 'that if Rome could be really given to the Pope with a solemn guarantee from all Europe his position would be a very good one – far better than it has ever been in latter times', though he doubted if the rising tide of Italian nationalism would permit Rome to remain outside Victor Emmanuel's kingdom.[24] Newman advocated a similar solution: 'I thought he might have Rome, and a slice of territory to the sea, or at least an honorary sovereignty.'[25] Such ideas foreshadowed the eventual solution arrived at in 1929.

The chief result of this crisis for Ireland was to widen the gulf between Monsell and the Catholic Whigs on the one hand, and Palmerston and the British Liberals on the other. In Parliament, Monsell condemned the Government's Italian policy.[26] Relations deteriorated steadily between the British and Irish Liberals throughout 1860 and 1861.[27]As Bernstein states, by November 1860 Cardwell, the Chief Secretary, told Palmerston that 'our position in Ireland was that we had no reliable support' and 'that the Italian question wd. continue to exercise an adverse influence'.[28] Palmerston himself wrote to the Chief Whip, Henry Brand, as late as 8 September 1864, that 'until the Roman question ... is finally settled, and hopelessly for the Pope, we shall have the Irish Catholics against us'.[29] However, the Prime Minister did little to reverse the trend, and did much to accelerate it. The bitterest blow of all was the appointment of Peel as Chief Secretary, a man whom even the Prime Minister himself had described in 1857 as having 'neither temper, tact, nor discretion suitable for the office'.[30] The period 1861–5, which marked Peel's term as Chief Secretary, and the last phase of Palmerston's rule, was the nadir of co-operation between the Irish and British Liberals. A sort of vicious circle developed throughout the late 1850s and early 1860s.[31] The administration's policies alienated Irish Catholic and Liberal opinion, which in turn made it very difficult for Irish Liberals appointed to office to be returned to Parliament.[32] However, the administration's reluctance to appoint Irish Liberals contributed to their alienation from their British colleagues. It was this unfortunate pattern that played the major role in keeping Monsell out of office from 1857 to 1866.[33]

It is not surprising perhaps that separatism enjoyed a strong revival in the 1860s.[34] Outside Parliament it took the form of Fenianism. Within the walls of Westminster Independent Opposition continued to flourish and doubts can be cast on Whyte's contention that the party disappeared in 1859.[35] In reality, the 1859 general election had seen the return of about ten independent Liberals in Ireland.[36] True, the Tenant League, which was the movement's formal extra-parliamentary institutional expression, did not meet again after 1858, but the Independent Opposition group established in the 1850s continued to operate in the Irish constituencies until 1866.[37] Its continued existence within and without Parliament posed a threat to Monsell and the Catholic Whigs, as well as providing a link between the Independent party of the 1850s and the Home Rule party of the 1870s. Its leading lights were John Francis Maguire and until 1865 Daniel O'Donoghue (1833–89), the O'Donoghue of the Glens, MP for Tipperary from 1857 to 1865.[38] Indeed, in the period from 1858 to the mid-1860s there was always the possibility of a national movement for self-government taking shape, due to the continued efforts of O'Donoghue, William Smith O'Brien (returned from Tasmania) and some others.[39]

Thus Monsell's position was an awkward one, and in May 1861 he contributed an article to the *Rambler* entitled 'Catholic Policy' in which he attempted to grapple with the issues of the day and set forth his current political beliefs.[40] Having soundly rejected the pro-Tory policies of Cardinal Wiseman, J.F. Maguire and the Independent Oppositionists, he outlined his own strategy. The problem, as he put it, was that 'the Tories are faithful, and the Liberals unfaithful to their principles when they wrong us'.[41] Nevertheless, he went on, 'carry out the principles of the one party to their logical results, and we have all we ask for or desire – liberty; a clear stage, and no favour; absolute and entire equality civil and religious; in foreign affairs, *bonafide* non intervention. Tory principles, on the other hand, involve privilege – exceptional favour towards the Established Church'.[42] The difficulty lay in the Liberal administration's failure to adhere to its principles, as Monsell saw them. He again attacked their Italian policy and complained that they had submitted the Irish Catholics, 'an influential portion of the Liberal Party, to insult and ostracism'.[43] Yet Monsell's solution to this dilemma was curiously unsatisfactory and came close to the position of Independent Opposition. Firstly, Catholics in both Britain and Ireland must be firmly united.[44] Secondly, they should not be weak, supine supports of the administration, but become truculent and obstreperous. They should vote against the Liberals, indeed even help to bring about their overthrow, for a temporary period of Tory rule might be necessary to bring them to their senses.[45] This 'involves no abandonment of Liberal principles, and no defection from the Liberal Party. They may turn out the government over which Lord Palmerston and Lord John preside, but they will not become Tories.'[46] They would only gain concessions by advertising to the British Liberals that they were not to be taken for granted.

Monsell was as good as his word. From 1861 to 1865 he was a most unreliable Liberal MP, and in practice was virtually indistinguishable from an Independent. In April 1861 Cardinal Wiseman demonstrated his appraisal of the situation when he advised the Conservatives to try and win Monsell to their side by virtue of his prominence within the Liberal party and his strong ties with the Irish bishops.[47] On the 24 May 1862 the Liberal Chief Whip, Brand wrote to the Irish Viceroy, Lord Carlisle: 'we have no more bitter enemies in the H. of C. than M. O'Ferrall, Monsell and Co.'[48] In January 1863 Monsell fiercely condemned Peel in the *Home and Foreign Review*.[49] In Parliament he regularly criticised the Government. On 17 August 1860 he blamed British policy for the massacres perpetrated on the Christian population of the Lebanon, and clashed with Palmerston over this matter.[50] On 7 May 1861 he criticised Government policy in the Ionian Islands, and on 10 May he returned to the Lebanese crisis.[51] On 30 May he opposed the Government on the repeal of the paper duty, and on 13 March 1862 he had a nasty row with Palmerston in the Commons on the question of the patronage in the hands of the Commander-in-Chief of the Army.[52] While the hostilities in Parliament between Monsell and the Government diminished somewhat in 1863 and 1864, his voting record continued to be most unreliable. An analysis of the voting records of Irish MPs demonstrates that Maguire, one of the leaders of Independent Opposition, showed greater loyalty to the Liberals than did Monsell![53] Of a total of thirteen vital parliamentary votes between 1857 and 1865, Monsell voted in favour of the Liberals on four occasions, against on three occasions, and was absent on six. Maguire's corresponding figures were six, three and four. Overall, Monsell's record throughout this period was more unreliable than the bulk of his Liberal colleagues.

The question of Catholic education preoccupied Monsell throughout the 1860s, although he differed from the Bishops on a number of issues. The central principle of the national schools system was that children of different religions would receive secular education together, but religious instruction separately.[54] By 1859 most national schools were in practice denominational. The Bishops were pragmatic enough not to condemn the national system, which conferred immense benefits, but they worked assiduously to bend it more and more to their will, while ultimately holding out for a *de jure* denominational system. On the other hand, Monsell was much more enthusiastic about the national system. On 22 July 1859 he told the Commons that 'the national system could hardly be said to be a failure, because there had been established under it schools in which 550,000 children were taught, and which, whatever may be the fault of some of them, were, compared with primary schools in other parts of the world, of a high order'. The Liberal Catholics in general – Dunraven, the de Veres and Bishop Moriarty – were also supportive of the National School System. Cullen and the Bishops continued their two-pronged policy of demanding a denominational system while agitating for changes to the national schools. While Monsell differed from them in theory, he tended to agree with their approach in practice.

It was otherwise with university education.[55] The Catholic University was now very weak and badly in need of both official recognition and endowment. Dr Woodlock, the new rector of the Catholic University, proposed extending the charter of Maynooth College to include the Catholic University, and his idea found support from Monsell and Moriarty.[56] Then, on 5 July 1862 Palmerston received a deputation from the Catholic University, which asked him for a charter. Monsell had attempted to smooth their way in a letter to Gladstone on 2 July, but

Palmerston flatly refused to grant the charter.[57] Monsell followed this up with an article in the *Home and Foreign Review* in January 1863 entitled 'University Education in Ireland'.[58] He fiercely denounced state education as it was practised in France before the Falloux Law, and in Ireland as represented by the Queen's Colleges, and the 'statesmen' promoting them, Palmerston and his 'intemperate and intractable Irish Secretary' Peel.[59] When he came to outlining his solution to the problem in Ireland Monsell was studiously moderate, stressing that Trinity College and other Protestant bastions would not be threatened by his three possible solutions. Firstly 'to give a charter to the unendowed Catholic University is perhaps the simplest mode by which this object might be attained'.[60] The second option was for 'all students who produced certificates of having completed their college course, whether at the Queen's Colleges, at the Catholic University, or at any other college, whether founded by government or by private munificence, might be entitled to enter for examination, and if found eligible, to receive degrees'.[61] This was similar to the systems in Belgium and France, to the federal universities of Oxford and Cambridge and to the University of London External System that had been founded in 1858. Thirdly, he referred to a proposal considered by Lord John Russell in the 1840s 'to make Cork and Galway Colleges Catholic, and the Belfast Presbyterian, in the same way as Trinity College belongs to the Established Church'.[62] On 22 May 1862 Monsell stated that ' a charter might be given to the Catholic University – or some central body in which all colleges were represented, might be established, and given power to appoint examiners and confer degrees'.[63] The first and third options outlined in 'University Education in Ireland' were incompatible with the Liberal creed of non-denominational education, but option two, which was already working smoothly on the continent of Europe, was the best way of squaring the circle.

At the end of 1864 Cullen and the Bishops were active in founding a pressure group called the National Association, which had as its three aims compensation for improvements for Irish tenants; disestablishment of the Irish Protestant Church; and freedom and equality of education.[64] This initiative was an attempt to counter the Fenian threat, but it met with limited success until its eventual demise in 1873. However, it played a role in the manoeuvres of John Blake Dillon (1816–66), MP for Roscommon 1865–6, in reconciling both the Irish Liberals and the Independent Oppositionists with the British Liberal party, a trend that culminated in Gladstone's election triumph of 1868.[65] Monsell did not join the National Association, probably due to the question of the oath taken by Catholic MPs, which precluded agitation against the Established Church.[66] However, he approved of the new association's policies, and they were to form the basis of Gladstone's reforms after 1868. The chief role of the National Association was to forge the alliance between the Irish Catholics and the English Nonconformists, whose Liberation Society was dedicated to disestablishment in Britain and Ireland. William O'Neill Daunt (1807–94), a lifelong supporter of self-government for Ireland and later secretary of Butt's Home Government Association, played a major role in establishing this link.[67]

On 20 June 1865 O'Donoghue asked for a charter for the Catholic University in the Commons.[68] The Government's counter-proposal was 'an enlargement of the powers of the Queen's University in Ireland by amending its charter so as to remove the restriction which now prevents it from granting degrees to any students except those who have passed through the course of instruction in one or other of the Queen's Colleges, and thus adopting a system analogous to that found to work satisfactorily in the University of London'.[69] Monsell welcomed this, saying that 'Her Majesty's government had conferred the greatest blessings upon Ireland.'[70] The Catholic MPs and the Bishops were reasonably satisfied, although Cullen feared 'the whole business may be an electioneering trick' in the forthcoming general election.[71]

On 7 July Monsell met Lord Wodehouse in Dublin and asked for a charter incorporating the Roman Catholic University as a college and outlining a governing senate of half ecclesiastics, half laymen, he suggested among others the Catholic Whigs Aubrey de Vere, the O'Conor Don, Thomas O'Hagan and Bishop Moriarty. This met with the approval of Wodehouse, who added the name of Monsell himself. It was now clear that their plans turned on the question of the grant of a charter to the Catholic University as a college of Queen's University.[72] Monsell was also firmly opposed to the Bishops' insistence on wanting a governing body of their proposed college exclusively composed of clerics.[73] At this point a rift between the Liberal Catholic desire for the laity having a major vote in running the Catholic University and the Bishops' desire for their absolute control was opening up. In 1865, following Monsell's involvement in the Oxford Hall scheme, Cullen told Kirby: 'Save us from our friends. No man living can do more mischief than Monsell if he go astray ... he is not thoroughly sound on the education question.'[74]

In the first week of August 1865 Monsell hosted a conference in Tervoe House on the education question.[75] It was attended by O'Hagan, Aubrey de Vere, Bishops Moriarty of Kerry and Butler of Limerick, Dr Woodlock, and H.A. Bruce, Vice-President of the Committee of the Privy Council for Education (in effect Minister for Education).[76] The devil was soon to be found in the details. On 11 February 1866 Monsell showed Cullen an incomplete draft of the charter of the Royal University (as the revised Queen's University was to be called).[77] The three Queen's Colleges, the Catholic University and possibly Magee College, Derry were to be affiliated to the university, which would have only two bishops in the senate of thirty-four. In the next week Monsell obtained the other provisions of the draft charter for Cullen, and this showed that the Catholic college would have to have lay membership in its governing body. Cullen was not at all pleased.[78] He felt annoyed that Monsell's allies, Moriarty and Butler, would take seats on the senate. Monsell in turn threatened to tell Chief Secretary Fortescue that there could be no deal.[79] He was standing for re-election after being appointed Vice-President of the Board of Trade, so Cullen acidly observed to Woodlock: 'Monsell wanted to be able to announce to the voters at his election that the education question was settled to the satisfaction of the bishops.'[80] Cullen now shifted in favour of an 'open system' in which the Queen's University would be open to students of all colleges and act as an examining board. In this way the Catholic University would retain its independence and still receive official degrees for its students.[81] At this stage he was convinced that Monsell was advising Fortescue not to yield to the bishops.[82] Eventually the Government issued a Supplemental Charter for the Queen's University, by which its degrees were thrown open to all students. Monsell accepted this as a solution and he and O'Hagan were among six new members appointed to the expanded senate of the Queen's University. They remained senators until the university's abolition in 1882. However, the Supplemental Charter was never put into operation as three graduates of the Queen's University obtained a court injunction preventing it from being put into effect and it was declared null and void in 1868.[83]

The Conservatives returned to office in 1866, and the Bishops now turned to them for official recognition for the Catholic University. Disraeli was still wooing the Catholic vote and the remains of Independent Opposition and on 19 February 1868 he told Manning that he was prepared to grant a charter for the Catholic University, but with no endowment and with laymen on the governing body. Manning pressed Cullen to accept the offer.[84] On 16 March Monsell rejected this proposal, largely because he did not want to see his Conservative opponents steal a march on the Liberals by solving the university question. In the meantime he moved to spike the Conservatives' guns. Bishop Moriarty had written to him on 2 March 1868 stating that the university question was not the means of curing discontent in Ireland, because 'it touches only a class which is not disaffected'.[85] It was disestablishment that would really cure popular discontent. Monsell gave this letter to Gladstone, who was thus influenced to bring his famous resolutions on the Church of Ireland before the Commons in an effort to outbid Disraeli for the Irish Catholic vote.[86]

As it happened, Monsell had nothing to fear, as the Bishops wanted to retain absolute control over the newly chartered university, while the Government insisted on laymen being included on the governing body. Consequently, the plan collapsed.[87] Nevertheless, this episode showed how Monsell, despite his desire to solve the university question, was prepared to help defeat a plan which would have given the Catholic University more than what was on offer in Gladstone's proposals of 1873, which he was to strongly support. Admittedly, the core of the 1873 bill was Monsell's own plan of making the University of Dublin a federal body, incorporating all the existing colleges in Ireland, but it must be remembered that the Liberals' supplemental charter was also less than the Conservative offer of 1868. However, Monsell's stance was logically consistent. He wanted a single federal university that would be non-denominational but could have denominational colleges affiliated to it, and he wanted the laity to be involved in its governing body. Thus, he supported the supplemental charter of 1866 and Gladstone's plan of 1873. However, the Catholic Bishops were lukewarm to the former, and actively opposed the latter. Also, Monsell was only prepared to accept the solution at the hands of a Liberal government. The 'one neutral university and denominational or other colleges' plan was not devised by Monsell as the solution to Ireland's university question, but he adopted it as his own, and became its leading advocate in the 1860s and 1870s.[88] Eventually it came to be known as 'Mr Monsell's scheme'.[89]

Monsell also took a major part in the controversy over university education for Catholics in Britain. On 5 May 1863 E.P. Bouverie introduced a bill in the Commons allowing non-Anglicans to join the teaching bodies of Oxford and Cambridge. Monsell wrote to Newman on 7 June stating that he would oppose this, as leading to mixed education, but would instead prefer a separate Catholic college to be established at Oxford to cater for the Catholic upper classes.[90] Newman replied on 10 June, agreeing to this proposal.[91] He agreed with Monsell that Catholic youths should benefit from attending what Monsell described as 'the training school for the social and political life of England' while avoiding contamination by the prevailing Protestant ethos that pervaded these institutions. The federal structure of Oxbridge allowed for this to be achieved relatively easily. However, Newman posed one problem for Monsell to solve: 'how can you, an Irish MP take part in such a movement without a pointed slight to the Catholic University of Ireland? Are Catholic Irish gentlemen to send their children to Oxford? ... who in the whole of Ireland can be expected to avail himself of the Catholic University, if such as you do not?'[92]

Monsell's reply, of 14 June, was an interesting one.[93] He answered Newman's query by stating that 'nothing could induce me to send my son there [i.e. the Catholic University]', because of the Ultramontanism of some of its professors, 'the class of students' and the nationalistic spirit exhibited there. He agreed that 'there was a large class ... who would be immensely benefited by sending their children there – in time all that would be an obstacle to me would probably be removed – civilisation – love of order and law will progress in Ireland – but that will not be during my lifetime.' This letter, which throws considerable light on Monsell's élitism and his belief that England was far superior in civilisation to Ireland, did not satisfy Newman, although not necessarily because he disagreed with Monsell's analysis of the shortcomings of the Catholic University. He replied on 16 June stating that Monsell could not 'become the advocate of an Oxford Catholic college without damaging the nascent hopes of the Catholic university to be recognised by government' precisely because he was 'a conspicuous Irish MP, the confidential friend of Dr Cullen'.[94] However, it is possible that Monsell may have involved Newman in the idea of going to Oxford to establish a hall or college or oratory for Catholics.[95] This idea gathered momentum in 1864, and Newman bought land in Oxford and attempted to put his plan into operation. However, the English Bishops met and laid down the rule that 'parents ought to be in every way dissuaded' from sending their sons to 'Protestant universities'.[96] This was the last significant act of the ailing Wiseman, who died on 15 February 1865.

The new Archbishop of Westminster was H.E. Manning, who was elevated to Cardinal in 1875 and ruled until his death in 1892. His accession was a further blow to the rapidly declining Liberal Catholic cause for he was an Ultramontane, an autocrat and a firm proponent of denominational education. He soon formed a close alliance with Cullen, and although he was an old friend of Monsell, he distrusted Newman, regarding him as a leading Liberal Catholic.[97] It was in these unpromising circumstances that Newman revived his Oxford plan, but it failed even more miserably the second time around, and its final collapse in August 1867 left a bitter taste in many mouths.[98]

The immediate cause of Monsell's biggest clash to date with the Ultramontanes was an article that appeared in the English Catholic newspaper the *Weekly Register* on 6 April 1867.[99] The offending article spoke of Newman's unsuitability for the Oxford mission, as it 'could not safely be entrusted to one who has compromised himself in the opinion of Rome'. This public attack made upon Newman by the Roman correspondent of a Catholic paper infuriated many English Catholics.[100] Monsell reacted swiftly, and on the same day a meeting of prominent Catholic laity was called by him in the Stafford Club. The following address was drawn up and presented to Newman:

> To the Very Rev. John Henry Newman,
> We, the undersigned, have been deeply pained at some anonymous attacks which have been made upon you. They may be of little importance in themselves, but we feel that every blow that touches you inflicts a wound upon the Catholic Church in this country. We hope, therefore, that you will not think it presumptuous in us to express our gratitude for all we owe you, and to assure you how heartily we appreciate the services which under God you have been the means of rendering to our holy religion.[101]

This address was signed by all the Catholic members of the House of Commons, by nearly all the Catholic peers and by the great majority of prominent laymen.[102] W.G. Ward, although he had very high regard for both Monsell and Newman, despite his theological differences with them, declined to sign on conscientious grounds, while Acton and Simpson were out of England and could not sign.[103] This was a serious setback to Manning, although it did not save Newman's mission at Oxford.[104] Manning himself took the news calmly, but his ally in Rome, the English convert Monsignor George Talbot de Malahide (1816–86), a personal friend of both the Pope and of Manning, was furious.[105] On 25 April he wrote to the Archbishop, 'now that a set of laymen with Mr Monsell at their head should have the audacity to say that a blow that touches Dr Newman is a wound inflicted on the Catholic Church in England, is an insult offered to the Holy See, to Your Grace, and all who have opposed his Oxford scheme ... They wish to govern the church in England by public opinion, and Mr Monsell is the most dangerous man amongst them.'[106] In reply on 3 May Manning again urged caution. The Bishops must remain united, for 'it would be fatal if the Stafford Club laymen could divide us, and get an Episcopal leader'.[107] He told the impetuous Talbot (who ended his days suffering from insanity) that 'the greatest prudence and circumspection is necessary'. He was right, of course, and final victory was to rest with him in this struggle, for soon after the English Bishops, under orders from Propaganda, issued instructions to the laity against attending Protestant universities.[108] As in Ireland, the Ultramontane emphasis on clerical control and the subordinate position of the laity played a major part in preventing a satisfactory solution to the problem of providing university education for Catholics. The Liberal Catholics were always determined that the laity should have a major role in Church life, and in particular, in the field of education.

The quarrel over university education in Ireland and Britain was but a part of the great world-wide struggle between Liberal Catholics and

Ultramontanes, which reached its climax in the 1860s. The former represented the most flourishing intellectual force in the Church.[109] In Britain the leading Liberal Catholics were Newman and Sir John Acton (1834–1902). They were two of the greatest men of the nineteenth century and the two outstanding figures in the development of Christian thought in the English-speaking world of the century.[110] Acton became a close friend of Monsell.[111] He was one of the greatest intellects of his time, and shared a number of Monsell's beliefs and attitudes. He had studied under Dupanloup in France, Wiseman in England and Dr Dollinger in Munich.[112] Like Monsell, he was as much at home on the continent of Europe as he was in England. In politics he was a Liberal, and sat as MP for Carlow from 1859 to 1865. His mother had married Lord Granville, one of Gladstone's chief political colleagues, and he became a close friend and confidante of the latter. Acton was a Liberal Catholic and, on his return to England in 1859, he saw it as his duty to introduce the isolated English Catholic community to progressive Catholic thought.[113] He had the Liberal Catholics' typical veneration of the English constitution, and was a close friend of Montalambert as well as of Dollinger. It was natural, therefore, that he and Monsell should become collaborators in this period.[114]

The chief Ultramontanes in Britain were Archbishop Manning and Monsell's former schoolfellow in Winchester, William George Ward.[115] The latter was a distinguished theologian and author, a contemporary of Monsell's at Oxford, and later an Anglican priest. He was an associate of Newman, and converted to Catholicism a short time before him, on 5 September 1845. He formed a close alliance with Manning and became one of the chief Ultramontanes in the country. As such, he became a great opponent of Acton, Dollinger and Montalambert. In Ireland, the battle lines were similarly drawn. On the side of the Liberal Catholics stood Monsell, Dunraven, the de Veres and their sole episcopal ally, Dr Moriarty, while Archbishop Cullen and the great phalanx of the bishops and clergy cleaved to the Ultramontane party.[116]

The two warring factions were represented by their respective periodicals. The *Dublin Review* had been founded in 1836 by the future Cardinal Wiseman and Daniel O'Connell.[117] Despite its name, it was always intended primarily as a learned journal for the rapidly growing Catholic population of England, and it was always published in London.[118] In 1862 Wiseman handed over proprietorship to Manning and in 1863 Ward became editor. He retained this position until 1878, and made it the chief organ of the Ultramontanes in Britain.[119] In this capacity it became one of the most influential periodicals in Europe. The *Rambler* had been founded in 1848 by Catholic converts, and soon developed into a Liberal

Catholic mouthpiece.[120] It clashed repeatedly with the Church authorities, especially after Richard Simpson became involved in 1854. After a stormy year as editor, Simpson was forced to resign in 1859, and Newman himself took up the post from May to July 1859. From 1858 to 1862 Simpson, Acton and Frederick Capes (brother of the magazine's founder) were the proprietors. In July 1859 Acton succeeded Newman as editor, and remained in this position until the magazine's demise in 1862. It was during this period that Monsell contributed his significant article 'Catholic Policy'. However, the *Rambler* had now become highly controversial and Acton and Simpson found themselves increasingly isolated and attacked. They were suspect in the Vatican, and threatened with censure unless they would come out in favour of temporal power.[121] The Church authorities, especially Wiseman and Manning, were deeply disapproving of the *Rambler's* supposed irreverence, its Liberal Catholicism and its refusal to bow to their authority.

In 1862 Acton and Simpson terminated the *Rambler* and replaced it with the *Home and Foreign Review*.[122] This was a quarterly magazine, which appeared from July 1862 until April 1864. Acton was the editor throughout its existence, and from December 1862, when Simpson ceased to be co-owner, he also was the sole proprietor. It soon came to be regarded as one of the most distinguished, well-written and influential journals in the country. It was the recognised organ of the Liberal Catholics, which prompted Cardinal Wiseman to revive the ailing *Dublin Review* as a counterweight, by putting Manning and Ward in control of it.[123] The following two years saw the most acute period of conflict between the parties. John Moore Capes, the founder of the *Rambler*, had written of the English Catholics in 1849, 'We are notoriously the most disputatious community in the kingdom, quarrelling with one another on every possible opportunity', and his strictures were never more applicable than to the period 1862 until 1864.[124] The new journal was to become even more controversial than the *Rambler*.

Monsell took fright at the new periodical's provocative articles. On 17 November he wrote to Newman saying that he wished that he had written to him before promising Acton an article, but in the January edition his contribution 'University Education in Ireland' appeared.[125] By 20 January 1863 he had reached the point of informing Acton that he would not contribute again, unless the dangerous tendencies in it ceased.[126] In fact, he never did contribute to it again, as the *Home and Foreign Review* ceased publication in April 1864, following a Papal Brief issued to the Archbishop of Munich following the controversial Malines and Munich congresses of 1863.[127] In July 1864 Monsell himself contemplated setting up a periodical to replace it, but had abandoned the attempt by 16 July.

Throughout this crisis Monsell, who knew intimately the chief players in both of the Catholic parties, had acted according to his usual tenets – adherence to Liberal and Liberal Catholic views, but in a pragmatic, realistic fashion, and in marked contrast to the brilliant Acton's intellectual arrogance and lack of tact.

Monsell was also involved intimately in the Ultramontane–Liberal Catholic struggle on the mainland of Europe, which also climaxed in 1863 and 1864. In August 1863 a congress of Belgian Catholics was held at Malines, the seat of the Belgian Primate (it is the Belgian equivalent of Armagh or Canterbury).[128] Montalambert delivered two very important speeches there on the 20th and 21st of the month. His first, on 'A Free Church in a Free State', urged that the Church should not be established, but that it should operate freely and without state support. His second, 'Liberty of Conscience', rejected religious intolerance in principle and condemned persecution in all its forms. However, he protected himself against theological criticism by making it clear that he was dealing, not with the 'thesis' of Catholic doctrine, but with the 'hypothesis' of its adjustment to the real world.[129] Because of this, and his previous defence of the Temporal Power, Cardinal Wiseman, who was present, prevented Ward from attacking Montalambert in the *Dublin Review*.[130] The importance of this exposition of Liberal Catholic political ideology by Montalambert was that it was an articulation of the same position as that held by both Newman and Monsell.[131] Monsell had condemned religious intolerance in Spain in the Commons on 17 July, and had stated that the Catholic Church in Ireland 'had no privileges, she had liberty. There was the source of her vigour, and of that zeal and energy which made her victorious over all her assailants.' On this occasion, even Palmerston applauded Monsell's speech.[132]

However, it was not Palmerston's good opinion that was uppermost in Monsell's mind. W.G. Ward coupled Montalambert's Malines addresses and Monsell's speech to the Commons in a fiercely critical pamphlet which he published soon after.[153] By January 1864 Monsell was seriously alarmed by denunciations of Montalambert's Malines speeches being made in Rome. On 22 January 1864 he wrote to Dunraven from Rome:

> On the one side are the Bishop of Orleans with whom I am with constantly [*sic*], and a few more obscure persons including myself – I have spoken in the strongest language to the Pope – on the other, a host of persons, among whom are many English, strange to say, denouncing Montalambert, and pressing as I am told, for his condemnation – as yet the blow has been averted, and I trust it will not fall. Have you read Ward's pamphlet? Berthe has been hard at work translating passages of it for the Bishop of Orleans.[134]

Eventually Pope Pius IX ordered Cardinal Antonelli to send private letters of complaint and censure to Cardinal Sterckx, Archbishop of Malines, where Montalambert had delivered his lectures, and to Montalambert himself.[135] In coming to this decision, the Pope also took into account the opinions of his friend, Monsell.[136] Wilfred Ward later wrote that

> Pio Nono expressly denied that his condemnation of the modern liberties [in the Syllabus of Errors] was aimed at Montalambert's speech ... the Pope stated, some months after the appearance of the encyclical, that he had not read the speech. 'Here it is,' he remarked to Mr Monsell, pointing to a presentation copy which he had received from Montalambert himself, 'it cannot be condemned if I have not read it, for I am the captain of the ship.'[137]

As with the case of Lucas's appeal to Rome in 1855, Monsell, in alliance with a powerful cleric, had again been successful in his intercession with the Pope. A public condemnation of Montalambert would have been disastrous, and both Newman and Monsell would have been tainted in the process.

Within a few weeks of the congress in Malines, a congress of Catholic scholars in Munich was addressed by Dollinger. In this speech he argued for the intellectual freedom of Catholics and exalted German theology and scholarship, which was destined to revitalise the Church, as it was not afraid of modern scientific and critical methods. This produced the Pope's brief to the Archbishop of Munich, which, as already mentioned, helped bring about the demise of the *Home and Foreign Review*.[138] If the demise of the latter ended the Liberal Catholic movement in England, the Pope himself moved decisively to crush it throughout the world.[139] He followed up his condemnations of the speeches of Montalambert and Dollinger by sending to the bishops of the world an encyclical *Quanta Cura* with an accompanying 'Syllabus of Errors'.[140] The latter caused a storm of protest everywhere when it appeared on 8 December 1864. A syllabus is a catalogue and this one was a list of eighty propositions that had already been condemned by the Pope in previous documents. However, the last proposition condemned was an exact statement of the Liberal Catholic creed, namely that 'the Roman Pontiff can and ought to reconcile himself to and come to terms with progress, liberalism and modern civilisation'.[141] The encyclical itself condemned the principle of freedom of conscience and worship, and the principle of 'the sovereignty of the people considered as supreme law independent of all human and divine rights'. It seemed as if the Pope was declaring war on the modern world. A later biographer of Pius IX has called it 'a gesture of defiance hurled by an outraged Pope against the nineteenth century'.[142] In particular, it caused consternation among the Liberal Catholics.[143]

Predictably, Monsell was horrified and told Newman on 10 January 1865 that 'our Catholic papers and the *Dublin Review* all seem to maintain that 80 new propositions are added to the creed ... but what are we to do in Parliament when the encyclical is thrown in our faces? Our respect for the Pope must tie our tongues ... The Bishop of Orleans is in despair.'[144] However, this same Bishop Dupanloup produced a pamphlet soon after in which he attempted to minimise the ill-effects of the Syllabus.[145] The latter was drawn up in the technical language of theology, and was intended only for the guidance of the bishops, so Dupanloup attempted to clear away the misrepresentations that had greeted its publication.[146] He wrote of the distinction between thesis and hypothesis; the Pope, he said, was speaking in terms of absolute principles and an ideal society; in the realm of hypothesis, the Liberal Catholic doctrines could still be followed.[147] Thus, Dupanloup virtually reduced the Syllabus to a nullity, but because he had included a defence of the Temporal Power in his work, he was officially thanked by over six hundred bishops, and in a half-hearted fashion, by the Pope.[148]

Despite this, *Quanta Cura* and the Syllabus were a major victory for the Ultramontanes.[149] The Munich brief and the Syllabus had sounded the death knell of Liberal Catholicism. It lingered on until 1870, however, as the Liberal Catholics struggled to keep their movement afloat.[150] Another sign of the times was the condemnation by the Vatican in 1864 of the Association for Promoting the Unity of Christendom, which had been established by Monsell's friend Ambrose de Lisle in 1857.[151] Monsell, a practical politician, had to soldier on, taking comfort from Dupanloup's pamphlet, but realising that, in the world of largely Protestant politicians in which he had his field of operation, the Pope's actions had made his task immeasurably more difficult.

Still, Monsell continued to campaign for Catholic issues at Westminster. He piloted two pieces of legislation through Parliament that remedied some of his co-religionists' grievances. The issue of the registration of Catholic marriages had been a problem for a number of years. England had a register of births, deaths and marriages since 1836, while Ireland had only a register of Protestant marriages since 1845, and none of births or deaths. During a debate on 19 February 1863 on a proposed bill to register births and deaths, Monsell advocated a register of all marriages, including Catholic ones, and was supported by Maguire.[152] His constituency colleague Colonel Dickson significantly stated that 'no two men in the world were more capable of expressing the real feelings of the Roman Catholics of Ireland' than Monsell and Maguire.[153] On 27

February Monsell 'rose to move for leave to bring in a bill to provide for the registration ... of marriages which were not at present registered – namely the marriage of Roman Catholics'.[154] It was simplicity itself, for 'the parties to the marriage would be bound, within three days after its celebration, to send a schedule to the registrar ... and the registrar would forward it to the registrar general'.[155] The bill received the royal assent on 28 July 1863, and on 22 April 1864 Cullen wrote to Monsell informing him that it was working smoothly and satisfactorily.[156] This legislation allowed for state records of Catholic marriages in Ireland to be kept for the first time and paved the way for the introduction of a full registration system for births, deaths and marriages in the following year. In 1868 the Burials Act allowed non-Anglicans to have their own religious rites at burials in parish graveyards. By an act of 1824 it was provided that 'every person, whatever his religion, should have a right to interment in the churchyard of the parish where he died', but no religious service could be provided without the permission of the Anglican minister. Monsell proposed abolishing this provision, and despite opposition by Newdigate and others, his bill was passed into law.[157]

Monsell also tackled the question of 'obnoxious oaths'.[158] He had already encountered this issue twice previously: on the first occasion when, following his conversion to the Catholic religion, he was obliged to take the oath prescribed for a Catholic MP; and in 1855, when he had forced a change in the oath taken by Catholic members of the Privy Council. Now he was also anxious to reform the oaths taken by MPs when entering Parliament. Under the Catholic Emancipation Act of 1829, Catholic and Protestant MPs took separate oaths. The Catholic oath bound Catholics to disclaim the right of the Pope to release subjects from their civil allegiance, and also to abjure any intention to subvert the Church Establishment or weaken the Protestant religion or Protestant government in the United Kingdom.[159] The whole question of Catholic oaths had to be dealt with before disestablishment could become practical politics for Roman Catholic MPs and holders of government offices, who, it was believed, could not campaign for disestablishment without violating their oaths.[160] The oath explains why a few prominent Catholic politicians like Monsell and a number of Catholic peers refused to join the National Association.[161] It was also considered that such provisions were grossly insulting to Catholics, especially as there was a longstanding and widespread Protestant belief that the Papists used equivocation and mental reservation as prescribed by St Alphonso De Liguori (founder of the Redemptorist Order) when taking oaths, a practice explicitly forbidden by the Catholic MPs' oath. On grounds both of expediency and of principle, therefore, the National Association commenced a campaign against 'obnoxious oaths' as one of its first acts.

Monsell himself considered disestablishment to be the most important measure of reform for Ireland and told Cullen: 'one preliminary step to effective agitation on the Established Church I propose to take next session, by introducing a bill for the abolition of the Catholic oath'.[162] In this action, he was supported by the National Association (of which he was not, of course, a member) and the Liberation Society, which approved of his bill at a meeting of its ruling council on 24 March.[163] On 21 March 1865 his speech introducing his private member's bill was, as usual, a moderate one.[164] He proposed substituting the Catholic oath for another one, which was much closer to the Protestant oath. He gave three reasons why the Catholic oath should be thus amended: firstly, the existing oath discriminated against the Catholic MPs; secondly, it was unnecessary and thus tended to trivialise the taking of oaths in general; and thirdly, it was equivocal and imprecise.[165] He also drew attention to the absurdity of Catholics having to make such affirmations, when the Nonconformist members such as Bright and Roebuck who desired the disestablishment of the Church of England (which Monsell personally had no wish for) did not have to do so.[166]

Sir George Grey, the Home Secretary, on behalf of the Government supported Monsell's bill.[167] The second reading, on 17 May, saw contributions by Chichester Fortescue in favour of Monsell's measure.[168] He referred to the curious circumstance that the Protestant oath had been amended in 1858, so that it was now, in fact, less offensive than the Catholic one. In the vote that followed, Monsell's bill was carried by 190 votes to 134. On 19 May it was discussed in committee and a proposal made that the Government should adopt it as their own measure. Speaking on behalf of the administration, the Chancellor of the Exchequer, Gladstone, stated that it was better for them not to get involved, as it might then become entangled in party politics. The measure had a better chance of success in the hands of a private member.[169]

In the meantime, Monsell was contending with difficulties outside Parliament concerning his proposal. Both the National Association and Sir John Gray, MP for Kilkenny, the owner and editor of the *Freeman's Journal* (himself a Protestant), favoured a single oath for all MPs. A more serious opponent was Archbishop Cullen. He preferred the single oath plan, but also deprecated Monsell's bill on theological grounds.[170] Two clauses which were retained in Monsell's amended oath obliged the swearer to defend the Protestant succession and to deny the Pope's temporal or civil authority, direct or indirect, in the kingdom. These were contrary to the Syllabus of Errors, which had condemned the notion that the Church had no temporal power. On 1 April Monsell wrote to Newman: 'I trust that Dr Cullen will keep quiet – an assertion of the temporal power of the Pope in this kingdom where bishops, priests, and students of Maynooth have been swearing, for the last seventy years he has none, would certainly have anything but pleasant results.'[171] Newman replied on 3 April: 'the common sense of mankind will decide, that you will have gained for Catholics, not all you wished to gain, but all you could'.[172] Cullen referred the matter to the Congregation of Propaganda in Rome, and its head, Cardinal Barnabo, replied, urging Cullen to try and stop the bill, and agreeing that it did not go far enough in removing Catholic grievances. Monsell was appalled at this, fearing that a Roman intervention would 'repeal the Emancipation Act'. It prompted him to move in the direction of Cullen and Gray's common oath idea. On 26 May he told Newman that he was negotiating with the Conservative party and hoped to frame a single oath to be taken by all members of Parliament equally.[173] 'If this is accomplished, it will be, I think, our greatest triumph since emancipation,' he wrote. 'It will establish our equality with Protestants, and it will relieve us from an odious and perplexing oath.' However, by 31 May he was telling Newman that negotiations with Disraeli had broken down.[174] The bill passed its third reading without amendments on 15 June.[175] However, while the Irish Catholic MPs had voted with Monsell in all the divisions, they had hardly spoken at all in the debate.[176]

On 26 June its second reading was debated in the House of Lords.[177] The Earl of Devon moved the bill, and was followed by the Conservative leader, the once and future Prime Minister, Lord Derby.[178] 'The Rupert of Debate', as he was known, was a fine orator, but inclined to be rash and sharp-tongued. On this occasion, his sarcasm was to lead him into employing what Roantree has called 'an astonishingly inelegant analogy'.[179] In the course of a very long address opposing the bill, he stated:

> if a man comes to me with a dog with a muzzle on, and says 'take the muzzle off this poor creature; he will do us no harm, he is quite harmless, and besides, the muzzle is half-rotten and affords no great protection', I understand him; but if he says 'this is a most vicious animal, and nothing prevents his pulling you and me to pieces except the muzzle which is put around his nose, and therefore, I want you to take it off', I am inclined to say 'I am much obliged to you, but I had rather keep the muzzle on.'[180]

He was followed by Earl Russell (formerly Lord John Russell), who argued strongly in its favour.[181] Even this endorsement by the author of the Durham letter and the Ecclesiastical Titles Act did not sway the Lords, who seemed much more inclined to join Derby in keeping the muzzle on the Papist dog. The bill was defeated by 84 votes to 63.

Among those who voted in favour of Monsell's measure were his neighbour Lord Monteagle, his old colleague Lord Panmure and Russell himself, while his opponents included his neighbours, Lords Clarina, Limerick and Inchiquin, six Anglican bishops and, of course, Derby.[182] Despite this defeat, Monsell's bill was an important measure. It paved the way for the final solution to the problem, which the Government adopted the following year, when it abolished the separate Catholic and Protestant oaths for MPs and replaced them with a single oath of allegiance.[183] Cullen approved of this act, a copy of which he sent to Cardinal Barnabo.[184] By an act of 1868 the remaining obnoxious oaths, taken by office-holders and Maynooth students, were abolished, and it was now permissible for a Catholic to hold the office of Lord Chancellor of Ireland, thus paving the way for the appointment of Monsell's friend and fellow Catholic Whig Thomas O'Hagan to that post.[185]

The debate on the disestablishment of the Church of Ireland was reaching its climax at the same time.[186] The chief issue amongst the proponents of disestablishment was how to dispose of the huge wealth of the Church. The British dissenters and radicals proposed disendowment, also called the voluntary principle and 'levelling down' under which the state would confiscate Church property and use it as it saw fit, while the Church of Ireland, like the dissenters and the Catholics, would be supported by its own congregations.[187] An opposing concept was that of 'concurrent endowment' or 'levelling up', which was 'the distribution of ecclesiastical property and state aid indifferently among competing religions, usually, and as in the suggested application to Ireland, according to their numerical proportions'.[188] The Irish Catholic bishops espoused the voluntary principle and in so doing they opposed the official teaching of their Church as set out in the Syllabus of Errors; that a secular, religiously indifferent state was an anathema.[189] A consensus emerged, due to the alliance between the Liberation Society and the National Association, which resulted in the Catholic hierarchy resolving, in October 1867, to renounce any endowment by the state, and instead declaring for the voluntary principle. Among Irish bishops, only Moriarty favoured concurrent endowment.[190] Bishop Butler also sympathised with this view, but did not express his feelings publicly on the subject. It was advocated by Aubrey de Vere, in several pamphlets published between 1863 and 1867, and in a celebrated letter to the *Times* in January 1865.[191]

Among the Irish MPs only Monsell favoured levelling up.[192] At a meeting of Irish Catholic MPs in December 1865 he told the convenor of the meeting, John Blake Dillon MP, that the Catholics 'lost instead of gained' by espousing voluntaryism. This was dismissed by W.J. O'Neill Daunt, with the caustic comment: 'Monsell is a Whig, and gives Whiggish counsel.'[193] Thus, concurrent endowment came to be associated with the Irish Liberal Catholics, and voluntaryism with the Ultramontanes, a curious reversal of the situation in continental Europe. When the Church was finally disestablished by Gladstone, he followed the path of 'levelling down'. The whole disestablishment debate shows the essential pragmatism of all the parties, who adopted policies at variance with their official ideologies. For Monsell, de Vere and Moriarty, disendowment would be an example of the vulnerability of private property in general to spoliation. Monsell himself was convinced that disestablishment was the greatest of all Irish reforms, eliminating the most serious barrier to Ireland's becoming a contented and equal partner in the United Kingdom.[194]

Monsell's involvement at this time in the question of the nationalisation of the railways of Ireland is an interesting aspect of his attitude to social and economic issues.[195] His interest in the railways was of long standing. On 17 December 1845 he spoke at a public meeting in Limerick city on the development of the railways.[196] He was a director of the Limerick and Ennis Railway, and later of the Waterford and Limerick Railway.[197] In 1865 he commenced an important campaign to have the Irish railways nationalised.[198] Under the Railways Act of 1844, the Government had the option of purchasing any railway by 1865, a provision known as Section Two, or the Gladstone Purchase Clause.[199] On 7 April 1865 Monsell moved in the Commons 'that the commission appointed to inquire into the railway system of the United Kingdom' should examine the possibility of nationalising the Irish railways.[200] The chief complaints against the Irish system were that the charges were too high and the multitude of small railway companies in Ireland were little monopolies and against the public interest. The nationalisation of the railways, by lowering fares and charges, would benefit the whole economy. Monsell remarked pragmatically that 'he was quite indifferent as to the means – the end he desired was low fares and more centralised management'.[201] In the meantime, a Commission of Enquiry chaired by the Duke of Devonshire and of which Monsell was a member was appointed to investigate the desirability of nationalising the British and the Irish railways, according to the provisions of the 1844 act.[202] The Devonshire Commission presented a majority report in 1867, which recommended that the railways should continue to be operated by private enterprise.[203] Monsell presented a minority report in which he proposed 'that the government should buy the Irish railways, consolidate them, and lease them to companies for limited terms and upon certain conditions as to rates and accommodation'.[204] On 11 May the *Freeman's Journal* praised Monsell's report and agreed with his proposals.[205] Nothing was done, although Irish opinion at this time was overwhelmingly in favour of the nationalisation of the Irish railways.[206] Monsell had enjoyed all-party support for his proposals, and in the 1870s Irish MPs continued to bring the matter before the bar of the House.[207] It was a measure ahead of its time, for the Irish railways were not to be nationalised until 1939, but Monsell's belief that 'of all measures for the improvement of Ireland, this is the one whose good effects will most permeate and filter through our whole social system' must surely sound Utopian to the modern observer.[208]

In retrospect, the most important political development in Ireland in the 1860s was the rise of the Fenian Movement. The republican and separatist tradition, absent between 1803 and 1848, and dormant in the 1850s, was henceforth to have a continuous, though sometimes tenuous existence until the 1916 Rising. Monsell detested the Fenians from the start, as he regarded them as communists and revolutionaries, dedicated to social upheaval. On 16 March 1868 he told the Commons that the Fenians 'were aggregated to the secret societies of Europe, and their object was to establish a democratic republic. They were the enemies of the priests, as well as landlords.'[209] In a letter to Cullen on 27 December 1869 he equated Fenianism with revolution.[210] The official Catholic Church, led by Cullen, took the same view. Even Newman wrote to Monsell on 16 October 1866: 'you will be somewhat exposed at Tervoe, if the Fenians are to invade you from America this year.'[211] However, Monsell was determined not to await this threat in a passive or unprepared manner. In 1864 he was appointed Colonel of the County Limerick Militia, a position which he held until his death and which entitled him to the appellation of 'Colonel Monsell', in the same manner as his grandfather. In this capacity, he took the initiative in organising Limerick city to defend itself against Fenian attacks. On 11 May 1867 Stephen de Vere wrote to Lord Dunraven:

> as long as real danger, and necessity for prompt action existed, W.M. [Monsell] almost lived at the club, and was the centre of all action, and by his wise, conciliatory, and at the same time energetic counsels, he restored and maintained confidence. When he came over, nothing was arranged, no precautions taken, a parcel of old women in command – the danger was imminent. He got proper people sent down, and [many] precautions taken and in a few days, all was safe. I believe there is not a single Limerick prisoner on trial. Politically and socially, he has done himself immense good.[212]

Monsell also urged that other measures be taken against the Fenians. When his friend, Bishop Moriarty condemned them in his notorious sermon on 17 February 1867 at Mass in Killarney Cathedral, stating that 'hell was not hot enough nor eternity long enough to punish these miscreants [the Fenian leaders]', even Cullen was annoyed at the intemperance of his remarks, saying that 'it had caused great offence' and 'I wish he could be called to an account for it.'[213] Cullen feared that such severity might alienate the people from their pastors, and, moreover, he suspected Moriarty of being a Liberal Catholic. Monsell took a different view, as Aubrey de Vere afterwards told Moriarty himself: 'Mr Monsell and I agreed that such plain and authoritative speaking was the only way in which the conscience of our people can be touched and that till that conscience is aroused as the duty of loyalty, no exhortation founded merely on the expedient can avail in any degree.'[214] On 22 March 1867 Monsell advocated the awarding of the Victoria Cross, Britain's highest military decoration, to the policemen who had taken part in the defence of the police barracks at Kilmallock and Ardagh (both in County Limerick) against Fenian attacks.[215]

The Fenian rising was seen by him as a serious indictment of the failure of British rule in Ireland. He made two powerful speeches to the Commons on 26 July 1867 and 16 March 1868, urging on the British government the need to enact timely reforms in order to prevent the mass of the Irish people from falling under the spell of the revolutionaries.[216] Significantly, Monsell wrote to O'Hagan following his speech of 26 July 1867 that 'when it was over, J.S. Mill, whom I know but slightly, came down from his place, sat down by me, thanked me, and said it was the best speech he had ever heard on Ireland.'[217] Monsell's programme to counter Fenianism consisted of action in the three great fields of grievance – education, land and religion. With regard to education, he proposed his usual university plan – one university, with several colleges affiliated to it. He proposed to tackle the land question in two ways; security of tenure should be promoted, by the granting of leases, and a certain amount of land purchase by tenants, as advocated by Bright, should be encouraged. Finally, on religion he advocated the disestablishment of the Church of Ireland.[218]

However, he also saw the Catholic Church playing an important role in eliminating Fenianism.[219] He believed that only condemnation of the Fenians by the Pope could bring this about, and on 29 January 1868 he wrote to the Chief Secretary, Lord Mayo: 'have you got the rules of the Fenian Association? If you can send their rules to me, I have strong reason to believe that we shall be able to get a stronger denunciation of Fenianism made by the highest authority in the world, that has ever yet been made.'[220] Nothing came of this, but Monsell urged the same course on Cullen in two letters that he addressed to him on 11 November and 27 December 1869, at the beginning of the Vatican Council.[221] In so doing, Monsell was in agreement with both the Irish hierarchy and the British government. On 27 December 1869 the Irish Bishops, meeting at Rome, decided to ask the Pope to condemn Fenianism and on 12 January 1870 Pius IX signed the Papal document condemning Fenianism by name in both Ireland and the USA. It was promulgated in Ireland in February, but like its successor, the Papal Rescript of 1888, it was to prove a dead letter.[222]

Monsell was not only an Irish, but also a British politician and took a wide interest in many British issues throughout the 1860s. His main interest, besides Irish and Catholic issues, was defence, and his long period at the Ordnance had made him one of the leading authorities on the subject in Parliament. In 1859–60 he sat on a select committee on military organisation, and in 1862 and 1863 he chaired select committees on Ordnance.[223] Monsell always defended his achievements in the Ordnance Department and his former colleagues, the Artillery and Engineers Corps, in a trenchant manner.[224] More significantly, he participated in the general debate on Britain's defences. In the 1860s the chief threat to British security was perceived to be the Second Empire of Napoleon III. The French army was considered to be the finest in the world, until the catastrophic defeat of 1870 showed what a paper tiger it really was. However, the rise of the French navy was, from the British point of view, a far more ominous development as this was one of four periods in modern history, when the French navy was the best in the world.[225] In 1859 the French built *La Gloire*, the world's first armour-plated, steam-powered battleship, which in theory could have sunk all the wooden ships of any opponent, without damage to herself, in a few hours.[226] British naval supremacy seemed threatened, and 1859 was the peak year of the fear of the French bogey. Nevertheless, the French threat informed the debate on Britain's defences throughout the 1860s. The argument largely centred around the issue of whether the country should rely on fixed fortifications, as Palmerston believed, or on a strong iron-clad fleet, as advocated by Monsell. On 23 June 1862 Monsell told the Commons that 'Britain ought to trust to her maritime resources, and to keep up a powerful channel fleet, and a number of moveable batteries.'[227] Palmerston even wanted to continue building wooden warships, a course of action opposed by both Gladstone and Monsell. In this debate Monsell was on the side of innovation and modernisation.

By 1866, despite his estrangement from the British Liberal administration, Monsell was regarded as one of the most prominent figures in Ireland and the leader of the Catholic Whigs. Disraeli wrote on 10 April 1863 of Monsell that 'both by position and talents, he is a leading man', and on 8 March 1866 he described him in the Commons as the 'recognised organ of the Roman Catholic members of the house'.[228] The revival of Monsell's fortunes, and those of the Irish Liberals, began with the death of Palmerston on 18 October 1865. O'Hagan wrote to Monsell on 27 October that 'you will be glad to hear what effect Lord Palmerston's death is likely to have on the making of the new government'.[229] He went on to say: 'I have no doubt that Peel will be called on to resign, and that Fortescue will succeed. This will, I know, be not only a matter of cardinal pleasure to you, but give sincere satisfaction throughout the Liberal party in Ireland.' Despite his poor record on Ireland, the new Prime Minister Russell was in fact prepared to be more conciliatory to the Irish Liberals than his predecessor. The Palmerstonian system could work as long as the Irish Catholics had no effective independent party and as long as British Liberalism did not mind being alienated from Irish Liberalism while relying on Tory support in the Commons.[230] These factors were now about to change. In the 1865 general election, which Palmerston had won handily, three months before his death, the Irish Independents had won about a dozen seats, but remained divided and without direction. However, the Liberal–Tory consensus that had been a major buttress of Palmerston's ascendancy did not long survive his death. Disraeli continued to woo the Catholic vote, causing Russell to reach out to the Irish Liberals. His appointment of the conciliatory Irish Liberal MP Chichester Fortescue as Chief Secretary was considered a major step in the right direction.[231]

This sudden revival in the fortunes of the Irish Liberals also benefited Monsell, whom Russell regarded as the 'most reasonable' of the Catholic spokesmen.[232] Gladstone asked Monsell to propose John E. Denison as the Speaker of the House of Commons. While the *Dictionary of National Biography* claims that this was a sign of Monsell's prominence, he himself took a somewhat bleaker view, asking O'Hagan: 'does this not look like telling me I have nothing to expect?'[233] Nevertheless, he carried out this task on 1 February 1866, and on 12 March, Russell appointed him as Vice-President of the Board of Trade, and Paymaster-General.[234] The Board of Trade was the government department charged with dealing with trade and commercial matters in general. The minister in charge was termed the *President*, but his deputy, the Vice-President, had little to do, so in 1848 the post of Paymaster-General (who made payments for the army, navy and civil service) had been attached to his position.[235] While his new role was a minor one, with a salary of £2,000 per year, Monsell did not enjoy it for very long. Russell's government was forced to resign on 10 July 1866, and Lord Derby and the Conservatives took office. The Liberals did not return to power until 1868, but by then the situation had been transformed. In 1867 William Ewart Gladstone, the greatest British statesman of the nineteenth century, had become leader of the Liberal party.

NOTES

1. For Palmerston, see Jasper Ridley, *Lord Palmerston* (London: Constable, 1970) and Donald Southgate, *The Most English Minister: The Policies and Politics of Palmerston* (London: Macmillan, 1966).
2. Hoppen, *Elections, Politics and Society in Ireland,* p.263.
3. Hoppen, 'Tories, Catholics and the General Election of 1859', p.52.
4. Ibid., pp.50–1. See also David Steele, 'John Francis Maguire (1815–1872)', in *Oxford DNB*.
5. For the English background see Dermot Quinn, *Patronage and Piety. The Politics of English Roman Catholicism 1850–1900* (Stanford, CA: Stanford University Press, 1993).
6. Newman, *Letters and Diaries*, Vol. 18, p.343, Monsell to Newman, 8 May 1858.
7. Ibid., p.359, Monsell to Newman, 6 June 1858.
8. Ibid., pp.452–3, Bowyer to Newman, 24 August 1858.
9. Hoppen, 'Tories, Catholics and the General Election of 1859', pp.65–7.
10. Ibid., pp.60–1. For Monsell's electoral performance in County Limerick between 1847 and 1874, see Walker, *Parliamentary Election Results in Ireland*, pp.293–4.
11. Hoppen, 'Tories Catholics and the General Election of 1859', p. 61. To 'plump' for a candidate meant to vote for him alone. Dickson, who sat from 1859 to 1865, was Monsell's only constituency colleague between 1847 and 1874 who was not a Liberal.
12. For an overview of the Tory resurgence, see Shields, *Irish Conservative Party*, pp.178–80.
13. A good account of the Unification of Italy is Derek Beales, *The Risorgimento and the Unification of Italy* (London: Allen and Unwin, 1971).
14. The best work on the church in Ireland at this period is Norman's *Catholic Church and Ireland in the Age of Rebellion 1859–1873*. For the crisis of 1859–60, see pp.33–5.
15. Their leader Myles O'Reilly (1825–80) capitalised on this to become an independent MP for County Longford from 1862 to 1879.
16. William Monsell, *A lecture on the Roman Question delivered at Limerick 1 December, 1859, to which is added the Report of the Count De Rayneval, French Envoy at Rome* (London: privately printed, 1860).
17. Ibid., p.5.
18. Ibid.
19. Ibid., pp.7–19.
20. Cullen to Monsell, 7 December 1859, in MP, MS 8319/3, and Cullen to Monsell, 25 January 1860, in MTP, MS 19337/57.
21. 'Temporal Prosperity a Note of the Church' (*sic*), in *Rambler*, 1 ns (May 1859), pp.1–15.
22. Dunraven to Monsell, 4 September 1861, MP, MS 8318/11.
23. Stephen De Vere to Monsell, 29 October and 6 December 1859, MP, MS 8317/7.
24. Newman, *Letters and Diaries*, Vol. 19, pp.483–4, Monsell to Newman, 16 March 1861.
25. MacDougall, *Acton–Newman Relations*, p. 65.
26. Hansard, CLVIII, 1771–3 (25 May 1860).
27. Bernstein, 'British Liberal Politics and Irish Liberalism after O'Connell', pp.57–9.
28. Ibid., pp.58–9.
29. Ibid.,p.58.
30. Ibid., p.59.
31. Ibid., *passim*.
32. Ibid., p.59.
33. Ibid., *passim*.
34. An outstanding work on the political situation in Ireland in the late 1850s and the 1860s is R.V. Comerford, *The Fenians in Context. Irish Politics and Society 1848–82* (Dublin: Wolfhound Press and Atlantic Highlands, NJ: Humanities Press, 1985).
35. See ibid., p. 142 for Comerford's contention that the party survived until 1866, when under the influence of John Blake Dillon, it became allied to the Liberal party.

36. Bernstein, 'British Liberal Politics and Irish Liberalism after O'Connell', p.57.
37. R.V. Comerford, 'Conspiring Brotherhoods and Contending Élites 1857–63', in Vaughan, *New History of Ireland,* Vol. 5, pp.416–17.
38. Comerford, *Fenians in Context*, pp.43–103.
39. Comerford, 'Conspiring Brotherhoods and Contending Élites 1857–63', p. 423.
40. (Monsell) 'Catholic Policy', pp.1–17.
41. Ibid., p.11.
42. Ibid.
43. Ibid., p.2.
44. Ibid., pp.16–17.
45. Ibid., pp.2 and 9–12.
46. Ibid., p.10.
47. Shields, *Irish Conservative Party*, pp.186–7.
48. Bernstein, 'British Liberal Politics and Irish Liberalism after O'Connell', p.60.
49. (William Monsell) 'University Education in Ireland', in *Home and Foreign Review,* 2 (January 1863), pp.34–5 and 39.
50. Hansard, CLX, 1479–80 (17 August 1860).
51. Hansard, CLXII, 1705–8 (7 May 1861) and CLXII, 1888–90 (10 May 1861).
52. Hansard, CLXIII, 298–302 (30 May 1861); CLXV, 1464–6 (13 March 1862).
53. Horgan, 'Irish Catholic Whigs in Parliament', pp.132–3.
54. For the national system, see, D.H. Akenson, *The Irish Education Experiment. The National System of Education in Ireland* (London: Routledge and Kegan Paul, 1970).
55. See T.W. Moody, 'The Irish University Question in the Nineteenth Century', in *History*, 43 (1958), pp.90–109.
56. Norman, *Catholic Church and Ireland*, p.79.
57. Ibid., p.81.
58. (Monsell) 'University Education in Ireland', pp.32–58.
59. Ibid., p.39.
60. Ibid., p.54.
61. Ibid., p.55.
62. Ibid., p.56.
63. Hansard, CLXVI, 2075–8 (22 May 1862).
64. Norman, *Catholic Church and Ireland*, pp.135–89.
65. R.V. Comerford, 'Gladstone's First Irish Enterprise 1864–70', in Vaughan, *New History of Ireland,* Vol. 5, pp.432–4 and Comerford, *Fenians in Context*, pp.139–42.
66. Norman, *Catholic Church and Ireland*, p. 293.
67. Ibid., pp.177–81. See also D.M. Cregier, 'William Joseph O'Neill Daunt (1807–94)', in *Oxford DNB.*
68. Hansard, CLXXX, 541–7 (20 June, 1865).
69. Ibid., 555.
70. Ibid., 565–8.
71. Norman, *Catholic Church and Ireland,* p.203, quoting Kirby Papers, Cullen to Kirby, no. 140, 27 June 1865.
72. Norman, *Catholic Church and Ireland*, pp.202–3.
73. Ibid., p.203.
74. See MacSuibhne, *Paul, Cardinal Cullen*, Vol. 4, p.173, Cullen to Kirby, 31 January 1865.
75. Norman, *Catholic Church and Ireland,* p. 204.
76. Ibid., pp.204–5.
77. Ibid., p.219.
78. MacSuibhne, *Paul, Cardinal Cullen*, Vol. 4, p.191, Cullen to Kirby, 23 February 1866.
79. Norman, *Catholic Church and Ireland*, pp.222–3.
80. Cullen to Woodlock, 28 February 1866, quoted in Norman, *Catholic Church and Ireland*, pp.223.
81. Norman, *Catholic Church and Ireland*, pp.222–3.
82. Ibid., p.224.
83. Ibid., pp.226–39.
84. Ibid., pp.256–7.
85. Moriarty to Monsell, 2 March 1868, GP, Ad. MS 44142. F–98.

86. Norman, *Catholic Church and Ireland*, pp.258–9.
87. Ibid., pp.264–81.
88. He used this term in a letter to Chichester Fortescue. See Monsell to Fortescue, 23 January 1869, in Carlingford Papers, Public Records Office of Somerset, Taunton, Cp.3/75.
89. Larkin, *Roman Catholic Church and Home Rule Movement*, pp.324–6.
90. Newman, *Letters and Diaries*, Vol. 20, pp.466–7, Monsell to Newman, 7 June 1863.
91. Ibid., pp.467–8, Newman to Monsell, 10 June 1863.
92. Ibid.
93. Ibid., p.472, Monsell to Newman, 14 June 1863.
94. Ibid., pp.473–5, Newman to Monsell, 16 June 1863.
95. Roantree, 'William Monsell and the Catholic Question', p.202.
96. Newman, *Letters and Diaries*, Vol. 21, p.XV.
97. For Manning, see Edmund Sheridan Purcell, *Life of Cardinal Manning, Archbishop of Westminster*, 2 vols (London: Macmillan, 1896), and V.A. MccClelland, *Cardinal Manning: His Public Life and Influence, 1865–92* (Oxford: Oxford University Press, 1962).
98. Newman, *Letters and Diaries,* Vol. 23, pp.XIII–XVI.
99. Ibid., p.XIV.
100. Purcell, *Manning*, Vol. 2, p.312.
101. Newman, *Letters and Diaries*, Vol. 23, pp.138–9.
102. Ibid., pp.XIV–XV and 145–7.
103. Purcell, *Manning,* Vol. 2, p.313. Ward was a very close friend of Monsell. See Ward, *William George Ward and the Catholic Revival*, pp.227–8.
104. Newman, *Letters and Diaries*, Vol. 23, pp.XIV–XV.
105. Judith F. Champ, revised Michael Peterburs, 'George Talbot (1816–1886)', in *Oxford DNB*.
106. Talbot to Manning 25 April 1867, quoted in Purcell, *Manning,* Vol. 2, pp.317–19.
107. Manning to Talbot 3 May 1867, quoted in Purcell, *Manning,* Vol. 2, pp.319–20.
108. Newman, *Letters and Diaries*, Vol. 23, pp.XV–XVI.
109. MacDougall, *Acton–Newman Relations*, p.2.
110. Ibid., p.IX.
111. Of the vast literature on Acton, two outstanding works are Roland Hill, *Lord Acton* (New Haven and London: Yale University Press, 2000) and Rocco Pezzimenti, *The Political Thought of Lord Acton: The English Catholics of the Nineteenth Century* (Leaminster, Herts: Gracewing and Rome: Millennium Romae, 2001).
112. MacDougall, *Acton–Newman Relations*, pp.6–8.
113. Ibid.
114. For Acton and Irish politics, see Colin Barr, 'Lord Acton's Irish Elections', in *Historical Journal*, 51, 1 (2008), pp.87–114.
115. See Sheridan Gilley, 'William George Ward (1812–1882)', in *Oxford DNB,* and K.T. Hoppen, 'William George Ward and Nineteenth-Century Catholicism' (unpublished Ph.D thesis, University of Cambridge, 1966).
116. For good accounts of the struggle between the two parties in Britain, see MacDougall, *Acton–Newman Relations*, Altholz, *Liberal Catholic Movement in England,* and Hill, *Lord Acton*, pp.108–225.
117. Walter E. Houghton (ed.), *The Wellesley Index to Victorian Periodicals,* 5 vols (Toronto: Toronto University Press and London: Routledge, 1966–89), Vol. 2, pp.11–19.
118. Ibid., p.12.
119. Ibid., p.15.
120. Houghton, *Wellesley Index*, Vol. 2, pp.732–41.
121. Ibid., pp.738–9.
122. Ibid., Vol. 1, pp.547–9.
123. Altholz, *Liberal Catholic Movement*, pp.189–90.
124. Houghton, *Wellesley Index*, Vol. 2, p.733.
125. Monsell to Newman, 17 November 1862, NP (M/2).
126. Ibid.
127. Altholz, *Liberal Catholic Movement in England*, p.223.
128. Ibid., pp.219–20.

129. Ibid., p.220.
130. Ibid.
131. Newman, *Letters and Diaries*, Vol. 20, pp.476–7.
132. Hansard, CLXXII, 1008–13 (17 July 1863).
133. (William George Ward) *Civil Intolerance of Religious Error. M. De. Montalambert at Malines* (London: privately published, 1863).
134. Monsell to Dunraven 22 January 1864, DP, D3196/F/10/43.
135. Newman, *Letters and Diaries*, Vol. 21, p.41.
136. Ibid.
137. Ward, *William George Ward and the Catholic Revival*, p.243.
138. Altholz, *Liberal Catholic Movement in England*, pp.220–3.
139. Ibid., p.228.
140. See Damian McElrath, *The Syllabus of Pius IX. Some Reactions in England* (Louvain: privately printed, 1964).
141. Altholz, *Liberal Catholic Movement in England*, p.231.
142. E.E.Y. Hales, *Pio Nono. A Study in European Politics and Religion in the Nineteenth Century* (London: Eyre and Spottisewoode, 1954), p.274.
143. Altholz, *Liberal Catholic Movement in England*, p.232.
144. Newman, *Letters and Diaries,* Vol. 21, p.383.
145. Altholz, *Liberal Catholic Movement in England*, p.232.
146. Ibid.
147. Ibid.
148. Ibid., pp.232–33.
149. Ibid., pp.233–4.
150. Ibid., p.235.
151. Pawley, 'Ambrose Lisle March Phillipps de Lisle (1809–1878)', in *Oxford DNB*.
152. Hansard, CLXIX, 549–51 (19 February 1863).
153. Ibid., 551.
154. Ibid., 855–6 (27 February 1863).
155. Ibid.
156. Norman, *Catholic Church and Ireland*, p.77.
157. Hansard, CLXCI, 1069–84 (22 April 1868) and 1454–5 (28 April 1868).
158. Norman, *Catholic Church and Ireland*, pp.291–6.
159. Ibid., p.291.
160. Ibid.
161. Ibid., p.293.
162. Monsell to Cullen, 15 December 1864, Cullen papers, Dublin Diocesan Archives, MS 320/7 / 75.
163. Norman, *Catholic Church and Ireland*, p.293.
164. Hansard, CLXXVIII, 24–31 (21 March 1865).
165. Ibid., 26–7.
166. Ibid., 30.
167. Ibid., 31.
168. Hansard, CLXXIX, 430–80 (17 May 1865).
169. Ibid., 611–20 (19 May 1865).
170. MacSuibhne, *Paul, Cardinal Cullen*, Vol. 5, pp.21–2, Cullen to Major Myles O'Reilly, 16 May 1865.
171. Newman, *Letters and Diaries*, Vol. 21, p.442, Monsell to Newman, 1 April 1865.
172. Ibid., Newman to Monsell, 3 April 1865.
173. Monsell to Newman, 26 May 1865, NP (N/4).
174. Ibid., Monsell to Newman, 31 May 1865.
175. Hansard, CLXXX, 325–30 (15 June 1865).
176. Roantree, 'William Monsell and the Catholic Question', p.218.
177. Hansard, CLXXX, 764–822 (26 June 1865).
178. Ibid., 772–92.
179. Roantree, 'William Monsell and the Catholic Question', p.222.
180. Hansard, CLXXX, 790 (26 June 1865).
181. Ibid., 792–8.

182. Ibid., 821–2.
183. Norman, *Catholic Church and Ireland*, p.294.
184. Ibid.
185. Ibid., p.296.
186. Ibid., pp.301–38.
187. Ibid., pp.282–5.
188. Ibid., p.285.
189. Ibid., p.287.
190. Ibid., pp.311–19.
191. Ibid., pp.305–11.
192. Ibid., p.332. See also his statement to the Commons on 16 March 1868, Hansard, CXC, 1696.
193. Entry for 5 December 1865 in Journals of W.J. O'Neill Daunt (MS 3041), NLI, P.779.
194. Hansard, CXC, 1693–7 (16 March 1868).
195. J.C. Conroy, *A History of Railways in Ireland* (London: Longmans, Green and Co., 1928), pp.38–70.
196. *Limerick Chronicle*, 20 December 1845.
197. *Thoms Directory* (1854–1861 inclusive) and *Munster News*, 21 April 1894.
198. Conroy, *History of Railways in Ireland*, pp.58–9.
199. Ibid.,p.58.
200. Hansard, CLXXVIII, 896–905 (7 April 1865).
201. Ibid., 902–25.
202. Conroy, *History of Railways in Ireland*, pp.45–50.
203. *Report from the Commissioners of the Railways of Great Britain and Ireland with Minutes of Evidence* , PP. 1867 (38), Part 1, 7 May 1867.
204. Ibid., pp.XCIII–CV, 'Report from the Rt. Hon. W. Monsell. M.P.'.
205. *Freeman's Journal*, 11 May 1867.
206. Conroy, *History of Railways in Ireland*, p.70.
207. Ibid.
208. Monsell, *Address to the Statistical and Social Enquiry Society 1869*, pp.68–9.
209. Hansard, CXC, 1690 (16 March 1868).
210. Monsell to Cullen, 27 December 1869, Cullen papers, MA 41/3, File 1, no. 41.
211. Newman, *Letters and Diaries*, Vol. 22, p.300.
212. Stephen de Vere to Lord Dunraven, 11 May 1867, DP, D3196/F/7.
213. Norman, *Catholic Church and Ireland*, pp.118–19.
214. Aubrey de Vere to Moriarty, 22 February 1867, De Vere papers, NLI, MS 13120/6.
215. Hansard, CLXXXVI, 415–17 (22 March 1867).
216. Hansard, CLXXXIX, 219–26 (26 July 1867); Hansard, CXC, 1688–98 (16 March 1868).
217. Monsell to O'Hagan, no date, Teeling papers, MS, NLI, 17871(4). See also Bruce L.Kinzler, *England's Disgrace? J.S. Mill and the Irish Question* (Toronto: University of Toronto Press, 2001).
218. Hansard, CXC, 1688–98 (16 March 1868).
219. Monsell to Cullen, 27 December 1869, Cullen papers, MA 41/3, File 1, no. 41.
220. Norman, *Catholic Church and Ireland*, p.129.
221. Monsell to Cullen, 11 November 1869, Cullen papers, MS 41/3, File 1, no. 36; Monsell to Cullen, 27 December 1869, Cullen papers, MA 41/3, File 1, no. 41.
222. Norman, *Catholic Church and Ireland*, pp.130–2.
223. *Report from the Select Committee on Military Organisation together with the proceedings of the committee, minutes of evidence and appendix*, PP. 1860(7); *Report from the Select Committee on Ordnance, together with the proceedings of the committee, minutes of evidence, appendix and index*, PP. 1862(8); *Report from the Select Committee on Ordnance, together with the proceedings of the Committee, minutes of evidence, appendix and index*, PP. 1863(11).
224. Hansard, CLII, 1332–3 (4 March 1859).
225. John de Courcy Ireland, 'The French Navy at the time of the Williamite War', in Old *Limerick Journal*, 28, 1690 Siege edition (winter 1990), p.23.
226. Ibid.
227. Hansard, CLXVII, 943 (23 June 1862).

228. W.F. Moneypenny and G.E. Buckle, *The Life of Benjamin Disraeli, Earl of Beaconsfield*, 6 vols (London: John Murray, 1910–20), Vol. 4, p.367, Disraeli to Lord Campden, 10 April 1863; Hansard, CLXXXI, 1720 (8 March 1866).
229. O'Hagan to Monsell, 27 October 1865, Teeling papers, NLI, MS 17871(1).
230. Bernstein, 'British Liberal Politics and Irish Liberalism after O'Connell', p.63.
231. H.C.G. Matthew, 'Chichester Samuel Parkinson-Fortescue, Baron Carlingford and second Baron Clermont (1823–1898)', in *Oxford DNB*.
232. Lord John Russell, *The Later Correspondence of Lord John Russell 1840–1878*, 2 vols (edited by G.P. Gooch) (London: Longmans and Co., 1925), Vol. 2, p.343.
233. Monsell to O'Hagan, 22 January 1866, Teeling papers, NLI, MS 17871(6).
234. Hansard, CLXXXI, 4–7 (1 February 1866).
235. J.C. Sainty, *Officials of the Board of Trade 1660–1870* (London: Athlone Press, 1974), pp.7–17 and 39–40.

CHAPTER SEVEN

Service under Gladstone

The advent of Gladstone to the head of the Liberal party transformed British politics.[1] Disraeli succeeded Derby as leader of the Tories and as Prime Minister at the beginning of 1868, and these two outstanding figures dominated British public life for the next twelve years.[2] The period of fluid party divisions and loose discipline that had begun with the Peelite split of 1846 came to an end, and with it the Palmerstonian consensus that had taken shape in the late 1850s. There now emerged two highly organised, disciplined political parties with recognisable ideological differences (although they were mild ones, compared to those of mainland Europe). Gladstone was a great moralist and reformer, and a sincerely religious man, but was also domineering, cunning, and was possessed of a rare political genius. His enemies frequently scoffed at the manner in which his crusading zeal often coincided with what was politically expedient at the time, and even one of his own supporters, Henry Labouchere, acidly commented that 'I don't object to the old man always having the ace of trumps up his sleeve, but merely to his belief that God Almighty put it there.'[3] In 1868 Gladstone reached the top of the 'greasy pole' in this typically masterful fashion. Although a devout Anglican, Gladstone came to believe that the Church of Ireland should be disestablished, but also realised that it was the one issue around which he could unite all the disparate elements of the Liberal party, so he fought and won the 1868 general election on this platform, securing a majority of 112 in the process. He became Prime Minister and inaugurated a six-year period of major Liberal reform (1868–74).

Monsell was delighted. At last a Liberal Prime Minister had emerged who was sympathetic to Ireland's grievances and prepared to tackle them. He had long regarded Gladstone as the great hope for the future. In his article 'University Education in Ireland' of January 1863, Monsell concluded his appeal for the resolution of Ireland's university question by directing it specifically 'to him whose political career is the flower of seed sown during his own brilliant university career – we should ask for justice at Mr Gladstone's hands'.[4] Monsell wrote that

> it was for the reconciliation of two hostile races – for the knitting together of two nations whom centuries of cruel oppression on the one side, and suffering unprecedented on the other, had divided – that three of our greatest modern ministers had laboured [Pitt, Fox and Peel] ... it cannot be a task unworthy of the foremost of our public men to preserve what they have achieved, and to perfect what they have left incomplete.[5]

Monsell's hopes were to be realised five years later as the new Prime Minister, unlike Palmerston and Russell, made Irish reform one of his main priorities. He intended dealing with the three great Irish problems of the Church, land and education. In addition, he had been an intimate friend of Monsell's for a quarter of a century, and they shared many political experiences and attitudes. Both had begun their careers as High Anglican Tories, both had revered Peel and seceded with him at the time of the Peelite split, and they shared a fundamental distrust of Palmerston. They had both found their way to Liberal principles after considerable soul-searching, and although their religious paths diverged after 1850, they continued to share an intense moral earnestness and religious fervour.

The general election of 1868, with its emphasis on Irish issues, and the resulting accession to power of Gladstone had sealed the reconciliation of British and Irish Liberals. The period 1865 to 1868 had seen the Irish and British Liberals draw closer together; John Blake Dillon had brought the Independent Opposition party back into alliance with the Irish Liberals in 1866, and the Irish Catholics were to form one of the chief elements in Gladstonian Liberalism. The period 1868 to 1873 was the high watermark of co-operation between British and Irish Liberalism, although cracks began to appear as early as 1870, with the rise of Home Rule and the disappointment engendered by the Land Act.[6] However, in 1868 it seemed to many that the two parties, and indeed the Irish and British political systems, had become permanently fused into one, and that the United Kingdom was finally becoming not merely tolerable, but desirable to the Catholics of Ireland. Indeed, Gladstone's ministry marked the culmination of the policies and influence of the Catholic Whigs. To the Fenians and separatists, it appeared that their hopes were entirely extinguished. In this heady atmosphere, Monsell's political hopes were high and his eyes were fixed on a Cabinet seat.

Gladstone's Liberal party consisted of several different groupings, including the English Whigs, the Radicals and the Irish Catholic Whigs, and he attempted to satisfy all of these elements when forming his government, by a judicious spread of the available posts among them. During the period leading up to the formation of the administration, representations were made to the Prime Minister by two of Monsell's friends, Dr Charles Russell (1812–80), President of Maynooth College, and Bishop Moriarty.[7] They both urged him to consolidate the Government's position in Ireland by appointing Thomas O'Hagan as Lord Chancellor of Ireland and Monsell to a seat in the Cabinet.[8] In the event, their hopes were only partially realised. O'Hagan did receive the Chancellorship, but Monsell only received a junior post – Under-Secretary for the Colonies, at a salary of £1,500 per year.[9] He was gravely disappointed, but continued to hope for promotion, as did his friends, including Cardinal Cullen and Montalambert.[10] On 21 May 1869 Cullen wrote to Monsell referring to newspaper reports that the Chief Secretary, Chichester Fortescue was to be raised to the peerage, and stating that if this were so, he hoped that Monsell would be 'promoted to his office. No Catholic has ever been as yet Secretary of State for Ireland.'[11] A few days later, Monsell told O'Hagan that Montalambert had 'entreated me to urge my claim to be in the Cabinet, that I had a right to it, that while France, and other Catholic countries had Protestant Ministers, after 30 years, England never had a Catholic one, and a great deal more to the same effect. I said to him, as I say to you, what can I do?'[12] However, nothing happened, and Monsell grew more discontented with his junior role in the administration.

In view of this, it is ironic that his period as Under-Secretary for the Colonies was one of his most productive periods. In 1868 the British Empire comprised some 8 million square miles of territories, a vast and heterogeneous entity even though the bulk of the immense African possessions were yet to be acquired. The Colonial Office was responsible for all of the Empire, (except for India, which was handled by its own department, the India Office) and was headed by a Secretary for State, who was always a Cabinet minister, and his deputy, the Under-Secretary.[13] The Colonial Office itself was a decrepit building at numbers 13 and 14 Downing Street, which was not replaced by proper accommodation until 1876.[14] The Secretary of State from 1868 to 1870 was George Leveson-Gower, fifth Earl Granville (1815–91), who was Acton's stepfather and a friend and political confidante of Gladstone. He was aristocratic, pleasant, easy-going and shrewd, and got along very well with Monsell. The chief civil servant in the Colonial Office was another old friend of Monsell's, Sir Frederick Rogers, who as Permanent Under-Secretary from 1860 to 1871 held real power in the department.[15] He was an intimate of Newman and a competent and experienced administrator. The Colonial Office had a relaxed and informal atmosphere, and was more like a social club than a place of work.[16]

It was an established practice that the Secretary of State and the Under-Secretary for the Colonies sat in different houses.[17] As Granville was in the Lords, Monsell's most important and most visible duty was to answer questions and defend colonial policy in the Commons. He was never a good speaker, so he did not shine in that role, but then colonial issues seldom attracted much attention in Parliament. The position of Under-Secretary was an anomalous one. 'He is neither fish nor fowl nor good red herring,' wrote Lord Buxton, 'his use and wont, his authority and responsibility, his enjoyment of, and interest in his post, depend in a very large degree on his chief.'[18] Usually, the Under-Secretary did not hold office long enough to familiarise himself with the workings of the office, or to make a significant contribution.[19] Monsell was fortunate in that he enjoyed a good relationship with Granville and was thus able to exercise considerable influence on policy. One of the main issues that confronted the Colonial Office at this time was the introduction of recruitment to the civil service by competitive examination. It was bitterly opposed by Rogers and the senior officials, but Monsell was an enthusiastic and energetic supporter and he urged Granville to implement it, which he did.[20]

However, Monsell's major achievement in the Colonial Office was to instigate important reforms in the educational systems of both Trinidad and Mauritius.[21] The West Indian island of Trinidad had been a British colony since 1802 and the vast majority of the population were Catholics. In 1859 a lavishly funded government college had been founded in the capital, Port of Spain, but it was boycotted by the Catholics as it provided non-denominational education and was staffed mainly by non-Catholics.[22] There was also a Catholic college in Port-of-Spain run by the Holy Ghost Fathers, called St Mary's College, which received no government funding and which was supported by the fees paid by the pupils. The Catholics urged the governor of Trinidad, Sir Arthur Hamilton Gordon (1829–1912), to provide them with a solution to this problem.[23] Sir Arthur Gordon was Governor from 1866 to 1870 and, like his father, the Peelite Prime Minister Lord Aberdeen, he was a just man, sympathetic to Catholic grievances.[24] He asked the Colonial Office to send an official inspector to Trinidad, 'to report to Parliament on conditions in the island as regards educational facilities, and to make recommendations towards a solution to their problem'.[25] Monsell immediately saw the opportunity to use Trinidad as a prototype for solving the education question in Ireland while also helping his fellow-Catholics in Trinidad. On 23 February 1873 he told Newman: 'when I was at the Colonial Office, I had the remodelling of the educational system of Trinidad – I took the greatest interest in this work, because it seemed to me the experiment tried there might, if successful, be applied to Ireland'.[26] Monsell sent Sir Patrick Keenan (1826–94), Chief Inspector of the Irish National Schools System, to Trinidad early in 1869, where he carried out an exhaustive investigation.[27]

The result was Keenan's report, entitled 'Colonies and Possessions: Papers on the State of Education in Trinidad', which appeared in 1870 and which recommended that a new royal college be established to which all other schools were to be affiliated in order to be eligible to avail of the financial and academic advantages of the system.[28] The royal college was to conduct public examinations, open to all candidates, whether or not they were students there. Each school was allocated financial support, in relation to the performance of its students at the state examinations. St Mary's stood to gain £10 per student presented at the examinations (a very substantial sum at the time) while retaining its independence and its denominational character.[29] Keenan described the royal college to Monsell as 'a West Indian University' which 'denominationalists and mixed educationalists alike may ... embrace'.[30] Gordon put the scheme into operation, and by 1873 Monsell could tell Newman that 'the new system, after three years experience has been found to work well – the Archbishop [of Trinidad] writes letters expressing his warmest satisfaction with it'.[31]

The 'Trinidad Scheme' had two further results. Firstly, Sir Arthur Gordon later served as governor of Mauritius (1871–4), a predominantly Catholic island in the Indian Ocean, and was able to integrate the Catholic college, St Louis, also run by the Holy Ghost Fathers, into the state system there in the same manner as he had done in Trinidad.[32] Father Jules Leman (1826–80), the French Holy Ghost priest who had founded Blackrock College near Dublin in 1860, acted as an advisor to Keenan and Monsell in both Trinidad and Mauritius, and like them he was a firm believer in the 'payments by results' system.[33] Monsell's initiative had brought about significant educational reform in two islands thousands of miles from each other, and from Ireland. Secondly, as Monsell had hoped, the Trinidad scheme was to act as a prototype for a possible solution to the Irish educational problem. Because the Royal College in Port of Spain was what Monsell called 'what answers to a university in Trinidad', he thought it might be of relevance during the debate over Gladstone's university bill of 1873. It was a practical application of 'Mr Monsell's scheme' for solving the Irish university question.[34] More significantly, it was to be a template for the Intermediate Education Act of 1878 (the chief authors of which were Keenan, Monsell and Leman) and the University Education (Ireland) Act of 1879.

Monsell's philosophy concerning the British Empire was typical of his time and generation. From 1815 to 1875 all of the great empires (Britain, Russia, France and the Netherlands) expanded continuously, but overt and conscious imperialism did not become fashionable until the 1880s.[35] Thus in 1869 Monsell advocated ceding the Gambia, in West Africa, to the French, as part of an exchange of territories that would consolidate their respective possessions in that area.[36] While he did not advocate aggressive imperial expansion, he was supportive of the continued existence of the Empire, which he made clear in a speech to the Commons on 26 April 1870.[37] He stated that 'they all desired to see the Colonies growing, not only in strength and power, but also in loyalty and affection to the mother country'.[38] He fully supported the policy inaugurated thirty years previously by the Durham Report, which was 'the system of giving to the Colonies complete and absolute control over their own affairs'.[39] The colonies of white settlement in Canada, Australia, New Zealand and South Africa were largely self-governing by 1870, with 'Home Rule' established and working smoothly and successfully. He concluded by stating:

> they are bound to us by no cords but those of affection and of interest. So sure as children become men, so surely will the days come when these great communities will develop into independent states. The desire of Her Majesty's government, and he believed of every party in the state, was to postpone that inevitable hour – to make the ties that bind us together so elastic that they may not burst, and ... to leave to each colony the fullest control over its internal concerns.[40]

There were two other aspects to Monsell's imperial ideology, his attitude to the native peoples, and his attitude to India. In his speech of 26 April he spoke at length about New Zealand and stated that a self-governing colony should not rely on imperial troops for its defence, but should cultivate its own self-reliance in this, as in other matters. Above all, a conciliatory policy should be adopted towards the natives, who should not be subject to 'unnecessary confiscation of land'. Indeed, the settlers 'should enter as far as they could into friendly relations with the Maoris' and would then have no need of imperial troops.[41] In 1857 Monsell had written of British rule in India that 'there is something so spontaneous in the growth of our Indian Empire, and there seems to be something so providential in its preservation that one cannot but expect the efforts of the Church there to be blessed', and he expressed a hope that the Catholic Bishops would make a greater effort to encourage missionary activity there.[42]

Monsell's period at the Colonial Office saw momentous events on the continent of Europe as well as in Ireland. On 19 July 1870 the Franco-Prussian War began, but Monsell went on holiday to France on 10 August and remained there until 12 September.[43] During his period in France, the French Army was defeated at Sedan, Napoleon III was overthrown, a republic declared, and Paris, 'then the world's largest city after London, and by far the most magnificent', came under siege.[44] The Monsells were horrified by these disasters, and by the savage violence of the Communard Rebellion that followed. Newman wrote to Monsell on 12 December 1870: 'how Mrs Monsell must suffer from what is going on in France!'[45] In 1869 Pope Pius IX convened a General Council of the Church in the Vatican which was to result in the proclamation of the doctrine of Papal Infallibility.[46] This was the last occasion on which the Liberal Catholics rallied in their losing battle against the Ultramontanes. They opposed Papal Infallibility and were known as Inopportunists, because while they tended to believe in the concept itself, they felt that it was inopportune to have it proclaimed a dogma of the Church at that moment. To them, it was a continuation of the retrograde policy of *Quanta Cura* and the Syllabus. On the other hand, the Ultramontanes enthusiastically supported it.

Newman, Monsell, Montalambert, Acton and Dollinger were among the most prominent Inopportunists.[47] Dupanloup and Moriarty were among the minority of bishops taking that line, while Cullen and Manning were among those who campaigned hardest for a definition.[48] Monsell played two major roles in the drama. Firstly, he unsuccessfully tried to persuade Newman to attend the Council as theological advisor to Dupanloup.[49] Secondly, Monsell was given a memorandum written in German by Dollinger which strongly opposed a definition of the Pope's personal infallibility.[50] Monsell translated it into English, Newman had it printed and it was then circularised among the English-speaking bishops due to attend the Council.[51] Its impact was difficult to measure, but Papal Infallibility became a dogma in 1870 and Monsell accepted it reluctantly, as he had already accepted the Syllabus of Errors.[52] Above all, the Vatican Council represented the final defeat of Liberal Catholicism. Soon after, in consequence of the Franco-Prussian War, and the resulting withdrawal of the French troops protecting the Papal States, Rome fell to the Kingdom of Italy, and the Temporal Power finally came to an end.[53]

In Ireland these years were also replete with crucial events. The Church of Ireland was disestablished in 1869 with the full approval of Monsell. The following year saw the passage of the Land Act that legalised tenant right and provided for a limited amount of tenant purchase. Monsell had long advocated these measures.[54] On 21 June 1864 he had spoken in the Commons of the huge emigration from Ireland, which was depriving the country of its population, and advocated 'security' for the tenants, while deprecating what he described as 'the extravagant views put forward by many persons' on the matter at the time of the Tenant League of the 1850s.[55] On 24 February 1865 he told the Commons that 'the people of Ireland did not want confiscation, but ... either that the landlord should provide permanent buildings for the tenant, or that if the latter erected them that he should have an occupation for such a number of years as would enable him to compensate himself out of the produce of the land, or that if the landlord wished to get rid of him, he should be compensated for them'.[56] On 16 March 1868 he again advocated 'stability of tenure by granting leases' and tenant purchase, although he qualified the latter by stating that 'he did not wish to see Ireland divided among small proprietors, but a small and occasional infusion of that class would be most beneficial to its social system'.[57] In consequence, Monsell's reaction to Gladstone's measure was very positive and he told the Commons on 10 March 1870 that the land bill was 'the greatest boon that had ever been offered' the people of Ireland.[58] He admitted that it did not contain the words 'security of tenure', but he maintained 'that it provided for security of tenure in substance, for it enacted that a heavy penalty should be paid by the man who violated the law of security of tenure by evicting his tenant'. He also applauded the encouragement it gave to landlords to grant 31-year leases. He concluded by warning that if this great measure on offer from England and Scotland were rejected, 'Ireland might go back to those evil days when England cared little for the interests of Ireland, but satisfied her conscience by the belief that Irish grievances were irremediable.' Worse still, 'his Right Hon. friend the Premier' might cease to 'take an interest in Irish affairs'. In Monsell's view, he and his Irish Liberal colleagues had been successful in their task of arousing in Britain's mind the need for Ireland's grievances to be remedied.[59]

As it happened, that which he most feared was about to happen. The revival of federalism, in the form of Home Rule, was one of the most paradoxical outcomes of Gladstone's reform programme in Ireland.[60] The tenant farmers did not agree with Monsell that the Land Act was a 'great act of justice', but were bitterly disappointed at its provisions. At the same time many Protestants and Conservatives regarded the disestablishment of the Church as a great betrayal, while the failure to grant freedom to the imprisoned Fenian leaders had led to the establishment of a massive Amnesty Association. Monsell himself advocated granting as wide an amnesty as possible to the Fenians, as he had earlier argued, on both practical and humanitarian grounds, against inflicting the death penalty on them. Isaac Butt, the ex-federalist who had gained national prominence as a result of his defence of the Fenian leaders, now channelled these three streams of discontent into a demand for Home Rule. The split between Catholic Whigs and Independent Oppositionists, never healed fully since 1866, now began to re-emerge.[61] J.F. Maguire was among those who came out in favour of Home Rule, and the former Independents were to be early recruits to Butt's cause.[62] Monsell was totally opposed to the Home Rule agitation, and was to observe its rise with anxiety throughout his remaining years in the Commons.

Monsell's period in the Colonial Office lasted just over two years. Despite his achievements in the field of colonial education (which were not widely known or appreciated), he was regarded as a very average holder of the office of Under-Secretary[63] He was growing increasingly restless, as he was now entering the autumn of his political career and was anxious to leave the Colonial Office because the easy-going Granville had been replaced by the anti-Catholic Earl of Kimberley (1826–1902) (who as Lord Wodehouse had formerly been Irish Viceroy). However, Granville contemplated having Monsell appointed his deputy at the Foreign Office, whither he had gone after leaving the Colonial Office.[64]

At last, in November 1870, Monsell's chance came when a vacancy was created in the Cabinet and he wrote to H.A. Bruce, the Home Secretary, canvassing for promotion. Bruce's reply on the 29 December stated that the ministerial reshuffle would result in Monsell's position being 'materially improved'. As to the Cabinet, Gladstone seemed determined to make no addition, as the number in it at present was 'inconveniently large'. However, Monsell was encouraged when his argument, that he would be a representative of the Catholic community in the Cabinet, was described by Bruce as 'a very strong one'.[65] Two motives determined Gladstone's policy at this time. Firstly, he had offended Catholic opinion in Ireland by publishing an article in the *Edinburgh Review* on 26 October, which, among other things, celebrated the recent fall of the Pope's temporal power.[66] Secondly, some commentators believed that Monsell did not possess the ability to be in the Cabinet. Lord Kimberley had confided to his diary in 1868 that 'we have no Irishman of our Party in the House of Commons, except C. Fortescue (and he is rather weak) fit for the Cabinet'.[67] Gladstone's aim was to satisfy Catholic claims without giving Monsell a position beyond his capacity.

The ensuing game of political musical chairs saw Chichester Fortescue appointed to the Board of Trade, Hartington going to Ireland as Chief Secretary and Monsell replacing the latter as Postmaster-General, but without a seat in the Cabinet.[68] Monsell's reaction was mixed and on 31

December 1870 he wrote to both O'Hagan and Gladstone. To O'Hagan he wrote 'of course I have accepted. It is a high office, and being generally a Cabinet one, brings me to the threshold.'[69] To Gladstone, he expressed thanks and told him that he would enjoy the work but also stated that 'of course, I should have liked to be in the Cabinet, and it seems to me ... that my presence there would have tended to promote objects you have very much at heart'.[70] Although Monsell was pleased at his promotion to the highest post attained by a Roman Catholic in a British administration since the Glorious Revolution, he still hankered after a seat in the Cabinet. Sadly for him, his term as Postmaster-General was to mark both the culmination and the end of his ministerial career, and he never made it to the Cabinet table.

Monsell's appointment was greeted by a profile in *Vanity Fair* on 11 February 1871. While it was a sign of prominence to be so honoured, the caption accompanying his portrait was far from flattering, describing him as being 'not one of those men whom a craving for notoriety has driven to rival the leader by gaining a world-wide, or even an England-wide reputation, through associating himself with any high-flown wonders done or said'. After sarcastically remarking that he owed his position in Government to his being a token Catholic, it concluded: 'every inhabitant of Great Britain must rejoice at his elevation; and if the Colonies mourn over the loss of so excellent an Under-Secretary, they may console themselves with the expectation that he will now have the opportunity of showing the great abilities which he has hitherto modestly kept in the background'.[71]

In the same year (1871) Monsell was appointed to the life position of Lord-Lieutenant of the city and county of Limerick, in succession to his brother-in-law, Lord Dunraven, who had died aged 59. This was an office of great importance, for he was now the chief civil and military official in Limerick.[72] The Lord-Lieutenant, officially styled 'Her Majesty's Lieutenant of the County and City of Limerick', was appointed by the Queen on the advice of the Government, and represented the Crown in his county. He was both a ceremonial figure and head of the magistry. He commanded the County Militia, appointed Deputy Lieutenants and recommended to the Lord Chancellor for appointments of all local magistrates. As Custos Rotulorum (Keeper of the Rolls), an office attached to that of Lord-Lieutenant, he was official guardian of the county records. His official uniform was similar to that of a general, and Monsell's portrait as Lord-Lieutenant, resplendent in scarlet trimmed with gold braid, hung in Tervoe House until 1951.

In 1871 the Post Office was both the largest employer in the United Kingdom and the biggest department in the British public service, with a staff of 38,000, of which 9,000 belonged to the newly acquired telegraphs section. Its gross annual revenue amounted to £4,880,000 and its annual expenditure to £3,611,000 (exclusive of the telegraph system). It had a national network of offices and officials throughout the length and breadth of the Kingdom and came into contact with the general public to a greater extent than any other Government department. The headquarters of the Post Office were housed in an imposing building at St Martin Le Grand, near St Paul's Cathedral, in the City of London. In some respects, the Post Office was undoubtedly a department of very great significance.[73]

Despite this, the office of Postmaster-General (PMG), the minister in charge of the Post Office, was not considered a significant one. In the nineteenth century the business of central government was perceived to lie chiefly in the prosecution of a vigorous foreign policy, for which strong armed forces and large financial resources were required. Consequently, the most important departments of state were the Treasury, the Foreign Office, the War Office and the Admiralty. By contrast, the dominant affairs of modern governments, such as management of the economy, health, education and social welfare, were regarded as being of less significance. It is not surprising that in such a climate of opinion the office of PMG was not highly regarded, and there are a number of indicators of its relative unimportance. Firstly, the Prime Minister, Chancellor of the Exchequer and other senior ministers each commanded a salary of £5,000 per annum, while the PMG only received £2,500.[74] Secondly, it did not carry with it an automatic seat in the Cabinet, and between 1835 and 1900 less than half the holders were included.[75] In 1866 a cynic remarked that the only reason for retaining the post was 'to pay a compliment to someone of high rank and give him a salary for doing nothing'.[76] Sir Herbert Samuel, PMG between 1910 and 1914 and again between 1915 and 1916, regarded it as being 'not one of the most onerous [positions] in the Government'.[77]

The PMG was the political head of the Post Office, responsible for the general supervision of the Posts and Telegraph systems of the realm. Perhaps his main task, and certainly his most visible one, was to represent his department in Parliament.[78] The degree of influence that an incumbent could exert over the day-to-day running of his office was constrained by several factors. The workload was enormous, but was conducted by a highly skilled staff led by the permanent head, the Secretary of the Post Office. The Secretary and his major subordinates usually held office for long periods, while the PMG held office for a very short period. Between 1835 and 1947 there were forty-four incumbents, of whom twenty-one held it for two years or less, so Monsell's two and a half years represented a fairly average tenure.[79] One commentator wrote that 'the part which a Postmaster-General takes in the control of the department depends very largely on his own inclination and strength of character. He is a bird of passage ... he usually comes to his duties without any experience of the technical work and routine of the department.'[80] Monsell came to the office with some of the necessary qualifications, for his long experience as a parliamentarian meant that he was able to defend his department in the Commons reasonably well, and he had seven years ministerial experience. While he totally lacked experience of the Post Office, this was also the case with virtually all PMGs. Monsell's greatest handicap was to be the very poor relations that he and his permanent secretary had with the Chancellor of the Exchequer and his staff, as the Post Office was a revenue department and was thus under Treasury control. The Treasury determined Post Office expenditure and by extension much of the general business of the department, so relations with the Treasury were thus of paramount importance to every PMG.

As PMG, Monsell found himself working with a set of very formidable colleagues. The permanent head of the Post Office from 1864 to 1880 was Sir John Tilley (1813–98), a man of patriarchal appearance and great experience, and a competent and professional administrator.[81] Frank Ives Scudamore (1823–84), who had become Second Secretary of the Post Office in 1867, was an eccentric and whimsical individual with a vast capacity for work, tremendous ability and a fierce, almost obsessive, determination to advance the telegraph service, for which he had special responsibility.[82] George Chetwynd, Receiver and Accountant General of the Post Office, had the task of monitoring and controlling the expenditure of the department, but was incompetent and credulous.[83] The all-important Treasury was headed by its First Lord, Prime Minister Gladstone, who was to blame Monsell for the disasters that befell the Post Office in 1873.[84] Second in command at the Treasury, and the real head, was the Second Lord, Robert Lowe (1811–92), Chancellor of the Exchequer. While his most notable achievement was to throw virtually the entire civil service open to public competition in 1870, he was brusque, arrogant and tactless, and was impatient with those who attempted to thwart his plans. He and Monsell became bitter opponents.[85] Finally, Sir Ralph Lingen (1819–1905) was the Permanent Secretary of the Treasury from 1869 to 1885, and thus chief of the entire British civil service. The *DNB* unctuously described him as 'an enemy of growing expenditure and a vigilant guardian of the public purse', but he was less flatteringly characterised by Tilley as a 'pedant'. Lingen worked well with Lowe, for they had previously been colleagues in the education department.[86]

William Monsell took up his new position officially on 14 January 1871 and was immediately confronted with three main issues.[87] The first was the newly acquired telegraphs system, purchased by the Government in 1870 in what had been described as the 'first significant experiment in nationalisation undertaken in modern British history'.[88] The second, largely resulting from the first, was the problem of labour relations difficulties within the department.[89] Thirdly, there was the question of the connection that the Post Office had with the Treasury, a long-simmering dispute that eventually flared into open warfare towards the end of Monsell's term as PMG.[90]

It was not long before the pattern of Monsell's style of management began to emerge. To begin with, he never succeeded in properly asserting his authority over his subordinates. He came into a department dominated by two strong personalities, Tilley and Scudamore, who had worked there since 1829 and 1841 respectively. Both of these men had served in a number of subordinate positions before reaching the top, both possessed enormous knowledge and experience, and both were strong-willed and opinionated. Monsell came to enjoy a good working relationship with Tilley, but he never came to an understanding with Scudamore.[91] Secondly, he was content to let the Post Office run itself with minimal interference from above. He worked diligently, and by his own lights, efficiently, but believed that a detached managerial style was best. Thirdly, he was by nature a comparatively diffident and scrupulous individual. Tilley himself wrote to Monsell that 'it will never be thought that you wish to be hard on people'.[92] In 1873 his friend Ralph Bernal Osborne, MP referred in the Commons to the 'meekness and gentlemanly feeling which characterised him'.[93] Edward McCabe, Archbishop of Dublin, characterised Monsell as being 'too much of the Christian gentleman to be uncivil to anyone'.[94] Eventually, Monsell allowed his subordinates to reduce his control at St Martin's Le Grand to a nullity, while his fellow-ministers came to treat him with less than the respect due to a holder of his position.

Monsell began well by presiding over the successful implementation of one of the major changes in British postal rates between 1840 and 1914.[95] When he announced these proposals in the Commons, S.R. Graves, Conservative MP for Liverpool, 'congratulated the Postmaster-General not only on the nature of the announcements he had made, but also on the tone and spirit, in which he had made them', and then went on to say that 'it augured well for the future of this Post Office that the right honourable gentleman [Monsell] thoroughly appreciated the responsibility of his post'.[96] Monsell, not normally a good performer in the House, enjoyed a triumph and while it would be absurd to suggest that he had any great influence on the formulation of the new policy, as he had only been PMG for two months, he fully appreciated its merits and was anxious to have it implemented as soon as possible. Above all, he had carried out very well one of the main functions of his office: to represent and defend the Post Office in Parliament. In addition, he used his position vigorously to bolster his local political base. He built a new General Post Office in Limerick city, which remained in use until its demolition in the 1960s.[97] He also was active in promoting Irishmen to positions in the Post Office to such an extent that J.T. Delane, the formidable editor of the *Times* from 1845 to 1877, acidly wrote that Monsell 'had put the whole patronage of the Post Office at the disposal of Manning and Cullen and there is not a letter carrier who does not speak with a brogue'.[98]

Monsell faced his first major conflict as PMG in the autumn of 1871. Frank Ives Scudamore had played the leading role in carrying through the nationalisation of the Telegraphs and subsequently directed the system with only nominal supervision from his superiors, the PMG and the Secretary of the Post Office.[99] He initiated and carried on a huge and expensive expansion of the system, which at its height resulted in the opening of thirty new telegraph offices per week. Scudamore worked with incredible energy and fanatical zeal on this project and soon came to regard the Telegraphs system as his own private fiefdom, over which he exercised autocratic control.[100] However, many of the former employees of the private telegraph companies had brought a tradition of militancy with them into their new working environment, and they soon complained about wages and working conditions. Scudamore became aware that an agitation was afoot. The ring-leaders of the nascent unrest communicated with each other using the telegraph wires, and Scudamore, by taking the drastic and astonishing step of tapping the lines, discovered their names and was able to draw up contingency plans to combat what he regarded as their insolent insubordination.[101]

In early December 1871 two hundred telegraphists and messengers in seven major cities of the United Kingdom, including Dublin and Cork, went on strike. This was the first strike in the history of the civil service, but Scudamore was more than equal to the occasion. He crushed the agitation with vigour and promptitude and inflicted severe penalties on the ring-leaders, in the form of instant dismissal with loss of pension rights. The rank and file of the strikers quickly scuttled back to work, and Scudamore rewarded the clerks who had remained at their posts with salary increases. Monsell was furious at this, for Scudamore had never bothered to consult him before sanctioning these increases.[102]

However, this was only the least of Scudamore's high-handed actions.

On the 7 and 8 December, when the strike was still in progress, Scudamore had delayed telegrams addressed to the *Times* and the *Daily News* concerning the progress of the dispute, fearing that such publicity would have caused it to spread. When this became known publicly, it caused a tremendous controversy. Monsell had been in Ireland for most of this episode, and on 11 December Tilley wrote to him suggesting that he should come over to London to supervise the conclusion of the dispute. 'It cannot be said that you did not personally take part in the matter,' Tilley wrote, obviously exasperated at having to recall the head of the department, in the throes of a major crisis.[103] While this is a glaring example of Monsell's detachment from the workings of the Post Office, he became incensed when he finally became aware of Scudamore's action concerning the Telegraphs. After all, a telegram was as 'sacred' as a letter, Tilley had told him, and no one but the recipient had the right to tamper with it.[104]

The controversy was raised in the Commons, where Monsell stated on 12 February 1872 that Scudamore's action had been taken 'without the knowledge or sanction of the Government'.[105] Monsell, enraged and embarrassed at the flagrant disregard with which Scudamore treated his authority, requested an explanation from Scudamore, whose defence was twofold. First, he claimed that he was justified in using any methods at his disposal to stamp out the strike, and second, he did not want to implicate the PMG or the Government by informing them of what he was doing. Monsell refused to accept this explanation and in a strongly worded rebuke, officially censured Scudamore for his unauthorised actions. The permanent heads of departments were 'responsible not to the public but to their political chief', Monsell told him angrily.[106]

Thus Monsell had reacted well to Scudamore's first challenge to his position and might have become *de facto* as well as *de jure* head of the staff of St Martin Le Grand had he persisted with such an assertive attitude. Unfortunately, he did not do so, and thus lost a major opportunity to avert the later disasters. Monsell soon lapsed into his previous inactivity, while Scudamore, having taken his superior's measure, continued to rule the Telegraphs like an independent despot. Henceforth, relations between the two were far from friendly. Soon after, Monsell was writing to O'Hagan about Scudamore's insolence and desperately asking advice as to how to deal with his unruly second secretary, thus showing that he had completely lost control of the situation. To make matters worse, Monsell became embroiled in similar disputes outside his department.[107]

The Treasury was the department with which Monsell as PMG had most dealings, so it was most unfortunate that relations between Robert Lowe and himself should have become soured. A serious clash was caused by the 'high-handed' refusal of Lowe to sanction Monsell's proposal to increase the wages of the letter-carriers (as postmen were then called) at Liverpool, Manchester and Birmingham. Tilley was furious at this rebuff and Monsell appealed to the Prime Minister himself on the matter. In his letter of 19 April 1872 Monsell emphasised to Gladstone that to refuse these wage increases would precipitate a strike and also cause letter-carriers to leave the Post Office permanently for more lucrative employment in the private sector. Even more alarming, Monsell warned Gladstone, was the prospect of a strike of the letter-carriers leading to a renewal of the telegraphists' dispute.[108] Monsell and Tilley and were at one in this battle with the Treasury, and the latter was particularly incensed at Lowe's jibe that the Post Office chiefs were afraid of the letter-carriers and were anxious to placate them with wage increases.[109]

In the meantime, Lowe had plunged into another controversy with the Post Office. For several decades the British Government had been in the forefront of efforts by the European powers to suppress the African slave trade and at this period was particularly concerned with the activities of the thriving slave market in the independent Sultanate of Zanzibar. Robert Lowe devised a plan, under which the Government would establish a regular mail service linking Zanzibar with Aden and the Cape of Good Hope, in return for the Sultan's co-operation in suppressing the slave trade. Lowe's plan would be less expensive than the alternative one, of deploying British warships on the East African coast. However, Monsell objected to the scheme, correctly pointing out that it was an expensive subsidised service, was being initiated for political reasons, would bring in little revenue and would do little, if anything, to improve mail services. Monsell voiced his objections in a letter to Gladstone on 22 September 1872, reminding the Prime Minister that he himself had frequently condemned 'the principle of postal ocean contracts' for long periods.[110] When Lowe heard of Monsell's opposition he was furious with what he regarded as the PMG's obtuse inability to appreciate the larger issues at stake and went ahead himself with his Zanzibar mail scheme. In effect, Lowe had usurped Monsell's role as PMG and eventually precipitated a major political crisis by his inept and irregular handling of the issue.[111]

Persistent demands for a wage increase by London letter-carriers touched off yet another wrangle. Monsell refused their demands, but instead recommended to the Treasury that they should be given a longer time-break, as compensation. The Treasury refused to sanction even this, although Monsell had recommended it to Gladstone. On 16 October 1872 Tilley wrote to Monsell pointing out that relations between the Treasury and the Post Office had always been very harmonious, until the advent to power of Gladstone's administration (which of course, had brought Lowe and Lingen, to the Treasury). Tilley recited a list of examples of Treasury high-handedness towards the Post Office, including their refusal to sanction Monsell's plan to reform the notoriously inefficient Dublin General Post Office, and also complained that there was widespread demoralisation and apathy at the Post Office because of Treasury officiousness. Most significantly, Tilley pointed out that as the PMG was directly responsible to Parliament for his department, his opinion should be given some weight by the Treasury and not, as was so often the case, 'hastily set aside'.[112]

On receipt of this communication, Monsell addressed a major letter of complaint to Gladstone in which he remarked bitterly that 'almost every proposal I make is considered by them [the Treasury] in a hostile spirit, and is very frequently refused'. Consequently, Monsell considered that he was 'degraded in the eyes of my subordinates' and all incentive to reform and improve the Post Office was stifled. He instanced the Dublin Post Office affair as an example of this. The PMG, 'a great officer of state', was now tied hand and foot by Treasury red tape. In conclusion, Monsell appealed to Gladstone to 'intimate to the Treasury the principle on which they ought to act, when proposals are submitted to them by the Post Office'.[113] However, Tilley after careful consideration now advised Monsell to let the matter drop and allow the Treasury to bear the blame for whatever industrial action the letter-carriers might take. Acting on this advice, Monsell again wrote to Gladstone, effectively withdrawing his complaint.[114]

Even so, industrial relations within the Post Office had not yet finished fuelling the flames. In late 1872 the Post Office surveyors, who played a vital role by acting as channels of communication between St Martin Le Grand and the Postmasters in the provinces, began agitating for wage increases. When Tilley told Lingen on 24 January 1873 that he thought their demands were well founded, he received a reply which he later described as 'simply astounding'.[115] In his ferocious letter, the Secretary of the Treasury sharply told Tilley that the surveyors' memorial should be rejected out of hand and then launched a fierce attack on the conduct of the heads of the Post Office, describing them as being 'mere delegates of your establishment, instead of being the advanced guard and bulwark of the Treasury' and even alleging that 'your men speak and write as if they had no masters'. Tilley, who had served for thirty-two years in the Post Office, was outraged by Lingen's remarks.[116]

By the beginning of 1873 a state of open warfare existed between the Post Office and the Treasury, with Monsell and Tilley now firmly aligned against Lowe and Lingen. Monsell and Tilley were desperately worried about the threat of strikes and were prepared to make judicious concessions to avert this threat, but Lowe and Lingen dismissed such fears as unfounded and upheld the doctrine of rigid economy. Monsell and Tilley's response was to ensure that when the great strike finally did occur, the Treasury should take all the blame for refusing to avert it.[117] Monsell's constant appeals to Gladstone had done little to alleviate these difficulties, and in the case of the Zanzibar mail contracts, had only served to infuriate the already irascible Lowe.[118] Also Gladstone was becoming increasingly weary of being called upon to referee the continual skirmishes. It is little wonder that a major scandal should have broken on such a clouded scene.

The Scudamore affair was one of the greatest financial scandals of late nineteenth-century Britain, attracting great public attention, which Gladstone described as 'mortifying'.[119] It broke on 21 March 1873 when it was revealed in the House of Commons that the Post Office had spent £812,000 on the Telegraphs in excess of the sums that Parliament had voted. A report of the Committee of Public Accounts stated that the position of the PMG was compromised because Monsell, 'as chief, is liable to account to the public' for these monies. The report also raised several other important issues, including the Post Office's undesirable control over large sums of money and the seeming inability of the Treasury to monitor their activities. Lowe promised the House that 'a thorough enquiry' into the whole affair would be held and the Treasury then established a Commission of Enquiry.[120] These revelations ushered in the worst period of Monsell's entire political career, but the origins of the scandal lay in a system established in 1854 to govern the finances of the Post Office. It provided for the entire revenue to be paid into the Exchequer, while expenditure would be provided by annual vote of Parliament.

This structure should have made any unauthorised expenditure by the Post Office impossible, but the institution of the Post Office Savings Bank in 1862 provided a new source of revenue to the Post Office.[121] The crux of the matter was that the rules governing the payment of the Savings Bank funds into the Exchequer had been drawn up by Scudamore, and it was he who was responsible for the expenditure of the extra £812,000. Before the nationalisation of the Telegraphs, a sum of £7 million had been allocated by Parliament, which Scudamore spent in his massive expansion programme. In June 1871 he informed Lowe that the initial grant had been overspent by £610,000, but the latter obligingly provided the Post Office with another £1,000,000. On this, as on every occasion between autumn 1869 and March 1872, Scudamore furnished no statistical justification for his requests for extra funds. By March 1872 expenditure on the expansion programme had been exceeded by £200,000 and

Scudamore again applied to Lowe for funds to defray that amount, plus £280,000 extra for other related expenses. Even Lowe was taken aback at this stage, and refused to provide the money. However, Scudamore, obsessed with the expansion programme, neither halted it nor did he inform the Treasury that his funds were exhausted. Instead, making use of his own regulations governing the payments of Savings Bank deposits into the Exchequer, he began holding back Savings Bank receipts to finance the Telegraphs expansion. By March 1873 he had held back £812,000 in this manner, disregarding both the regulations of 1854 and Parliament's control over the telegraphs system.[122] George Chetwynd, Receiver and Account General, proved himself to be totally incompetent at his task of watchdog of Post Office funds, and it was clear that his ability 'to monitor and control expenditure was minimal'.[123]

The significance of this whole affair for Monsell was that he was totally unaware of what was happening. Lowe held Monsell in contempt, but admired Scudamore as a man of ability and energy. Both Scudamore and Lowe were impatient with procedures and bureaucracy, and had regularly communicated with each other, by-passing Monsell completely since he had come to St Martin's Le Grand. This was totally contrary to official practice, as department heads were supposed to communicate with each other, not with each other's civil servants. Thus, Monsell was dumbfounded when the full extent of the irregularities became known. The whole affair was attracting a great deal of public interest by the time the Commission of Enquiry reported, in July 1873. This report was most damning for Monsell and Lowe, but Scudamore also came in for some criticism. Monsell was accused of having failed to acquaint himself with the workings of his department, and of allowing his civil servants to do as they pleased in collusion with the Chancellor of the Exchequer.[124] There was a widespread belief among the public at large that Scudamore was only a very zealous civil servant, while Monsell, as political head of the Post Office, was held to be responsible for his staff's misdeeds.[125]

In response, Monsell sent Gladstone a long *apologia* on 18 July 1873 defending his actions as PMG. He began by denying that the 'errors and irregularities' at the Post Office were his responsibility, as he had been systematically deceived concerning them, or that he had been 'content to be in the dark' by his subordinates. He maintained that his predecessors, the Duke of Montrose and Lord Hartington, had allowed Scudamore to 'assume an exceptional and abnormal' authority over the Telegraphs, and that this had been sanctioned by Lowe. He further maintained that the pernicious system of Scudamore communicating directly with the Chancellor had begun in 1861, and that Savings Bank deposits had been used to finance telegraph operations as far back as 1869. The heart of

Monsell's defence was that he had inherited an undesirable situation from his predecessors and was unable to take corrective action due to systematic deception by Scudamore and Lowe. As examples of this, he mentioned Lowe's mishandling of the Zanzibar mail contract and the manner in which three letters sent to him by the Treasury in late 1872 concerning the Post Office Capital Account had never reached him. This part of Monsell's defence had more than a grain of truth in it, but he was on much shakier ground when he maintained that the accounting role of the PMG could never be more than a nominal one and that he had to rely on his subordinates, especially the Receiver and Accountant General, to bring irregularities to his attention. Indeed, Monsell never seemed to think that the PMG ought to familiarise himself thoroughly his department, but saw his role as essentially passive, totally reliant on his civil servants, and content to accept that his predecessors' actions were correct practice.[126]

Gladstone's reaction was volcanic. In his diary entry of 26 July 1873, Lord Kimberley noted that the Prime Minister was furious with Monsell and was initially determined to dismiss him, but was persuaded not to do so. Kimberley himself described Monsell's conduct as being 'really indefensible, his neglect of this office and total incapacity have largely been the cause of the Telegraphs and other scandals'. The Treasury was also to blame, Kimberley believed, but he noted sarcastically that Monsell wasn't even aware of the situation 'and would have gone on contentedly at the Post Office, as if nothing had happened'. Kimberley also mentioned that Monsell would have to resign, but would receive a peerage.[127]

Meanwhile, the Conservative MP for South-West Lancashire, Richard Assherton Cross, had moved a resolution recording the House's disapproval of the conduct of the Post Office in this affair, and expressing an opinion that the control of the Treasury over the Post Office, having proved inadequate, would in future have to be 'more watchfully exercised'. This resolution was debated in the House on 29 July, when Cross sharply criticised Monsell for not properly supervising Scudamore or checking his misdemeanours, though he also criticised Lowe. The Government brought forward a counter-resolution, which contained no censure of any of the parties involved, although Sir John Lubbock, in moving this resolution, blamed Scudamore and Chetwynd for misleading the PMG. He was followed by Monsell himself, who having listed the achievements of the Post Office during his tenure (the reduction of postage rates, the development of the telegraph service and of the money order system, improvements in the parcel post) defended himself by using the same arguments that he had presented to Gladstone in his letter of 18 July. His remarks at this point concerning his predecessors' alleged shortcomings annoyed both Gladstone and Hartington. Monsell concluded by expressing his sincere regret for what had happened, and thanked the House for its kindness to him. Monsell's point of view found support from two subsequent speakers, one of whom, his friend Bernal Osborne (who roundly blamed Lowe for all the mischief) described him as 'a very ill-treated person' and even 'a sort of paschal lamb'. The debate was concluded by Gladstone, who said nothing to defend Monsell, but pointedly said of Scudamore that his undoubted errors were balanced 'by still greater services'. Cross's motion was defeated by 161 to 111, and the Government's motion was adopted instead.[128]

While it is clear from Kimberly's diary that Monsell was to resign and receive a peerage as compensation, it is doubtful whether his career in the House of Commons would have lasted much longer, even without Scudamore. The position of Catholic Whigs had come under increasing threat since the beginning of the Home Rule movement in 1870. A series of by-elections in Ireland between 1870 and 1873 saw the return of nine Home Rule MPs. Three of these were particularly alarming to Monsell, as he had been in close touch with the anti-Home Rule elements in each case. In June 1871 his friend and confidante, J.A. Dease withdrew as the Liberal candidate in the Westmeath by-election, and left the field open to the Home Rule candidate; Isaac Butt himself was returned unopposed for Limerick City in September 1871 and in February 1872 J.A. Dease was defeated by the Home Rule candidate, Rowland Blennerhassett, in a by-election in Kerry.[129] Also, the introduction of the secret ballot in 1872 is believed to have facilitated the rise of Home Rule. Even Monsell's own constituency was not safe, and in August 1872 his close friend Stephen de Vere wrote to him, stating that he wished that the PMG was out of active politics, as the rise of the nationalist movement and the introduction of the secret ballot would lead to expensive, contested elections resulting in the return of Home Rule MPs. He expressed a desire to see Monsell made a peer, and accurately predicted that Gladstone's proposed Irish university reform would not be acceptable to the Irish Bishops and would thus leave Monsell, as a Catholic member of the Government, in an impossible position.[130] Also Bishop Butler of Limerick told Monsell on 18 March 1873 that he wished to see him raised to a position (a peerage) away from 'the miseries of contested elections'.[131]

The crisis in Monsell's position as an MP broke at the same time as his downfall as a minister. Early in 1873 Gladstone introduced his long-awaited and very significant Irish university bill.[132] Gladstone himself saw it as the third, and by no means the least important, part of his Irish reform programme. He and his High Church supporters wanted to encourage 'the efforts of Irish Liberal Catholics to develop a distinctly national, rather than Ultramontane, religious culture. Liberal Catholic control of education, especially higher education, was perceived to be the most important precondition of such a development.'[133] However, Gladstone and Acton made the mistake of grossly overestimating the importance of the Irish Liberal Catholics, who were a minority, while the mass of Irish Catholics were prepared to take their direction on educational matters from the bishops.[134] The Catholic Whigs also feared the manner in which the rising Home Rule party made the demand for denominational education one of its chief means of winning support.

Gladstone's bill was ultimately based on 'Mr Monsell's Scheme', thus demonstrating the latter's important role in the university question.[135] On 23 January 1869 Monsell had told Fortescue that Cullen was receptive to his plan of 'one neutral university, and denominational or other colleges', and this was passed on to Gladstone, who was thus convinced that the hierarchy would accept his proposals.[136] The *Freeman's Journal* of 3 September 1869 carried a report of resolutions passed by the Bishops in Maynooth in which they stated that while their preference was for a Catholic university, they would be prepared to accept a Catholic college within one national university.[137] In 1871 they repeated this in a pastoral letter. On 1 April 1872 Professor David Dunne of the Catholic University had written to Woodlock: 'Monsell's scheme is now the name by which the transfer to Ireland of the London University System is known.'[138] This same hostile observer told Woodlock on 8 May 1872: 'I hear from some quarters that Gladstone is favourable to "indirect" endowment, if it can be accomplished. But indirect endowment may mean Mr Keenan's plan, or as it is now (to make it more acceptable, I presume) called "Mr Monsell's scheme?"'[139] The Cabinet began work on the problem in November 1872. At the same time Gladstone adamantly refused to consult with the Bishops, fearing that it would lead to their asking too much.[140] On 4 February 1873 Monsell forwarded a petition to the Prime Minister from 'the leading men of County Limerick', stating that intermediate education should also be tackled, but Gladstone ignored it.[141]

On 13 February 1873 Gladstone unveiled his proposals to the Commons, which in Norman's summary consisted of the following:

> the University of Dublin was to be separated from Trinity College to become an Irish National University. It would have the exclusive privilege of granting degrees, and would be federal, with affiliated colleges. These were to be Trinity, the Queen's Colleges of Belfast and Cork, the Catholic College in Dublin, Magee College in Londonderry, and any others to be determined by Parliament in the first instance, and afterwards by the governing body. The Galway

> Queen's College was to be suppressed. The university was to be an examining body, but it was also to be nominally a teaching body with a staff of professors. The teaching of theology, modern history and ethics was not to be by the university, however, but by the constituent colleges, which were to be denominational, although there were to be no religious tests for the university. The university was to be 'open'; anyone would be able to present themselves for examination and degree without attendance at the colleges.[142]

Other provisions were for Trinity College to retain its buildings, but to abolish all religious tests. Magee and the Catholic College were to receive no endowment. Any teacher or any other person of authority in the new university might be suspended if he offended the religious convictions of any member of the university.

It was an ingenious and complicated measure, but it was opposed from all sides. Protestants were furious at the dismantling of Trinity's independence and resented the recognition of the Catholic University. The Queen's University was similarly vexed at the suppression of Galway and the recognition of the Catholic College. British Liberals and secularists resented even the slight improvement in the position of the Catholic University. Supporters of denominational education of all religions deplored the establishment of a secular university and the creation, in the shape of the non-denominational Trinity, of a powerful non-religious college at the heart of the system. The Irish Catholics were very disappointed at the lack of endowment for the Catholic University and felt that it would be unable to compete with its well-endowed rivals. They saw in the abolition of the religious tests in Trinity the creation of a powerful new Queen's College, and they resented the continued existence of the colleges in Belfast and Cork.

Monsell and O'Hagan were strong supporters. On 7 March Monsell wrote to Cullen:

> if the University Bill is thrown out ... the alliance between Catholics and the Liberals will be dissolved ... in the present aspect of the world, it would be dangerous for us to have both the great parties in the state our enemies. I have been in the House of Commons for a quarter of a century, and never felt in such low spirits as to public affairs as I do now. The separation between the Catholics and Liberals in 1851 was made by an attack by the Liberals on the Catholics. In this case the Liberal party will feel that we have thrown them over, when they were trying to serve us.[143]

Earlier, he had written to another correspondent that he had used the

Trinidad scheme as a template for Irish educational reform. In Trinidad 'the new system, after three years experience, has been found to work well. The Archbishop writes letters expressing his warmest satisfaction with it. Can that which is right in principle in Trinidad be wrong in principle in Ireland?'[144] He was shocked when Newman, of all people, condemned Gladstone's Bill in a letter to him on 21 February. Newman wrote: 'I don't think Cardinal Cullen has a chance of accepting it, unless he is very hard up.' If the Catholic Bishops accepted it having opposed mixed education since the Synod of Thurles, it would be a 'great scandal' and 'will do immense harm'. 'What is mixed education,' he asked, 'if this proposed plan is not, since its advantages cannot be obtained except through professors who must not recognise Catholicism as true?'[145]

On 27 February the Bishops condemned the bill at a meeting in Dublin, at which only Dr Butler of Limerick spoke in its favour.[146] Cullen had scant sympathy for Monsell and O'Hagan and told Kirby on 5 March: 'some of our Catholics are for the Bill, because they fear the loss of their places if Gladstone should be defeated – if the Ministry go out, Lord O'Hagan loses £4,000 per an., and Mr Monsell loses his office in the Ministry, and his salary, whatever it is. However, the Catholics who lose are very few, and in any case, the faith of the people cannot be sacrificed to their interests.'[147] As early as 3 March, Monsell had told Newman that 'my belief is that the government and the bill will both disappear'.[148]

In this he was correct. Irish Catholic opinion was strongly opposed, even before the Bishops' disapproval became known. In Britain there was also widespread opposition.[149] Gladstone himself reported much opposition from his own supporters.[150] Monsell had wanted to speak in Parliament in its favour, but Gladstone wrote to Fortescue on 6 March telling him not to allow this, as it would annoy Liberal backbenchers.[151]On the 11 March, on the second reading, the bill was defeated by 287 votes to 284. Of the 64 among the 103 Irish members who usually voted with the Liberals, 37 voted against the Government, 11 voted for and 16 were absent. Of the 37 who voted against, 26 were Catholics and 11 were Protestants; of the 11 who voted for, 4 were Catholics and 7 Protestants; and of the 16 absentees, 6 were Catholics and 10 Protestants.[152] The four Catholics who voted for the bill were Monsell himself, George Gavin, MP for Limerick City, Sir Dominic Corrigan, MP for Dublin, and Sir Rowland Blennerhassett, MP for Galway.[153] None of the four contested their seats at the 1874 general election.[154] There is no doubt that it was the Irish vote, influenced by the Bishops, that had been the decisive factor.[155] However, the impact of their defection was mitigated by the fact that Irish Liberal MPs had been very lax in giving support since the general election due to indifference rather than from any ideological opposition to the Government and in continuation of a tradition dating back to the 1840s.[156]

Nevertheless, the defeat was a turning point. It marked the end of Gladstone's alliance with the Catholic Church in Ireland, irretrievably weakened his government and immensely strengthened the Home Rule movement. Above all, it spelt the end of the Irish Catholic Whigs, whose policy of attaching themselves to the British Liberals in order to win concessions was totally discredited. Many of the sitting Liberal MPs now moved closer to Home Rule in order to prepare themselves for the general election that was now imminent. Gladstone was full of resentment towards the Irish Bishops, and used this grievance to fuel his anti-Papal campaign in 1874 and 1875.[157] For Monsell personally, it was a bitter disappointment. His standing with all parties, the Bishops, Gladstone, the Liberals, his electorate, was damaged. He was seen to be ineffectual and inept, and many years later Archbishop Walsh of Dublin characterised him to Kirby as 'an over busy layman' who had 'misled Gladstone on the views of the Irish Bishops on education, which led to the fall of the ministry'.[158] On 24 November 1874 Monsell was to tell the Statistical and Social Enquiry Society 'that the greatest misfortune which has happened to Ireland during the last twenty years ... was the rejection last year of the University Bill'.[159]

On the 5 August 1873 Gladstone drafted a letter to Monsell, dismissing him as PMG but cancelled it when he received the latter's letter of resignation dated 6 August.[160] In his letter Monsell stated that he would have to contest his seat if he wanted to retain it, and as he had no intention of doing so, he was resigning as PMG. He cited the same reason in a letter to O'Hagan on 18 August, and moreover, stated that all his friends concurred with his opinion.[161] Clearly, Monsell could not afford to contest his seat, nor was he hopeful of success. On the other hand, Stephen de Vere's diary entry for 6 August claimed that Monsell was informed by Gladstone that he would have to step down, and would be raised to the peerage, but was to return to his constituency, and having ascertained that his position there was very weak, should cite this as the cause of his resignation. This version implied that Monsell's electoral weakness was only the pretext for his departure from St Martin's Le Grand.[162]

Probably both factors were equally important. Monsell was unlikely to ever hold Government office again, after his farcical tenure in the Post Office, especially as Gladstone continued to maintain that Monsell had been a total failure as PMG.[163] His contempt for Monsell was illustrated when he wrote to Bright on 14 August: 'we have emerged from the discredit and disgrace of the exposures by an administration of mild penal justice, which will be complete all round when Monsell has been disposed of'.[164] It is equally true that Monsell's chances of retaining his seat in County Limerick were minimal. He had been returned unopposed at every election since 1859, and had neither the stomach, nor the financial resources, for the rough and tumble of a bitterly fought electoral contest.[165] His annual income of £2,500 was totally inadequate to finance a contested election, which could cost up to £6,000.[166]

Also, he correctly forecast that his chances of success were slight. In the 1874 general election the Irish Catholic Whigs were annihilated and Home Rule swept the country.[167] In County Limerick, Monsell's nominee James Kelly, who also received the support of Bishop Butler and the clergy, sustained a crushing defeat at the hands of the advanced Home Rule candidate, W.H. O'Sullivan.[168] The election as a whole was marked by the abandonment of the Liberal label in favour of Home Rule by many new and sitting MPs. Of the sixty Home Rule MPs elected in 1874, twenty-six were former Liberals and twelve newly elected members were closet Liberals.[169] Of course, as an office-holder in the Gladstone administration, Monsell could not have credibly jumped on the Home Rule bandwagon, even had he so wished, which, given his subsequent career, is highly unlikely. Monsell's resignation took effect on 18 November 1873, and his departure from the Commons occurred on 12 January 1874. Gladstone's administration was defeated at the 1874 general election, and Disraeli became Prime Minister at the head of a Conservative administration (1874–80).

The results of the Scudamore scandal were many. Gladstone's great administration, already in decline, was dealt another blow, which hastened its demise in 1874.[170] The Post Office underwent internal reforms to prevent a recurrence of the misdeeds of the Monsell era, resulting in tighter Treasury control over St Martin's Le Grand.[171] The Treasury became much less enthusiastic for further experiments in nationalisation, and there occurred no further attempts to extend the Government's rule in that field until 1912, when the telephone system was purchased. Perhaps the most important result of the affair was that it marked a milestone in the accountability of ministers. Henceforth, a minister was to be held responsible for his civil servants' misdeeds.[172] John Tilley continued as Secretary of the Post Office until 1880 and emerged relatively unscathed, as did Lingen, who remained Secretary of the Treasury until 1885 and continued to enjoy a reputation for efficiency and economy.[173] On the other hand, Scudamore, although he came out of the crisis with his reputation apparently untarnished, did not remain long at the Post Office. He resigned in 1875, after being defeated in an internal bureaucratic dispute, and died a disappointed man in 1884.[174] Robert Lowe was transferred to the Home Office in late 1873, and after the 1874 general election never held government office again.[175]

As far as Monsell is concerned, there is little doubt that his career at St Martin's Le Grand ended in abject failure. Gladstone, Kimberley and Lowe were at one in their belief that Monsell was primarily responsible for the disasters of the Scudamore affair. An able and efficient minister would have stamped his authority on the department at an early stage and curbed the excesses of Scudamore, but Monsell never succeeded in doing this. He allowed Scudamore complete discretion in the running of the Telegraphs, did not succeed in informing himself of the full workings of his department, and believed that it was incumbent on his staff to draw his attention to such problems as might arise, thus becoming overly dependent on them. In addition, he was unable to win the respect of his government colleagues, who often disregarded his viewpoint. Nevertheless, there is also much to be said in Monsell's defence. He was most unlucky, to say the least, to have had Lowe and Scudamore as colleagues whose correspondence was highly irregular and unusual. Scudamore was eccentric, obsessive and crankish, and his determination to carry out his self-appointed mission in the Telegraphs section led him into all sorts of outlandish behaviour. Lowe was tactless and irritable, quarrelled fiercely with many other colleagues besides Monsell, and even tried Gladstone's patience with his superior attitude.[176] He behaved in a high-handed and bungling manner in his handling of the Zanzibar postal contract, and in his general dealings with postal matters. Chetwynd, who should have alerted Monsell to the financial irregularities, was totally incompetent and ineffective. Scudamore and Chetwynd deceived their political chief and kept official correspondence from him. There is no doubt of Monsell's honesty and application (by his own standards) to his duties as PMG, but it would seem he was undertaking a task beyond his capacity throughout his tenure, which eventually became a shambles.

The sorry end to his career as an office-holder is in sharp contrast to his performance at the Board of Ordnance, where he had shown himself to be a masterful politician by winning the support of his superiors and carving out a position of great authority. There he had carried through major changes of policy against much opposition, and his success had been acclaimed by Gladstone, Panmure and even Queen Victoria. On the other hand, he had played a very poor hand at the Post Office, quarrelling with Lowe and Scudamore, becoming a nonentity, achieving very little and departing in circumstances of shame and failure. There would appear to be three reasons for this strange deterioration in his performance. Firstly, he seems to have made a better subordinate than a chief.

Secondly, he lacked the colossal energy of Gladstone, who remained Prime Minister until he was 85. Thirdly, and perhaps most importantly, he hoped to be promoted from the Post Office throughout his period there, and probably did not devote himself to the task in hand with the necessary enthusiasm. Clearly, the zeal and abilities that he had displayed in the 1850s seem to have been entirely absent in the 1870s. However, Monsell's career was by no means finished and the last twenty years of his life were to be full of activity and achievement.

NOTES

1. Among the best lives of Gladstone are John Morley, *Life of William Ewart Gladstone*, 3 vols. (London: Macmillan, 1903); Sir Philip Magnus, *Gladstone* (London: John Murray, 1954); Richard Shannon, *Gladstone*, Vol. 1, *1809–1865* (London: Hamish Hamilton, 1982); Roy Jenkins, *Gladstone* (London: Macmillan, 1995); and the two-volume biography by H.C.G. Matthew, *Gladstone, 1809–1874* (Oxford: Clarendon Press, 1986) and *Gladstone, 1874–1898* (Oxford: Oxford University Press, 1995). The main work dealing with the creation of Gladstone's Liberal Party is John Vincent, *Formation of the Liberal Party, 1857–68* (London: Constable, 1966).
2. For a dual biography, see Richard Aldous, *The Lion and the Unicorn: Gladstone vs Disraeli* (London: Hutchinson, 2006).
3. Angela Partington (ed.), *The Oxford Dictionary of Quotations* (Oxford: Oxford University Press, 1992), p.404.
4. (Monsell) 'University Education in Ireland', pp.57–8.
5. Ibid., p.57.
6. For the best account of the rise of Home Rule, see Thornley, *Isaac Butt and Home Rule*.
7. Ambrose Macaulay, *Dr Russell of Maynooth* (London: Darton, Longman and Todd, 1983).
8. Russell to Gladstone, 25 November 1868; Moriarty to Gladstone, 28 November 1868, both in GP, Ad. MS 44416, ff. 273–8.
9. For O'Hagan, see John McEldowney, 'Lord O'Hagan, 1812–1885', in *Irish Jurist*, new series, Vol. 14 (1979), pp.360–77, and John F. McEldowney, 'Thomas O'Hagan, first Baron O'Hagan (1812–1885)', in *Oxford DNB*.
10. Monsell to O'Hagan (undated), O'Hagan Papers, PRONI, D2777/9/81/24.
11. Cullen to Monsell, 21 May 1869, MP, MS 8317(3).
12. Monsell to O'Hagan, 23 May 1869, Teeling Papers, NLI, MS 17871(5).
13. For the Colonial Office, see Henry L. Hall, *The Colonial Office–A History* (London: Longmans, Green, 1937); John W. Cell, *British Colonial Administration in the Mid-Nineteenth Century; the Policy-Making Process* (New Haven and London: Yale University Press, 1976) and Brian L. Blakely, *The Colonial Office 1868–1892* (Durham, NC: Duke University Press, 1972).
14. Cell, *British Colonial Administration*, pp.3-4; Hall, *Colonial Office*, pp.48–9; Blakely, *Colonial Office*, p.18.
15. For Rogers, see H.C.G. Matthew, 'Frederic Rogers, Baron Blachford (1811–1889)', in *Oxford DNB*, and Warwick Perceval Newell Tyler, 'Sir Frederick Rogers, Permanent Under-Secretary at the Colonial Office 1860–1871' (unpublished Ph.D. thesis, Duke University, 1963).
16. Blakely, *Colonial Office*, pp.17–18.
17. Hall, *Colonial Office*, p.50.
18. Ibid., p.51.
19. For the role of Under-Secretary see Tyler, 'Sir Frederick Rogers', pp.69–71.
20. See Blakely, *Colonial Office*, pp.30–1 and Monsell to Granville, 22 February 1870 in Colonial Offices Papers CO 323/297, Public Records Office, Kew.
21. See Sean P. Farragher, 'Père Leman. A French Contribution to Ireland' (unpublished Ph.D.

thesis, University College Galway, 1985), pp.383–405 and Seán P Farragher, *Père Leman (1826–1880). Educator and Missionary, Founder of Blackrock College* (Dublin and London: Paraclete Press, 1988).
22. Farragher, 'Père Leman', p.38.
23. Ibid., p.389.
24. J.K. Chapman, *The Career of Sir Arthur Hamilton Gordon, First Lord Stanmore 1829–1912* (Toronto: University of Toronto Press, 1964), pp.45–102.
25. Farragher, 'Père Leman', p.389.
26. Newman, *Letters and Diaries*, Vol. 26, p.262, Monsell to Newman, 23 February 1873.
27. For Keenan, see S.M. Parkes, 'Sir Patrick Joseph Keenan (1826–1894),' in *Oxford DNB*; M. O'Doherty, 'Patrick Keenan, Educator and Administrator: A Study of the Influence of Sir Patrick Keenan on Key Developments in Nineteenth-Century Education' (unpublished M.Ed. thesis, University College Dublin, 1998) and Fiacra S. O. Dubhtaigh, 'A Review of the Contribution of Sir Patrick Keenan (1826–1894) to the Development of Irish and British Colonial Education' (unpublished M.Ed. thesis, Trinity College Dublin, 1974).
28. Farragher, 'Père Leman', p.390 and p.630, note 16.
29. Ibid., p.390.
30. Keenan to Monsell, 24 February 1869, MP, MS 8317(3).
31. Newman, *Letters and Diaries*, Vol. 26, p.262.
32. Farragher, 'Père Leman', p.391 and Chapman, *Arthur Hamilton Gordon*, pp.134–6.
33. Farragher, 'Père Leman', *passim*.
34. Newman, *Letters and Diaries*, Vol. 26, p.262, Monsell to Newman, 23 February 1873.
35. D.K. Fieldhouse, *The Colonial Empires. A Comparative Survey from the Eighteenth Century* (London: Weidenfeld and Nicolson, 1966), pp.177–80.
36. Hall, *Colonial Office*, p.177.
37. Hansard, CC, 1876–90 (26 April 1870).
38. Ibid., 1877.
39. Ibid., 1880.
40. Ibid., 1890.
41. Ibid., 1883–89.
42. Monsell to Newman, 28 December 1857, NP, M/2.
43. Entries for 10th August to 12th September 1870 in the diary of Stephen de Vere, Vol. 11, DVP, Trinity College, MS 5067–72.
44. Ensor, *England 1870–1914*, p.7.
45. Newman, *Letters and Diaries*, Vol. 25, p.245.
46. For the Irish bishops at the Council, see Larkin, *Roman Catholic Church and Home Rule Movement*, pp.XVII–XVIII and 3–26.
47. See Dermot Roantree, 'William Monsell and Papal Infallibility: The Workings of an Inopportunist's Mind', *Archivicum Hibernicum*, 43 (1988), pp.118–34.
48. Larkin, *Roman Catholic Church and Home Rule Movement*, pp.4–7.
49. Roantree, 'William Monsell and Papal Infallibility', pp.123–4.
50. Ibid., p.125.
51. Anon, *Is it opportune to define the infallibility of the Pope? Memorandum addressed to the Bishops of Germany. Respectfully offered in translation to the Bishops of the United Kingdom and its Colonies and to the Bishops of the United States* (London: Privately published, 1869).
52. Roantree, 'William Monsell and the Catholic Question', p.243.
53. Newman, *Letters and Diaries*, Vol. 25, p.245.
54. See E.D. Steele, *Irish Land and British Politics. Tenant Right and Nationality 1865–70* (Cambridge: Cambridge University Press, 1974) and Paul Bew, *Land and the National Question in Ireland 1858–82* (Dublin: Gill and MacMillan, 1978).
55. Hansard, CLXXV, 72–4 (21 June 1864).
56. Hansard, CLXXVII, 707 (24 February 1865).
57. Hansard, CXC, 1693 (16 March 1868).
58. Hansard, CXCIX, 1703–7 (10 March 1870).
59. Ibid., 1706.
60. Thornley, *Isaac Butt and Home Rule*, pp.62–176.
61. Comerford, *Fenians in Context*, pp.161–3.

62. Ibid., p.197.
63. See Tyler, 'Sir Frederick Rogers', p.71, and *Vanity Fair*, 11 February 1871.
64. Agatha Ramm (ed.), *The Political Correspondence of Mr Gladstone and Lord Granville 1868–1876*, 2 vols, in Camden Third Series, Vol. CXXXI (London: Royal Historical Society, 1952), Vol.1, pp.102–3, Granville to Gladstone 29 June 1870.
65. Bruce to Monsell, 22 December 1870, Teeling Papers, NLI, MS 17871(2).
66. Parry, *Democracy and Religion*, pp.315–16.
67. John Wodehouse, 1st Earl of Kimberley, *A Journal of events during the Gladstone Ministry 1868–74* (edited by Ethel Drus), in Camden Miscellany XXI (London, 1958), p.2.
68. Gladstone to Monsell, 30 December 1870, GP, Ad. MS 44152, no. 114.
69. Monsell to O'Hagan 31 December 1870, Teeling Papers, NLI, MS 17871(6).
70. Monsell to Gladstone, 31 December 1870, GP, Ad. MS 44152, no. 116.
71. *Vanity Fair*, 11 February 1871.
72. For accounts of the duties of this office, see William F. Bailey, *Local and Centralised Government in Ireland. A Sketch of the Existing Systems*, (Dublin: Hodges, Figgis and Co., 1888), p.51 and Virginia Crossman, *Local Government in Nineteenth-Century Ireland* (Belfast: Institute of Irish Studies, Queen's University of Belfast for the Ulster Society of Irish Historical Studies, 1994), pp.15–23.
73. *Annual report of Postmaster General, 1872*, p.18; Howard Robinson, *Britain's Post Office* (Oxford: Oxford University Press, 1953).
74. Gladstone to Monsell 16 June, 1886, GP, Ad. MS 44152, no. 264.
75. M.J. Daunton, *Royal Mail. The Post Office since 1840* (London: HMSO, 1985), p.308.
76. Ibid.
77. Daunton, *Royal Mail*, p.310.
78. Ibid., p.308.
79. Ibid., p.317.
80. Ibid., p.306.
81. See C.R. Perry, 'Sir John Tilley (1813–1898)', in *Oxford DNB*.
82. For Scudamore see C.R. Perry, 'Frank Ives Scudamore (1823–1884)', in *Oxford DNB*, and Charles Perry, 'Frank Ives Scudamore and the Post Office', *Albion*, 12 (1980), pp.350–67.
83. Daunton, *Royal Mail*, pp.319–20.
84. Ramm, *Gladstone–Granville Correspondence*, Vol. 2, p.434 and Kimberley, *Diary*, p.41.
85. For a good biography, see James Winter, *Robert Lowe* (Toronto: University of Toronto Press, 1976).
86. For Lingen, see *DNB*, Vol. 1, pp.467–9, and Gillian Sutherland, 'Ralph Robert Wheeler Lingen (1819–1905)', in *Oxford DNB*.
87. For a good survey, see C.R. Perry, *The Victorian Post Office: The Growth of a Bureaucracy*, Royal Historical Society Studies in History, no.64 (London: Royal Historical Society, 1992).
88. Perry, 'Frank Ives Scudamore', p.350.
89. Ibid., pp.356–7.
90. Monsell to Gladstone 4 March, 1873, GP, Ad. MS 44152 (178)
91. Monsell to O'Hagan, Undated, Teeling Papers, NLI, MS 17871(6).
92. Tilley to Monsell, 5 January 1873, Tilley Papers (hereafter referred to as TP), Post Office Archives, London, Post 101(13), 189.
93. Hansard, CCXVII, 1225 (29 July 1873).
94. McCabe to Butler, 13 November, 1879, MTP, MS 20676(4).
95. Robinson, *Britain's Post Office*, p.193.
96. Hansard, CCIV, 2003–23 (14 March 1871).
97. Potter, *Catholic Unionist*, p.102.
98. Parry, *Democracy and Religion*, p.384.
99. Perry, 'Frank Ives Scudamore', pp.353–7.
100. Ibid., pp.353–7.
101. Ibid., pp.356–8.
102. Ibid., p.357.
103. Tilley to Monsell, 11 December 1871, TP, Post 101 (12), 214.
104. Tilley to Monsell, 20 December 1871, TP, Post 101 (12), 227.
105. Hansard, CCIX, 212–14 (12 February 1872).

106. Monsell to Scudamore, Feb 1872 in the PO Archives, Post 30/125 E 225/1871.
107. Monsell to O'Hagan undated. Teeling Papers, NLI, MS 17871(6).
108. Monsell to Gladstone 19 April, 1872. GP, Ad. MS 44152, 143.
109. Tilley to Monsell, 23 April 1872, TP, Post 101(13), page 75.
110. Monsell to Gladstone, 22 September 1872, GP, Ad. MS 44152, 151.
111. Winter, *Robert Lowe*, pp.288–91.
112. Tilley to Monsell, 16 October 1872, GP, Ad. MS 44152, 157.
113. Tilley to Monsell, 18 October 1872, GP, Ad. MS 44152, 153.
114. Tilley to Monsell, 5 November 1872, GP, Ad. MS 44152, 169.
115. Lingen to Tilley, 25 January 1873, GP, Ad. MS 44152, 181.
116. Tilley to Monsell, 26 January 1873, TP, Post 101(13), pp.193–5.
117. Ibid.
118. Tilley to Monsell, November 1872, TP, Post 101 (13).
119. Morley, *Life of Gladstone*, Vol. 2, p.461.
120. Hansard, CCXIV, 2055–63 (21 March 1873).
121. Winter, *Robert Lowe*, pp.285–7 and Daunton, *Royal Mail*, pp.318–20.
122. Daunton, *Royal Mail*, pp.318–21and Perry, 'Frank Ives Scudamore', pp.358–61.
123. Daunton, *Royal Mail*, p.320.
124. *First report from the Committee of Public Accounts, together with ... the proceedings of the committee, minutes of evidence and appendix* (PP 1873(7)).
125. Daunton, *Royal Mail*, pp.320–1.
126. Monsell to Gladstone, 18 July 1873, GP, Ad. MS 44152, 194–211.
127. Kimberley, *Diary*, pp.40–1.
128. Hansard, CCXVII, 1189–1232 (29 July 1873).
129. Thornley, *Isaac Butt and Home Rule*, pp.113–32.
130. Stephen de Vere to Monsell, 10 August 1872, MP, MS 8317(7).
131. Butler to Monsell, 18 March 1873, MTP, MS 20677(1).
132. Parry, *Democracy and Religion*, p.4.
133. Ibid., pp.192–6.
134. Ibid.
135. For good accounts of this crisis, see Larkin, *Roman Catholic Church and Home Rule Movement*, pp.157–78; Parry, *Democracy and Religion*, pp.353–68 and Norman, *Catholic Church and Ireland*, pp.444–54.
136. Monsell to Fortescue, 23 January 1869, CP 3/75 and Fortescue to Gladstone 21 October, 1872, CP/1/176, Carlingford Papers.
137. *Freeman's Journal*, 2 September 1869.
138. David Dunne to Dr Woodlock, 1 April 1872, quoted in Larkin, *Roman Catholic Church and Home Rule Movement*, p.324.
139. Ibid., p.326, Dunne to Woodlock, 8 May 1872.
140. Norman, *Catholic Church and Ireland*, pp.446–7.
141. GP, Ad. MS 44152, f.172, 4 February 1873.
142. Norman, *Catholic Church and Ireland*, pp.448–9.
143. Monsell to Cullen, 7 March 1873, quoted in Larkin, *Roman Catholic Church and Home Rule Movement*, p.171.
144. Newman, *Letters and Diaries*, Vol. 26, pp.261–3, Monsell to Newman, 23 February 1873.
145. Ibid., pp.251–2, Newman to Monsell, 21 February 1873.
146. Norman, *Catholic Church and Ireland*, p.451.
147. Cullen to Kirby 10 March 1873, quoted in Larkin, *Roman Catholic Church and Home Rule Movement*, p.169.
148. Newman, *Letters and Diaries*, Vol.26, p.264, Monsell to Newman, 3 March 1873.
149. Parry, *Democracy and Religion* , p.361.
150. Ibid.
151. Ibid., p.161. See also Fortescue to Gladstone, 6 March 1873, GP, Ad. MS 44123, fo. 37.
152. Larkin, *Roman Catholic Church and Home Rule Movement*, p.173.
153. Ibid., pp.173–4.
154. Ibid., p.174.
155. Ibid.
156. Parry, *Democracy and Religion*, p.197.

157. Ibid., pp.369–70 and p.423.
158. Patrick J. Corish, 'Irish College Rome: Kirby Papers', in *Archivium Hibernicum*, 32 (1974), pp.1–63.
159. William Monsell, 'Inaugural Address of the Rt. Hon. Lord Emly 24th November, 1874', in *Journal of the Statistical and Social Enquiry Society of Ireland*, Part XLVI (November 1874), p.365.
160. Gladstone to Monsell 5 August, 1873, GP, Ad. MS 44152, no. 221; Monsell to Gladstone 6 August, 1873, GP, Ad. MS 44152, no. 224.
161. Monsell to O'Hagan, 8 August 1873, Teeling Papers, NLI, MS 17871(5).
162. Entry in the diary of Stephen de Vere, Vol. 12, 8 August 1873, DVP, Trinity College, Dublin, no. 5071.
163. Ramm, *Gladstone–Granville Correspondence*, Vol.2, p.434.
164. Gladstone to Bright 14 August, 1873 quoted in Morley, *Life of Gladstone*, Vol. 2, p.65.
165. Walker, *Parliamentary Election Results in Ireland 1801–1922*, pp.293–4.
166. John Bateman (ed.), *The Great Landowners of Great Britain and Ireland* (Leicester: Leicester University Press, 1971; facsimile reprint of the edition of 1883), p.152; Stephen de Vere to Monsell, 13 February 1872, MP, MS 8317(7).
167. Thornley, *Isaac Butt and Home Rule*, pp.176–204.
168. Ibid., pp.191–4.
169. Comerford, *Fenians in Context*, pp.197–8.
170. Gladstone to Monsell, 5 August 1873, GP, Ad. MS 44152, no. 221.
171. Daunton, *Royal Mail*, pp.321–4.
172. Perry, 'Frank Ives Scudamore', p.351, and Henry Parris, *Constitutional Bureaucracy: The Development of British Central Administration since the Eighteenth Century* (London: Allen and Unwin, 1969), pp.103–5.
173. DNB, Supplement, Vol. 1, pp.467–9.
174. Perry, 'Frank Ives Scudamore', p.364 and Daunton, *Royal Mail*, p.324.
175. Winter, *Robert Lowe*, pp.94–8.
176. Ibid., p.295.

CHAPTER EIGHT

The Elysian Fields

On the 12 January 1874 William Monsell was raised to the peerage of the United Kingdom, with the title of Baron Emly of Tervoe. The title of Baron is the lowest of the five orders of the British nobility, but as a peer of the United Kingdom, he was automatically entitled to a seat in the House of Lords, unlike a peer of Ireland (such as his neighbour Lord Clarina), unless he was elected as one of Ireland's twenty-eight representative peers.[1] The usage of 'Emly' by Monsell caused some puzzlement, as he had no connection with that part of County Tipperary. As 'Limerick' had already been taken as their designation by the Perys, and as Monsell was such a zealous Catholic, the place-names that he considered for his title may have included 'Tervoe' (his residence), 'Mungret' (the site of an ancient monastery nearby), or 'Kilkeedy' (the parish in which he resided). However, it was Stephen de Vere who finally made the choice, as he wrote in his diary: 'The title Emly was chosen and suggested by me. It is derived from the historically famous diocese of Emly, which occupies one third of County of Limerick.' Thus it was as Lord Emly that William Monsell was known for the rest of his life.[2]

Lord Emly now found himself in the rarefied atmosphere of the magnificent House of Lords, which, with its lavish decorations in an ornate Gothic style, plush red seats and the elaborate Sovereign's throne, was an appropriate setting for the deliberations of 'the most exclusive club in the world'. Disraeli, raised to the peerage in 1876 with the title of Earl of Beaconsfield, compared it to the Elysian Fields.[3] Consuelo, Duchess of Marlborough, described the Lords in the following memorable account:

> The English language never seemed so rich and so beautiful as when spoken by these cultivated men who owed their education to the Universities of Oxford and Cambridge. The polished elegance of their phrases, the purity of their diction, and the pleasant pitch of their voices made of these debates something more than the mere

> expression of political loyalties. It was as if a standard of excellence had to be maintained and a forum created for the perfect presentation of any opinion.[4]

The Wykehamist and Oxonian Monsell was perfectly at home in this atmosphere. He took his seat on the 19 March 1874 and played an active role in the Upper House for the next sixteen years.[5]

In the same year, Emly became involved in a controversy over Papal Infallibility. Gladstone had been appalled by the proclamation of this dogma and sparked off a major row in Britain and Ireland by attacking it in a number of publications, the first of which was his article 'Ritual and Ritualism' in the *Contemporary Review* of October 1874.[6] In an angry outburst, he wrote of the activities of the Papacy in the nineteenth century, 'when Rome has substituted for the proud boast of "semper eadem" a policy of violence and change of faith ... when no-one can become her convert without renouncing his moral and mental freedom; and placing his civil loyalty and duty at the mercy of another'.[7] On 3 October Lord Emly sent a letter of rebuke to Gladstone in which he informed him that 'the charge of renouncing our mental and moral freedom, and placing our civil loyalty and duty at the mercy of another, is at least as grave as any contained in the Durham letter'.[8] Newman thought that Emly should expand his letter into a pamphlet publicly replying to Gladstone.[9] Emly began to work on one, while conducting an acrimonious correspondence in private with Gladstone, who expanded his attack in a pamphlet entitled *The Vatican Decrees in their bearing on Civil Allegiance*.[10] Eventually it was Newman who published a public reply to Gladstone's attacks in *A Letter to the Duke of Norfolk*, which won widespread praise. Emly assisted Newman by researching Irish matters for this work.[11] For Emly, the main result of the controversy was to further impair his friendship with Gladstone (already seriously damaged by Scudamore), although they were never to become completely estranged.

In the late 1870s Lord Emly turned his attentions once more to the Irish educational question. On 3 July 1874 he told the Lords that he considered the failure of the 1873 university bill to have been the greatest misfortune to have befallen Ireland in his time.[12] His sense of disappointment was felt by his close friend and collaborator on the Trinidad scheme, Sir Patrick Keenan, who had become Resident Commissioner (in effect Head) of the National Schools system in 1871. Both men were exasperated by the Bishops' stiff policy on education and were in turn distrusted by the hierarchy for favouring payment-by-results rather than direct endowment. The failure of Gladstone's bill had temporarily removed third-level education from the political agenda, while primary education did not appear to be a burning issue (the hierarchy accepted the state system *de facto*, if not *de jure*, and most of the other interested parties were quite satisfied with it), with the result that secondary education (invariably known as intermediate education at this period) came to the fore for the first time. Thus Emly and Keenan were able to use their Trinidad scheme to good effect in framing the Intermediate Education Act of 1878, which marked the foundation of the present system of secondary education in Ireland.

In 1874 Richard O'Shaughnessy, MP for Limerick City, at the instigation of Father Leman, brought a motion before the Commons 'that the present state of intermediate education in Ireland is unsatisfactory and requires the immediate and serious consideration of Her Majesty's government', and went on to propose a system similar to the Trinidad scheme.[13] Then Emly himself made an important move when in his inaugural address as President of the Statistical and Social Enquiry Society of Ireland on 24 November 1874 he advocated an intermediate education system approximating to the Trinidad scheme.[14] Father Leman was delighted with this address, as he too wanted to encourage intermediate education in Ireland along the lines of Trinidad.[15] The three principal players in the scheme, Emly, Keenan and Leman, were thus reunited in support of an initiative in intermediate education along the same lines. Emly gathered much material from Keenan, Leman and others concerning the deplorably low standards in Catholic secondary schools in Ireland.

At the end of 1875 the masters, students and parents of students of Blackrock College presented a petition to the Chief Secretary, Sir Michael Hicks-Beach, requesting that the Trinidad scheme be introduced to Ireland.[16] Hicks-Beach, a friend of Woodlock, was favourably impressed by the growing demand for a solution to the problem of intermediate education, and he entrusted the drawing-up of the reform scheme to Sir Patrick Keenan.[17] This commission was known only to Keenan's close confidantes, Lords Emly and O'Hagan, and also to Fathers Leman and Reffé of Blackrock College.[18] Keenan worked on it from 1875 to 1876, while in constant correspondence with Emly, reporting progress and consulting him in matters of detail.[19] The scheme received the approval of both Cardinal Cullen and of the Cabinet.[20] It formed the basis of the Intermediate Education Bill, which was warmly welcomed in the House of Lords by Emly on its second reading there on 28 June 1878.[21] Under its provisions, based on the Trinidad scheme, the Intermediate Education Board was set up, which organised public examinations open to all secondary schools of every denomination. Lord O'Hagan was later appointed vice-chairman of the first board. Funds were allocated to schools, based on the performance of their pupils at the public examinations and Catholic schools thus received indirect endowments with the warm approval of the hierarchy. The payments-by-results system had a very harmful effect on Irish education and was heavily criticised by many educationalists, including Padraig Pearse, until its abolition in 1924. Nevertheless, while Sir Patrick Keenan was its chief instigator, Lord Emly, as well as Leman and Hicks-Beach, can also be regarded as founding fathers of Ireland's secondary school system.[22]

The Intermediate Education Act set a precedent of indirectly subsidising denominational educational institutions using the machinery of the Trinidad scheme, which was next employed to tackle the even more vexed question of university education. All of the interested parties believed that the university question should logically form the next step in educational reform. Father William Delaney (1835–1924), headmaster of the Jesuit secondary school of St Stanislaus, Tullabeg (outside Tullamore) in County Offaly, was the first to use the Trinidad scheme to provide Irish students with tertiary education.[23] In 1876 he began preparing his senior boys to be external students of the University of London, which was a purely examining body.[24] The success of Delaney's pupils proved that Catholic Irish students could compete at university level. Father Delaney, like Emly and many other Irish educationalists, had come to despair of the feeble Catholic University, as had even the Catholic Bishops.[25] The result of the confluence of these events was the University Education (Ireland) Act of 1879. Again, the Trinidad scheme (payment-by-results) was the preferred solution.[26] The Queen's University was to be abolished and replaced by the Royal University, which was to be purely an examining body and to which the three former Queen's Colleges were to be affiliated. However, students from outside the three colleges were free to sit for its examinations and to obtain its degrees, which would result in students of the Catholic University obtaining recognised degrees for the first time.

Initially, many Catholics, including Emly, were disappointed at the lack of endowment for their university, the retention of the government-funded Queen's Colleges and the continued existence of Trinity College with its vast resources. However, one clause in the bill, which allowed for the provision of 'exhibitions, scholarships and fellowships', made a crucial contribution to the acceptance of the bill, by providing indirect funding for Catholic university education.[27] In addition, the Senate was to be the key factor in determining the scope of the new university.[28] The first Senate was appointed by the Government on 27 April 1880 with a total membership of thirty-six (half Catholic and half Protestant).[29] Among the Catholic members were Edward McCabe, the new

Archbishop of Dublin, Dr Woodlock and Lord Emly, while Lord O'Hagan became the first Vice-Chancellor. The Royal University was housed in Earlsfort Terrace, in the building that now contains the National Concert Hall. A standing committee, of which Lord Emly was a very active member, was formed to work out the details of programmes for examinations, scholarships and the allocation of fellowships.[30] Significantly, twenty-eight fellowships (paid lectureships), each worth £400 a year, were allocated to the new university, and their distribution was perhaps the most explosive matter discussed by the standing committee. On 16 October 1880 Newman learnt from another correspondent that Emly had high hopes for the Royal University, which might in time 'be developed (a) into a true university and (b) into what will, to all practical intents and purposes be a truly Catholic university – a university mixed, indeed, in name, but denominational in fact, like our present system of national schools'.[31] Eventually it was decided to grant thirteen fellowships to the Queen's Colleges, one to Magee College in Derry and all fourteen reserved for Catholic colleges to the Catholic University, which was taken over by the Jesuits in 1883. This brought substantial funds to the latter and saved it from extinction. The Royal University survived until 1908, and while it was considered an interim solution to the Irish university question by almost all the parties concerned (including Emly himself), it was nevertheless from the official Catholic point of view a major improvement on the despised Queen's University (1850–82).

In 1878 a particular era in the history of the Catholic Church came to an end with the deaths of Pope Pius IX on 7 February and Cardinal Cullen six months later. Lord Emly was saddened by the deaths of these two old friends, although he had been more distressed by the death, in the previous year, of Bishop Moriarty of Kerry. (He had even wanted to write a biography of Dr Moriarty, and had began collecting correspondence for this project, but it never came to fruition.[32]) One of the first acts of the new Pope, Leo XIII (1810–1903), was to make the 78-year-old Newman a Cardinal. Lord Emly was overjoyed at his old friend's elevation and shed tears of joy at a reception held in honour of the new Cardinal in Norfolk House, London.[33] The new Archbishop of Dublin, Edward McCabe (1816–85), was a Catholic Whig and a close friend of Emly.[34]

The course of Irish history also changed decisively at this time. The Land League was founded in 1879, pledged to achieve the three Fs and ultimately to bring about the total overthrow of Irish landlordism. At the same time, the Home Rule movement, which under Butt's feeble leadership had become virtually moribund in the late 1870s, was revitalised by Charles Stewart Parnell (1846–91). By 1880 Parnell had united the two movements into the most formidable nationalist agitation that Ireland had seen since the 1840s. He rid the party of the crypto-Catholic Whigs who had survived in its ranks into the early 1880s, and thus prevented a recurrence of the drift back to mainstream Liberalism that had been a feature of Irish independent or nationalist groups since the time of O'Connell. Lord Emly was profoundly alarmed by these developments. Everything that the Catholic Whigs stood for – the Union, the sanctity of private property, the rule of law – seemed about to be swept away. What was even more shocking was the attitude of the Church to this 'socialistic' agitation.[35] After Cullen's death there was no one to give firm direction to the bishops and clergy. Archbishop McCabe and the Archbishop of Armagh, Daniel McGettigan (1815–87) were both Catholic Whigs, but were not commanding figures.[36] They were both overshadowed by the new Archbishop of Cashel, Thomas Croke (1824–1902), who was enthroned in 1875 and was an outspoken supporter of both the land agitation and of Home Rule.[37] Many of the other bishops, (including even Emly's old friend, Butler) were swept along by public opinion and supported Croke in these stands, while priests formed a significant element in the rank-and-file organisation of both the land and Home Rule agitations.

On 5 March 1880 Emly told the Lords: 'we have agitators preaching undisguised Socialism, and setting against the race and religion of Ireland the feelings of the people of England and Scotland.'[38] He believed that the masses of the Irish people were sound but were being led astray by socialist agitators, who drew much of their inspiration from the United States. Thus, Emly took refuge in a conspiracy theory which Buckland has identified as commonplace at this period: 'in the main, the Southern Unionists tried to explain away the nationalist movement largely in terms of an agrarian conspiracy theory: a few self-seeking or misguided individuals, including most notably priests and shopkeepers, spurred on by the Irish in America, playing on the greed of an ignorant and semi-literate Irish peasantry'.[39] As Buckland writes, this conspiracy theory 'was the only way they could reconcile the obvious fact of a Home Rule movement with their own view of their social and political role in Ireland. They could not throw off centuries of tradition and persisted in believing in their good relations with their tenants.'[40] In line with this thinking, many of the Southern Unionists drew comfort from the restoration of good relations between landlord and tenant after the Land War of 1879–82. Thus, on the occasion of the marriage of Emly's daughter, the following occurred: 'on Tuesday evening, a deputation of the tenancy of the Limerick and Clare estates ... presented the bride with a massive gold bracelet, on which was inscribed – "presented to the Hon. Mary O.

Monsell, by her father's tenancy in Clare and Limerick, on the occasion of her marriage, June 1st, 1881"'.[41] The continuation of these good relations between Emly and his tenants into the 1880s and 1890s confirmed him in his belief in the conspiracy theory.

Also, the association of Home Rule with the land agitation was to destroy any hankering after federalism amongst the ranks of the landlords, for it could only result in the destruction of their social position.[42] Although Emly had flirted with federalism in the 1840s, there was no possibility of his adopting a similar sympathetic attitude to this far more formidable social and political agitation, which threatened the entire social system. Also, Home Rule and the land agitation propagated a nationalist ideology that excluded the Anglo-Irish from the Irish nation and the governing myths of twentieth-century Irish nationalism – of an Ireland Gaelic, peasant, Catholic – were taking shape in the 1880s and 1890s. This was completely antagonistic to Lord Emly's belief in an Ireland that was Anglicised, ruled by an enlightened gentry, made up of all classes and creeds, Liberal, and above all part of the United Kingdom. Emly's response to the crisis was twofold. Firstly, he reluctantly supported sweeping concessions to the tenant demands in order to stave off social revolution. He carried an amendment in the Lords on 5 August 1881 during the debate on the land act, deleting a clause providing for the necessity of three-quarters of the tenants on an estate consenting to purchase it before it could be sold. He told the Lords on this occasion: 'there could be no real peace and contentment in Ireland until the basis of property was extended by largely increasing the number of proprietors'.[43] On 1 August 1882 he told the Lords that there were two reasons why Parliament had passed the 1881 land act legalising the three Fs:

> there was, in the first place, a large cottier tenantry in Ireland living upon very small farms, and these persons were in a miserable and hopeless state under the system of land competition that prevailed ... and in the second place, there were ... a large number, though happily only a small minority of the whole, of the landlords in Ireland who took advantage of the poverty and misery of those cottier tenants, and of their having no means of subsistence except the land, to screw them down to the payment of exorbitant rents, and confiscate their improvements.[44]

His second response was to work to detach the Catholic clergy from their support of the nationalist movement. His attitude was well summarised in the petition against the second Home Rule bill, which he signed in 1893: 'Home Rule, if imposed upon Ireland, would, under the peculiar conditions of the country, foster a revolutionary spirit disastrous to the true interests of our religion.'[45] In France, in Italy, in Latin America, revolution had led to anti-clerical legislation, confiscation of church property, even the murder of priests and bishops, so the folly of the Irish clergy in supporting revolution would have to be counteracted. In the 1880s and 1890s Lord Emly was one of a group of Catholic Unionists, British and Irish, who attempted to influence the Church to act against nationalist and land agitation.[46] The leader of this counter-revolution was his close friend, Henry Fitzalan-Howard, fifteenth Duke of Norfolk (1847–1917), the premier peer in England, Earl Marshal, a Tory, a Catholic Unionist, and a man of immense wealth.[47] Lords Emly and O'Hagan were his chief Irish allies. George Errington (1839–1920), a Catholic Whig gentleman who sat as MP for Longford from 1874 to 1885 as a pseudo-Home Ruler, was another valuable ally. Their clerical friends included Herbert Vaughan (1832–1903), Bishop of Salford from 1872 to 1892, Archbishop of Westminster in 1892 and Cardinal in 1893, and Edward Henry Cardinal Howard (1829–92), a cousin of Norfolk who was a powerful contact based in the Vatican.[48] On the other hand they were strongly opposed by Archbishop Croke and by Cardinal Manning, who was sympathetic to Irish grievances.

The situation at the Vatican favoured this Catholic Unionist offensive. Pope Leo XIII had ascended the throne in 1878 when the Church was locked in battle with the two newly created states of Italy and Germany, and in the 1880s he also found himself in conflict with the Third Republic of France. The Pope was determined to restore the power of the Papacy by diplomatic means, and to this end he ended the quarrel with Bismarck in the 1880s and tried to prod the French Catholics into a *Raillement* with the Third Republic, but with less success. He was also anxious to establish diplomatic relations with the British Empire, a powerful potential ally against the anti-Papal Italian government and ruler of millions of Catholic subjects all over the world.[49] The British government responded favourably to feelers from the Vatican and hoped to use the Pope's desire for better relations to enlist him in the battle against Irish sedition. In a game of diplomatic chess between the world's strongest state and its most powerful religious figure, Ireland counted as a very small pawn on the board.

The first task that the Catholic Unionists set themselves was to provide assistance to Dr McCabe in his struggle with the obstreperous Croke. Contact with the Vatican was made originally through Lord Emly and his friend Cardinal Howard. On 1 November 1880 Emly wrote to Lord Granville suggesting that he (Granville) might ask the British Ambassador in Paris to speak to the Papal Nuncio there about the situation in Ireland. Emly thought that it would be necessary to suspend *habeas corpus* in Ireland to restore order there. Also, the British representations to the Nuncio in Paris might counteract the bad influence of Archbishop Croke, who had set off for Rome. However, Gladstone vetoed this idea.[50] Lord Emly had tried a similar approach in October 1879, but the Nuncio's attempts to have the Irish Bishops condemned were firmly scotched by Cardinal Manning.[51]

These contacts were proving fruitless, so from 1881 to 1885 George Errington served as an unofficial envoy to the Vatican. The Unionists wanted to bolster McCabe's authority by having him appointed Apostolic Delegate in Ireland and also by having him raised to the Cardinalate.[52] In 1882 the Pope created McCabe a Cardinal, but this only made him *primus inter pares* amongst his fellow Irish bishops and his comparatively diffident personality meant that he was still unable to impose his authority on them. In 1884, indeed, they entered into an alliance with the Home Rule party, which undertook to represent their educational and other demands at Westminster. Then, Cardinal McCabe's death on 11 February 1885 touched off the greatest battle to date between the Catholic Unionists and their clerical opponents. The main candidate to succeed was William Walsh (1841–1921), President of Maynooth College and a supporter of Home Rule and the land agitation.[53] Norfolk and Errington lobbied tirelessly against him, while Manning championed his cause. Eventually he was appointed Archbishop of Dublin, to the great dismay of Emly and his allies. Now the Catholic hierarchy was dominated by two staunch nationalists, Walsh and Croke, while since the late 1870s even Lord Emly's own friend, Bishop Butler of Limerick, had moved decisively into the Home Rule camp.[54] The appointment of Walsh marked the final defeat of the Errington mission, and he returned from Rome in 1885.

The Home Rule crisis of 1885–6 brought tensions to a climax. On 11 June 1885 Emly wrote to Stephen de Vere:

> the Home Rule on which the present government has agreed is not only county elective boards, but a central elected board in Dublin to manage education and other matters with taxing power. Fancy education taken from the National Board and placed in such hands ...The work which the best men in Ireland have been perfecting would be shattered in a day. Dark indeed and hopeless seems our future.[55]

Lord Emly deplored the Home Rule bill itself, and considered its provision excluding Irish MPs from Westminster to be disastrous, as he told Newman: 'I am horrified at Gladstone's proposals. They exclude Catholics practically from the legislature which governs our great empire. They deprive Irishmen of their status as citizens.'[56] The Home

Rule bill created a sensation, the great Liberal party split and both the Whigs led by the future eighth Duke of Devonshire and the Radicals led by Joseph Chamberlain seceded. These became known as the Liberal Unionists and they allied themselves with the Conservatives but retained their separate identity until the two parties merged in 1912. Lord Emly and the Irish Catholic Whigs also seceded and became Liberal Unionists. Ironically, Emly now found himself back in alliance with the Tory party which he had left in the 1840s and which he had opposed with vehemence for nearly forty years. The Home Rule bill was defeated in the Commons by the combined votes of the Conservatives and the Liberal Unionists, who won a great victory in the ensuing general election and remained in office until 1892. The Prime Minister throughout this period was Lord Salisbury and the Chief Secretary for Ireland was his nephew, Arthur Balfour (1848–1930). In 1886 Cardinal Manning for the first time declared himself in favour of Irish Home Rule.[57]

The new Conservative administration had to confront the next phase of the Land War, known as the Plan of Campaign, which was launched in 1886 with the support of Walsh and Croke.[58] The Salisbury administration was anxious to persuade the Pope to condemn this activity. In 1887 the Catholic Unionists formed a dining club to discuss Irish affairs.[59] Its president was Lord Emly, the Secretary was Wilfred Ward (1856–1916), son of William George Ward, who was later to be the biographer of Newman, and members included the Duke of Norfolk, Aubrey de Vere, Sir John Ross of Bladensburg and Edwin de Lisle, a Conservative MP and son of Emly's old friend Ambrose. Sir John Ross of Bladensburg (1848–1926), a Catholic landowner from Rostrevor, County Down, was to play a leading role in the British diplomatic initiatives at the Vatican over the next few years. The Pope was receptive to the British feelers, and in response to the efforts of the Catholic Unionists, he sent Ignatius Persico (1823–95), Archbishop of Damietta, a senior figure in the Curia and later a Cardinal, to Ireland to investigate the situation. He arrived in Ireland on 7 July 1887 and travelled around the country collecting information. He distrusted Norfolk and Ross and was inclined to be sympathetic to Irish grievances, but in his efforts to be impartial, he annoyed both sides. On 26 July he went to Limerick and stayed with Lord Emly at Tervoe, but infuriated Croke when he bypassed his diocese. 'It would, I think, be more in order and look better in the public eye, if instead of going to Lord Emly, and passing Thurles by, his Excellency came to visit the Archbishop of Cashel,' Croke wrote to Walsh on 31 July.[60] On 4 August he told the same correspondent: 'great indignation loudly expressed here, and generally felt in the South at Monsignor Persico's extraordinary manoeuvre in passing me by here and going to meet Lord Emly and his gang'.[61] However, Errington wrote shortly afterwards: 'my fears that his mission was a very imprudent step and that he is almost certainly in the hands of the violent clergy are, I am sorry to say, confirmed. He has been asked to many of the best houses, Catholic and Protestant: so far he has only been to Tervoe, and only pays an occasional afternoon visit to the others as he goes around.'[62] Persico remained in Ireland until January 1888 and then returned to Rome via England.

As a result of the numerous representations made by Norfolk and Ross in Rome, and Persico's gloomy reports about the situation in Ireland, the Vatican formally condemned the Plan of Campaign and the practice of boycotting in a Papal Rescript which was dated 20 April 1888.[63] Manning, Walsh and Croke were horrified, Irish nationalists were furious, while Persico was surprised at its appearance, fearing that he would be blamed for something that he had neither instigated or anticipated. On the other hand Emly and the Catholic Unionists were delighted, believing that they had struck a mortal blow to the Plan of Campaign, but their joy was short-lived. The Irish hierarchy, led by Archbishop Walsh but with the exception of Bishop O'Dwyer of Limerick, did not enforce the Rescript, and it became a dead letter. Lord Emly was appalled. 'Is this not monstrous?' he commented to Ross concerning this manoeuvre.[64] He told the same correspondent that 'nothing will come right until we have a Papal Delegate in Ireland with ample authority not only to inquire but to act'.[65] This did not happen, and the Papal Rescript was, from the Unionist point of view, a complete failure.

In December 1888 Balfour appointed Norfolk the sole channel of communication between the British government and the Vatican.[66] He was given the liberty to select his own team, and at the beginning of 1889 he wrote to Cardinal Rampolla, the Secretary for State, that 'Lord Emly and Captain Ross are quite in my confidence, and through me in that of the government, *but no other person is in this position* [writer's emphasis].'[67] The Catholic Unionists' main interest now was to help secure a Catholic university for Ireland. They were pleased when a relatively moderate nationalist, John Coffey, was appointed Bishop of Kerry on 27 August 1889, as they had actively supported his candidature in Rome.[68] Another bishop whom they supported was John Healy (1841–1918), who became co-adjutor bishop of Clonfert in 1884, Bishop of Clonfert in 1896, and Archbishop of Tuam in 1903. Healy was a close friend of Emly and the de Veres, as was the new Bishop of Limerick, Edward Thomas O'Dwyer, who had been appointed in 1886.[69] Both these bishops, who had attended Maynooth together and were close friends, were moderate nationalists who remained on good terms with the Catholic Unionists and disapproved of the Plan of Campaign. In 1893 the Catholic Unionists won their last major victory when Ross and Norfolk helped influence the Pope's decision to confer the Red Hat on Michael Logue, Archbishop of Armagh, instead of their *bête noir* Dr Walsh.[70] The Irish cardinalate thus moved from Dublin to Armagh for the first time.[71] The leading authority on the Catholic Unionist counteroffensive has concluded that while they had gained some successes, 'their principal aim – that of achieving the withdrawal of the Irish clergy from involvement in the national movement – was not realised'.[72]

The battle between the Catholic Unionists and the nationalist bishops was also fought in the Senate of the Royal University, where Lord O'Hagan as Vice-Chancellor and Lord Emly as a member of the Senate were in conflict with Dr Walsh.[73] Although these quarrels were not a straightforward Whig versus nationalist fight, the coincidence of the opposing personalities in both sets of rows is highly significant.[74] In 1884 there was a quarrel over the allocation of a Royal University fellowship when Dr Walsh, who favoured the dispersal of the fellowships among various Catholic colleges, proposed Father Reffé of Blackrock College. Lord Emly favoured concentrating them in the Jesuit-run University College on St Stephen's Green, and proposed Father Gerard Manley Hopkins (1844–89), the distinguished Jesuit poet. In the election the indecisive Cardinal McCabe actually proposed Reffé and was seconded by Walsh, while Lord Emly proposed Hopkins. The election took place at a meeting of the Standing Committee of the Senate on 30 January 1884 and Hopkins won by twenty-three votes to three. On 29 May a second attempt to have Reffé granted a fellowship was defeated, and Walsh resigned from the Senate. During the controversy Dr Walsh had criticised Lord Emly and declared him unsuitable to be a senator of the Royal University. Bishop Butler defended Emly. He wrote to Walsh: 'I am puzzled by your reference to Lord Emly in connection with neglect of duty as a senator or committee man. I think you will find on enquiry that he has been constant in his attendance at senate and committee meetings.'[75] Henceforth, Walsh was to be hostile to the Royal University. He was replaced on the Senate by Emly's friend, Dr Healy, while another ally, Father Delaney SJ of Tullabeg College, also became a senator at this time. In 1885 Lord Emly became Vice-Chancellor on the death of Lord O'Hagan, but Walsh's simultaneous appointment as Archbishop of Dublin caused considerable apprehension in the Royal University. On 24 November 1886 the newly appointed Bishop O'Dwyer of Limerick was appointed to the Senate, and though Walsh put strong pressure on him to resign at once, Lord Emly and Dr Healy urged him to remain, which he did.[76] However, a later attempt by Lord Emly to have the Bishop of Waterford nominated to the Senate was scotched by Walsh.[77]

In 1882 Lord Emly became one of the founders of Mungret College, situated outside Limerick city.[78] A model farm and agricultural school had been established there in 1858, but it never prospered and closed in 1878.[79] The board of trustees of the defunct school, of which Emly was chairman, decided to establish a secondary school in its place, but this required a change in the trust.[80] Lord Emly was instrumental in having an act of parliament passed which 'enabled the Lord Lieutenant, with the consent of the Treasury, to apply the whole property vested in the trustees of the agricultural school to any educational purpose he thought fit, provided that the agricultural sciences were still included in the subjects taught'.[81]

The first secondary school there, run by a diocesan priest, Father Joseph Bourke, only lasted from 1880 to 1881.[82] Lord Emly and Dr Butler then offered it to the Holy Ghost Fathers. Father Francis X. Libermann from that order has left an interesting pen picture of Emly, who he met in this connection, describing him as

> a typical English diplomat, a former minister of Queen Victoria, of a practical and direct mind, phlegmatic and tenacious in character. He is, besides, a fervent and zealous Catholic, although with a Liberal strain. He belongs to the school of Falloux, Montalambert, de Broglie, and he is not all Irish, which is one of the reasons why he prefers us. He is also very generous, to judge by what he has already done for the college, and what he intends to do.

Father Libermann also noted that 'he has great influence', and for the Holy Ghost Fathers in general, 'there would be a great advantage in setting up constant relations with the noble Lord'.[83] However, the Holy Ghost Fathers refused the offer to take over Mungret. Father Morrissey has speculated that this 'may have inclined Lord Emly at a later stage to favour the Jesuits rather than them in the field of university education' (later exemplified in the row over Reffé versus Hopkins).[84]

It was Lord Emly who was instrumental in arranging for the Jesuits to take over Mungret and establish their college there on 14 September 1882.[85] His chaplain, the Abbe L'Heritier, approached Father William Ronan (1825–1905), the actual founder of the Jesuit college at Mungret, to inform him that the site was available to him.[86] It was run by the Jesuits as a university college, whose students were prepared for the examinations of the Royal University, and no students were entered for the Intermediate examinations until 1905.[87] It also incorporated the Limerick diocesan seminary until Bishop O'Dwyer removed this to St Munchins College in 1888, and lay students then arrived at Mungret instead.[88] Emly proved to be a 'powerful protector and generous benefactor' of the infant college.[89] On 31 October 1888, as Vice-Chancellor of the Royal University presiding at the conferring of degrees at their buildings at Earlsfort Terrace, he said:

> a new college that I happen to take a particular interest in has been founded at Mungret, in the south of Ireland, and is, I believe, the only Catholic College outside Dublin which confines itself altogether to university education ... From the fact of this dawn being so bright, may we not hope when the full day comes, Mungret may occupy again in the province of learning that position, which, on this very spot, it had occupied twelve hundred years ago.[90]

Lord Emly was still chairman of the trustees who nominally ran the school and the Jesuits were merely leasing it from them until 1892, when they were allowed to buy it out for £2,500.[91] It continued as a university college until 1912, but failed to gain recognition by the newly established National University in 1908, and was to continue as a secondary school until its closure in 1974.[92] Had it continued as a university college, it might have formed the nucleus of the University of Limerick, which was only to be established in 1972. The role of Lord Emly in Mungret College was a decisive and an interesting one. He was the chief founder of the college, and took a personal interest in it for the rest of his life. The fact that many of the Jesuits who originally staffed it were French, fleeing from the anti-clerical measures of the Third Republic, and that his own chaplain Heritier taught science there from 1882 to 1905, made it especially close to his heart.[93] It was also an attempt by him to found a denominational Catholic university and 'University College Mungret' was one of his most unusual legacies. Despite its failure as a university after 1912, it still played a major role in the educational life of Limerick for nearly a century. Thus, Lord Emly has thus the unique distinction of helping to found two of Ireland's most famous secondary schools – one Protestant (St Columba's) and one Catholic (Mungret).

Lord Emly's popularity diminished somewhat in the 1880s and 1890s due to his opposition to Home Rule and the land agitation. A progressive figure while in the Commons, he was now increasingly regarded as reactionary and out of touch. As a peer, he was at least spared the humiliation meted out to other landlords, such as Art McMurrough Kavanagh, of being ignominiously routed at the polls and suffering the loss of his Commons seat.[94] However, Emly was subjected to a similar indignity at a local level. At the height of the Land War, Parnell called on the electorate to vote for Land League candidates at the forthcoming annual elections to the Poor Law boards.[95] This was a reflection of their campaign against the landlord control of local government.[96] Initially, however, there was no change in the Limerick Union, of which Emly had been chairman since 1857.[97] Following the 1882 elections William Abraham, a 'daring Nationalist', was elected a guardian while in prison and on 28 March he defeated Lord Emly for the chairmanship of the Limerick Board.[98] The *Limerick Reporter* stated that the guardians had no objection to Lord Emly as such, but wanted to exhibit their opposition to the coercion legislation under which Abraham had been jailed.[99]

Indeed, as Lord Emly grew older it seemed that his *via media* was crumbling everywhere. In Ireland, Unionism and landlordism were on the defensive. Within the Church, Liberal Catholicism had been eliminated and did not revive even under the comparatively benign rule of Leo XIII.[100] The Catholic Church faced anti-clerical attack from Bismarck's *Kulterkampf*, the kingdom of Italy, and above all from France under the Third Republic, where from the late 1870s Emly's beloved second homeland had taken a sharp turn in the direction of republicanism and anticlericalism.[101] In the early years of the Third Republic his friends Bishop Dupanloup and the Duc de Broglie had been active in politics, working for the restoration of the French monarchy, but as a parliamentary, not an absolutist, regime.[102] Broglie was a French 'Whig' who served as prime minister very briefly in 1877 after being appointed by the Royalist President McMahon, who had dissolved Parliament in an attempt to gain a Royalist majority. Broglie presided over the ensuing general election, which resulted in a disastrous defeat for the Royalists.[103] The Republicans swiftly took command of the government and embarked on an anti-clerical campaign against the Catholic Church and in particular its role in education.[104] These conflicts raged on throughout the 1880s and 1890s. On the instructions of the Pope, Emly's friend, Cardinal Lavigerie, attempted to promote a reconciliation known as the *Raillement* between church and state in the early 1890s, but to no avail.[105] Emly's residence in Montoire gave him a unique insight into the turbulent French politics of the time. In the department of Loire-et-Cher 'Republican lawyers and doctors seized the initiative in the 1870s by playing on peasant fears of war, neo-feudalism, and clericalism in a department where religious practice fell 50% between 1850 and 1900.'[106] There was even a land war there in the 1880s and 1890s, where rents declined by 44 per cent causing agricultural depression and friction between landlords and tenants.[107]

Lord Emly's relatively happy family life continued to be a consolation for him. In 1881 both his children married into the de la Poer family of Gurteen le Poer, Kilsheelan, County Waterford. On 1 June his daughter Mary Olivia married the Count de la Poer (1841–1915), who had received his title from Pius IX in 1864 and had sat as a Catholic Whig MP for County Waterford from 1866 to 1873.[108] On 5 September his son and heir Gaston married the Count's sister Frances (1851–1925).[109] The question of an heir to Tervoe again became acute in the 1880s. Gaston's only child, a son named William (1883–6), died on 19 February 1886 and it appears that Gaston and Frances were unable to have any more children, because in 1887 Lord Emly altered his will. By its new terms, the Monsell properties were to pass to his grandson Edmund (1883–1964), second son of his daughter Mary Olivia (who incidentally was always styled the Honourable Mrs de la Poer, rather than Countess), but with the stipulation that the boy would be obliged to assume the surname Monsell as a condition of inheritance.[110]

Thus, Lord Emly's last years were clouded by the knowledge that the title would die with his son as well as by the latter's impetuous and eccentric behaviour. Gaston Monsell shared his father's pious Catholicism, but favoured more extreme measures to obtain civil rights for Catholics and created silly scenes in the Limerick Grand Jury.[111] He also contrived to make himself foolish at the Viceregal Court at Dublin Castle, where he held the positions of State Steward (1880–2) and Gentleman Usher (1882–5). In the latter capacity, his duty was to announce the names of guests at functions, but at a levee he once announced a member of the prominent English family of Sclater-Booth as 'Mr Scatter-Boots'. Such blunders were a frequent occurrence.[112] Later, when Cardinal McCabe's death coincided with a Court Ball, Monsell refused to attend and was threatened with dismissal.[113] Gaston's shambling period at Dublin Castle did little for his reputation or that of his family.

In 1890 Lord Emly suffered the loss of the two people that he loved the most. On 11 August Cardinal Newman died, aged 89, and Emly travelled to Birmingham for the funeral. On 4 November his wife Berthe died, aged only 55. He spoke for the last time in the Lords on 5 June 1890.[114] He continued to be one of the most prominent figures in Ireland, Lord-Lieutenant of Limerick, Colonel of the Limerick Militia, Vice-Chancellor of the Royal University and a member of the Privy Council. He was also offered the Order of St Patrick (the Irish equivalent of the Garter) on a number of occasions, but declined the honour.[115] In the early 1890s Emly was heartened by the fall of Parnell, the resulting split in the Home Rule party and the vigorous policy of Arthur Balfour, who, as Chief Secretary (1887–92) quelled the land agitation. Indeed, Lord Emly welcomed Balfour to his home at Tervoe during this period. On 21 September 1892 Lord Emly celebrated his eightieth birthday in Tervoe House and Wilfred Ward left a charming description of the event.

> We kept Emly's 80th birthday with pomp on Wednesday, and in the evening, the picture was quite a memorable one. We sat in the

> Music Room which they have made really beautiful, with furniture from Lady Emly's French chateau. Bishop Healy, a huge wild Celt telling Irish legends, pagan and Christian, and Aubrey de Vere and Emly on each side of him listening, looked more Irish than words can tell, Emly taking snuff as he drank in each word, and de Vere, the picture of refinement dressed better than usual, but exactly as our grandfathers dressed, fired by the poetry of the legends but a little startled at the uncouthness of the narrator, who is out and out Celtic barbarian.[116]

Indeed, Ward also described the sprightly old gentleman as 'Evergreen Emly'.[117]

However, in the same year Gladstone became Prime Minister for the fourth and final time and early in 1893 brought his second Home Rule bill before Parliament, to Emly's great dismay and disgust. A massive Unionist agitation was organised throughout Ireland and Lord Emly made his final public appearance when he addressed a great Unionist meeting at the Theatre Royal in Dublin on 8 April, and in the presence of Arthur Balfour, strongly denounced Gladstone's proposals.[118] He joined with fellow Catholic Unionists in petitioning Parliament because

> as a false impression has been created that the contrast upon the Home Rule Bill is, in reality, only a contrast between a Roman Catholic majority and a Protestant majority, we have thought it right, in order to make the position clear, that Irish Roman Catholic Unionists should have an opportunity of joining in a separate and distinct petition to Parliament against the bill ... we believe that Home Rule, if imposed upon Ireland, would under the peculiar conditions of the country, foster a revolutionary spirit disastrous to the true interests of our religion.

The petition stated that they regarded the maintenance of the Union as a necessary safeguard of the 'full civil and religious liberty' that they enjoyed under the British constitution. Home Rule would be 'most prejudicial to our religion and disastrous to the best interests of Ireland'.[119] However, due to ill-health Lord Emly was not present in the House of Lords when the bill was heavily defeated there on 30 September 1893.

This was Emly's last bout of political activity, as his health had begun to fail at the beginning of 1893.[120] He hardly ever left Tervoe House for the last six months of his life and 'for the last three weeks, he was unable, through physical weakness, to go upstairs, and his library, on the ground floor was fitted up as a bedroom'.[121] Father Flanagan, parish priest of Adare and Bishop O'Dwyer attended him devotedly in his last days. Just two hours before his death, he received a telegraph from the Vatican, in which Pope Leo XIII gave him a final blessing. He died at 11 o'clock at night on 20 April 1894 in his library at Tervoe, in the presence of members of his family.[122] His funeral to Ballybrown Church was by far the most splendid ever seen in that church. It was wet and windy on the 24 April, when the immense funeral procession left Tervoe House for Ballybrown Church, at 9.30 a.m. The coffin was placed on a special funeral car and drawn by the tenants and labourers of Tervoe. The whole regiment of the Limerick County Militia and forty policemen marched in the procession, along with a throng of mourners. The cortège arrived at the church, where the aisle floor was covered with Persian rugs and the coffin was placed on a huge catafalque, draped in black velvet and with massive black and gold candelabra on either side. The attendance at the funeral included the Mayor and Corporation of Limerick, the chief officials of County Limerick, Lord Clarina, Sir Stephen and Aubrey de Vere, Sir Charles Barrington of Glenstal, Sir David Roche of Croom, the Countess of Dunraven and her daughters and many others. The chief mourners were Gaston and his wife, Count de la Poer and his wife and Sir Hunt Allen-Walsh of Ballykilcavan, cousin of the deceased. Three bishops (Limerick, Clonfert and Waterford) and forty priests con-celebrated Requiem Mass. The burial took place in the family vault at Kilkeedy graveyard in the shadow of Carrigogunnell Castle, where his two young sons (who had died in 1837 and 1845 respectively) and his two wives were already interred.[123]

The panegyric on Lord Emly delivered by Bishop O'Dwyer at the conclusion of Mass in Ballybrown Church was a remarkable tribute, for he described the deceased as 'one of the most loveable, one of the most beautiful, and one of the noblest characters I ever met'. He said of Emly that 'there was about him a wonderful charm, a grace of courtesy as of the olden times, an overflowing goodness of heart', as well as a 'deep and profound faith'. While he conceded that Emly 'did not occupy as prominent a place in public and political life' in his latter years, as he had done previously, the Bishop continued that 'as he advanced in years, he was growing in authority, until in the end, the leaders of Catholic thought in these countries looked to him with the most unbounded confidence and the deepest respect'. O'Dwyer himself paid him the highest compliment when he asked: 'Amongst the Catholics in Ireland that have survived him, who is his equal? He is gone and I know no man who can take his place.'[124] Lord Emly had indeed been a unique figure in Irish and British public life, a figure with 'a European reputation'.[125]

NOTES

1. Burke, *Dictionary of the Peerage and Baronetage*, pp.347–8 (the 3rd Lord Clarina held one of these seats from 1849 to 1872, and the 4th Lord held one from 1888 to 1897).
2. Diary of Stephen De Vere, Vol.12, 26 December 1873, DVP, Trinity College, MS 5061–72.
3. Partington, *Oxford Dictionary of Quotations*, p.249.
4. Consuelo Vanderbilt Balsan, *The Glitter and the Gold* (London: Heinemann, 1953), pp.79–80.
5. Hansard, CCXVIII, 25 (19 March 1874).
6. W.E. Gladstone, 'Ritualism and Ritual', in *Contemporary Review*, 24, 5 (October 1874), p.674.
7. Ibid.
8. Emly to Gladstone 3 October, 1874, GP, Ad. MS 44152, ff. 235–8.
9. Newman, *Letters and Diaries*, Vol. 27, p.124, Newman to Emly, 2 October, 1874.
10. W.E. Gladstone, *The Vatican Decrees in their Bearing on Civil Allegiance: A Political Expostulation* (London: John Murray, 1874).
11. Newman, *Letters and Diaries,* Vol. 27, pp.160 and 165.
12. Hansard, CCXX, 977 (3 July 1874).
13. Hansard, CCXIX, 1271–82 (9 June 1874).
14. Monsell, 'Inaugural Address of the Rt. Hon. Lord Emly', pp.364–5.
15. Farragher, 'Père Leman', p.476.
16. Ibid., p.488.
17. Ibid., pp.488–9.
18. Ibid., p.493.
19. Farragher, *Pére Leman (1826–1880)*, pp.402–4.
20. Farragher, 'Peré Leman', p.494.
21. Hansard, CCXLI, 435–9 (28 June 1878).
22. Farragher, 'Père Leman', *passim.*
23. Thomas J. Morrissey, *Towards a National University: William Delaney S.J. (1835–1924)* (Dublin: Wolfhound Press and Atlantic Highlands, NJ: Humanities Press, 1983).
24. Ibid., pp.25–7.
25. Ibid., pp.47–51.
26. Ibid., p.53 and Fergal McGrath, 'University Education', in Patrick Corish (ed.), *A History of Irish Catholicism* (Dublin: Gill, 1967), Vol. 5, pp.109–10.
27. Morrissey, *Towards a National University*, pp.54–5.
28. Ibid., p.57.
29. Ibid., p.58.
30. Farragher, 'Peré Leman', pp.545–6.
31. Newman, *Letters and Diaries*, Vol. 29, p.302, John Woulfe Flanagan to Newman, 16 September 1880.
32. Roantree, 'William Monsell and the Catholic Question,' pp.306–7.
33. Ward, *Life of John Henry Newman*, Vol. 2, p.472.
34. See C.J. Woods, 'The Politics of Cardinal McCabe of Dublin', in *Dublin Historical Record*, 26 (1973), pp.101–10.
35. Hansard, CCLIV, 1867 (2 August 1880).
36. See Larkin, *Roman Catholic Church and Home Rule Movement*, pp.214–19.
37. See Mark Tierney, *Croke of Cashel: The Life of Thomas William Croke 1823–1902* (Dublin: Gill and Macmillan, 1976).
38. Hansard, CCLI, 416–17 (5 March 1880).
39. Patrick James Buckland, 'Southern Unionism 1885–1922 with Special References to the Period after 1914' (unpublished Ph.D thesis, Queen's University Belfast, 1969) , p.82.
40. Ibid., pp.83–8.
41. Sheehan, *Corner of Limerick*, p.126.
42. Buckland, 'Southern Unionism', pp.41–4.
43. Hansard, CCLXIV, 978–82 (5 August 1881).
44. Hansard, CCLXXIII, 332–6 (1 August 1882).
45. Anon., *Irish Roman Catholic Protest against Home Rule* (Dublin: Irish Unionist Alliance Publications, 1893).

46. The chief account of this episode is Father Edward Patrick O'Callaghan, 'English Catholics and the Irish Question 1870–93' (unpublished Ph.D thesis, University College Galway, 1983). See also three volumes of Emmet Larkin's history of the Catholic Church in Ireland: *The Roman Catholic Church and Creation of Modern Irish State 1878–86*, (Philadelphia and Dublin: Gill and Macmillan, 1975); *The Roman Catholic Church and the Plan of Campaign 1886–88* (Cork: Cork University Press, 1978); and *The Roman Catholic Church and Fall of Parnell 1888–91* (Chapel Hill, NC: University of North Carolina Press, 1979). For the Unionist perspective, see Biggs-Davison and Chowdharay Best's *Cross of St Patrick*, pp.193–270.
47. See Anon., revised K.D. Reynolds, 'Henry Fitzalan–Howard, fifteenth Duke of Norfolk (1847–1917)', in *Oxford DNB*.
48. See Robert O'Neil, *Cardinal Herbert Vaughan, Archbishop of Westminster, Bishop of Salford, Founder of the Mill Hill Missionaries* (Tunbridge Wells: Burns and Oates, 1995), and Thompson Cooper, revised G. Martin Murphy, 'Edward Henry Howard (1829–92)', in *Oxford DNB*.
49. See Duffy, *Saints and Sinners*, pp.235–44.
50. Larkin, *Roman Catholic Church and Creation of Modern Irish State*, pp.55–6.
51. O'Callaghan, 'English Catholics and the Irish Question', pp.72–7.
52. Ibid., pp.136–40 and 170–5.
53. Revd P.J. Walsh, *William J. Walsh: Archbishop of Dublin* (Dublin and Cork: Talbot Press, 1928). It has now been superseded by Thomas J. Morrissey, *William J. Walsh, Archbishop of Dublin (1841–1921)* (Dublin: Four Courts Press, 2000).
54. Larkin, *Roman Catholic Church and Creation of Modern Irish State*, pp.24, 55, 61–2.
55. Emly to Stephen de Vere, 11 June 1885, DVP, Trinity College MS 5053/ 158.
56. Emly to Newman, 11 April 1886, NP, M/7.
57. O'Callaghan, 'English Catholics and the Irish Question', pp.288–95 and 549–51.
58. See L.M. Geary, *The Plan of Campaign 1886–91* (Cork: Cork University Press, 1986).
59. Ward, *Aubrey de Vere*, p.315 and O'Callaghan, 'English Catholics and the Irish Question', pp.314–15.
60. Croke to Walsh, 31 July 1887, quoted in Larkin, *Roman Catholic Church and Plan of Campaign*, pp.117–18.
61. Ibid., p.118, Croke to Walsh, 4 August 1887.
62. Ibid., p.335.
63. Ibid., pp.381–417.
64. Larkin, *Roman Catholic Church and Plan of Campaign*, p.287.
65. O'Callaghan, 'English Catholics and the Irish Question', pp.403–4.
66. Ibid., pp.418–22.
67. Ibid., p.420.
68. Ibid., pp.427–9 and 437–9.
69. See P.J. Joyce, *John Healy, Archbishop of Tuam* (Dublin: M.H. Gill and Son, 1931) and O'Callaghan, 'Bishop O'Dwyer'.
70. O'Callaghan, 'English Catholics and the Irish Question', pp.493–505.
71. Dublin was not to have another resident cardinal until Archbishop Desmond Connell received the Red Hat in 2001.
72. O'Callaghan, 'English Catholics and the Irish Question', pp.559–60.
73. For an account of the fellowship controversy see Morrissey, *Towards a National University*, pp.79–88.
74. Ibid., pp.85–6 and Morrissey, *William J. Walsh*, p.38.
75. Morrissey, *William J. Walsh* , p.39.
76. Morrissey, *Towards a National University*, pp.124–7.
77. Larkin, *Roman Catholic Church and the Fall of Parnell*, pp.154–7.
78. Morrissey, 'Some Jesuit Contributions to Irish Education', pp.111–262.
79. Ibid., pp.113–20.
80. Ibid., p.123.
81. Ibid., p. 24.
82. Ibid., pp.125–6.
83. Ibid., pp.128–9.
84. Ibid., p.130.

85. Ibid.
86. Ibid., p.135.
87. Ibid., p.223.
88. Ibid., pp.183–6.
89. Ibid., p.138.
90. *Freeman's Journal*, 1 November 1888.
91. Morrissey, 'Some Jesuit Contributions to Irish Education', p.211.
92. Ibid., pp.222–3.
93. *Mungret Annual* (Limerick, 1907), pp.27–8.
94. Buckland, 'Southern Unionism', pp.40–1.
95. For an examination of the background to Emly's departure from the chairmanship, see William Leo Feingold, 'The Irish Boards of Poor Law Guardians 1872–86. A Revolution in Local Government' (unpublished Ph.D thesis, University of Chicago, 1974) and William R. Feingold, *The Revolt of the Tenantry: The Transformation of Local Government in Ireland, 1872–1886* (Boston: Northeastern University Press, 1984).
96. Feingold, 'Irish Boards of Poor Law Guardians', pp.142–5.
97. Ibid., p.154.
98. Ibid., p.196.
99. *Limerick Reporter*, 31 March 1882.
100. Altholz, *Liberal Catholic Movement in England*, p.244.
101. Cobban, *History of Modern France*, Vol. 3, pp.24–6.
102. G. W. Brogan, *The French Nation. From Napoleon to Petain 1814–1940* (London: Hamilton, 1957), pp.158–9 and Magraw, *France 1815–1914*, p.63.
103. Cobban, *A History of Modern France*, Vol. 3, pp.19–21.
104. Ibid., pp.24–6.
105. Brogan, *French Nation*, p.192; Magraw, *France 1815–1914*, pp.271–2 and Cobban, *History of Modern France*, Vol. 3, pp.38–9.
106. Magraw, *France 1815–1914*, p.352.
107. Ibid., pp.324–5.
108. For a charming picture of the de la Poers at home, see Mark Bence-Jones, *Life in an Irish Country House* (London: Constable, 1996), pp.130–47.
109. Sheehan, *Corner of Limerick*, p.126.
110. Ibid., pp.126–7.
111. *Thom's Irish Who's Who* (Dublin: Thom, 1923), p.73.
112. Mark Bence-Jones, *Twilight of the Ascendancy* (London: Constable, 1987), p.51.
113. *Thom's Irish Who's Who*, p.73.
114. Hansard, CCCXLV, 6–7 (5 June 1890).
115. *Munster News*, 21 April 1894.
116. Maisie Ward, *The Wilfred Wards and the Transition*, Vol. 2, *Insurrection Vs. Resurrection* (London: Sheed and Ward, 1937), p.53.
117. Ibid., p.54.
118. Monsell, *Roman Catholic Liberal Peer on the Irish Home Rule Bill.*
119. *Irish Roman Catholic Protest Against Home Rule.*
120. *Munster News*, 21 April 1894.
121. Ibid.
122. Ibid.
123. Ibid.
124. Ibid.
125. Ibid.

CHAPTER NINE

Conclusion

After the death of Lord Emly his son Gaston succeeded as second baron, but he soon became notorious for his odd and whimsical behaviour. His political views were decidedly unorthodox for a peer of the realm. He declared in favour of Irish nationalism, and made so many inflammatory speeches that he was removed as a magistrate of County Limerick in 1899 and was not reinstated until 1913, an extraordinary fate for the son of a previous Lord-Lieutenant of the county.[1] Even more unusual was his fervent embrace of the cause of Labour. He became chairman of the County Limerick Land and Labour Association and instigated an agitation to end the contract system, under which local authorities contracted out public works to private enterprise, which usually resulted in the labourers being harshly exploited. Instead, Lord Emly advocated 'direct labour' by which the local authorities would directly employ their own labourers to carry out the works.[2] Within a few years this method was universally adopted, a reform for which Lord Emly deserved great credit. He was a member of Limerick County Council from 1899 to 1920, and became Chairman of the Limerick County Committee of Agricultural and Technical Instruction.[3] He campaigned for a Catholic university and was a member of the Athenaeum Club.[4] Despite his comparative radicalism and his Pythonesque displays of oddness (he often travelled to public meetings and other functions by bicycle), he was not popular. He was distrusted both by nationalists as an opportunistic and insincere convert to their cause, and by Unionists for his apostacy. In addition, the old landlord system was crumbling fast, his wife died in 1925, and he survived until 1932, a sad figure who had long outlived his social and political relevance.

Gaston's death brought about the extinction of the title, and Tervoe passed to his nephew, Commander Edmund de la Poer Monsell (1883–1964), who resided there until 1948, when he made over the estate to his son John (1916–89) and retired to a house in Rosbrien, near

Limerick City.[5] John Monsell was unable to keep up the large old house and estate, and in September 1951 the contents of Tervoe House were auctioned and the treasures accumulated over three centuries were dispersed.[6] The house itself became a ruin in 1953 and was totally demolished in 1985, although in 1951 the portico was re-erected at the main entrance to Mungret College, where it still stands. Captain Monsell and his family sold the Tervoe demesne to Irish Cement Ltd and went to live in the beautiful seaside town of Ilfracombe in Devonshire, so by a curious irony they had returned to their West Country origins after a 300-year 'interlude' in Ireland.

Meanwhile, the English branch of the family, descended from Archdeacon Thomas Monsell, had flourished. William Monsell's first cousin, the Reverend John Samuel Bewley Monsell (1811–75), was one of the greatest Victorian hymn-writers, the author of 'Fight the Good Fight' and the latter's grandson, Bolton Meredith Eyres Monsell (1881–1969) had the most brilliant political career of any Monsell. He was Conservative MP for South Worcestershire from 1910 to 1935, and held a succession of posts culminating in that of First Lord of the Admiralty (1931–6), thus attaining the Cabinet seat that William Monsell had always craved. One of his daughters was married to the distinguished British travel writer, Sir Patrick Leigh-Fermor. Bolton was created Viscount Monsell in 1935, but his son, the second Viscount, died unmarried in 1993, so the title became extinct.[7] Curiously, both Monsell peerages lasted fifty-eight years (1874–1932 and 1935–93 respectively) and for two generations. Another famous grandchild of John Samuel Bewley Monsell was Bolton's first cousin Elinor Mary Monsell (1879–1954), the celebrated portrait painter and engraver. A graduate of the Slade School of Fine Art, she enjoyed a long and distinguished career and was married to Bernard Darwin, a grandson of Charles Darwin. Elinor was a close friend of Lady Gregory, W.B. Yeats and Jack Yeats, and designed the famous logo of the Abbey Theatre, which depicts Queen Maeve and an Irish wolfhound.[8]

The political career of William Monsell was one of the most remarkable and at nearly sixty years (1835–93) one of the longest in nineteenth-century Ireland. His local legacy was considerable. Limerick owes to his zeal and dedication the Redemptorist Church and Monastery at Mount St Alphonsus, the Good Shepherd Convent in Clare Street (now home of the Limerick School of Art and Design) and the contribution of the Sisters of Mercy to St Camillus Hospital. He donated two prominent statues to St John's Cathedral, facilitated the establishment of Mungret College, and ordered the construction of a General Post Office in Limerick city. In his own parish he built two primary schools at Tervoe (one for boys and one for girls), which remained in use until 1976. During the Great Famine he promoted the development of the present main road from Limerick to Kildimo via Clarina and the Ferrybridge (the current N-69).[9]

His national achievements were also considerable. His reforms at the Board of Ordnance were of enormous significance. He introduced competitive examinations into the Royal Military Academy at Woolwich and reorganised the armaments industry by greatly increasing the role of government establishments. He did much to advance the civil rights of his Catholic co-religionists. He played a major role in reforming the parliamentary oath in 1865–6, and facilitated the registration of Catholic marriages in Ireland, thus paving the way for the present system of registering births, deaths and marriages. Monsell pioneered the introduction of Catholic nuns into the public health system in Ireland and reformed the law on Catholic burials.[10] He advanced the civil and political rights of Catholics by his own example, and facilitated their absorption into British public life. When he became Postmaster-General in 1871, he was the highest-ranking Catholic office-holder since 1689. By so doing, he paved the way for the appointment of the first Catholic Cabinet minister – the convert Marquess of Ripon in 1886.[11]

However, it was in education that Monsell's impact was most significant. He helped found two great secondary schools in Ireland and set up primary schools in his own locality. He reformed the entry requirements for Woolwich Academy, thus transforming the education of a significant section of the British Officer Corps. Above all, he played a central role in tertiary education in a number of ways. First, he was instrumental in bringing about the reform of the educational systems of Trinidad and Mauritius; second, he provided the blueprint for Gladstone's momentous university bill of 1873; thirdly, despite this setback, he saw his 'Trinidad scheme' play a vital role in the Intermediate Education Act of 1878 and the Royal University of 1879; fourthly, he helped build up the Catholic University by supporting the concentration of the fellowships of the Royal University there in the 1880s, and, finally, he founded an embryonic university at Mungret, which endured for thirty years.

As a political figure he was successful because he held a seat in Parliament for a quarter of a century; became one of the significant statesmen in Ireland and the leading Catholic Whig, and established himself as the chief link between the Catholic hierarchy and the British government. His influence was substantial and his prominence was shown by his inclusion in every Liberal administration between 1853 and 1873 (except under Palmerston). He gained the respect of figures as diverse as Gladstone and Disraeli; Queen Victoria and Gavan Duffy; Montalambert and Cullen. He was the ultimate insider and pillar of the establishment, as can be illustrated by Manning when he wrote: 'I was walking in 1861 with Monsell, and in the passage between the Horse Guards and Downing Street, met Gladstone on his way to the House of Commons.'[12] Monsell also forged links with prominent figures in France, Italy and Germany, and this gave his career an international dimension.

Monsell's political skills were of a high order. In 1847 he was elected to Parliament due to his uncanny ability to straddle the opposing parties of Repeal and Unionism, Catholic and Protestant, Liberal and Conservative, and had to face only one further contested election in 1859, which he easily won. Again, in the 1870s he gauged the shift of public opinion towards Home Rule, and avoided the fate of less astute colleagues by withdrawing gracefully rather than fighting what he knew to be a losing electoral battle. He cultivated his constituency base assiduously and his reading of the public mood was always acute. Yet he combined this cunning and guile with a real adherence to a coherent and sincerely felt ideology.

His record as an administrator was a more mixed one. His period as Clerk of the Ordnance saw him take advantage of the Crimean War to advance to a position of great power and influence, by using his personal friendship with Newcastle and his close working relationship with Panmure to gain authority and influence, which he then used to effect reforms of a significant nature. Similarly, he employed his influence at the Colonial Office to advance his educational ideas in the Colonies, and ultimately in Ireland. However, his period at the Post Office was a complete failure, and his shortcomings as a full minister were mercilessly exposed – lack of initiative, timidity and a tendency to excessive delegation.

The final verdict on his political career must be that it was a failure. His whole ideology was based on a *via media*, and in nearly every instance this was to prove untenable. The Catholic Whigs, of whom he became unofficial leader, were an interesting attempt to combine Irish Unionism and Catholicism and enjoyed a certain success in the 1850s and 1860s.[13] After all, 40 per cent of Irish landlords in 1861 were Catholics, and it is reasonable to suppose that the great majority of them were Catholic Whigs.[14] However, they were living on borrowed time and they suffered from the neglect and disregard of their British Liberal colleagues. In this regard, the period of Palmerston's ascendancy was a particularly wasted opportunity.[15] While the political legacy of the Great Famine was bitter and, for Irish nationalists at home or in exile, rich in recriminations, directed especially at the stewardship of Lord John Russell's Whig government after 1846, it can not be taken as inevitable that Catholic Unionism was a politically impossible position in post-famine Ireland.[16] Had Gladstone's reform programme of 1868–70 been enacted even ten years earlier, it is at least plausible that a significant constituency of Irish Catholics might have become reconciled to the Union. However, the crucial Palmerstonian interlude enabled Fenianism to take root, and in the aftermath of 1867 the seeds of Home Rule were sown, so that ultimately the Catholic Whigs were squeezed between British indifference and insensitivity on one side, and the growth of Irish political and social radicalism on the other. They were unable to survive their electoral rout in the 1874 general election and never made the transition from an old-fashioned political connection to a party with a broad popular support-base and organisation, like the Home Rule movement under Parnell.

Similarly, Monsell's simultaneous espousal of Unionism, Liberalism and Irish patriotism was a position that did not survive the transition of the 1880s and 1890s. The Irish Liberals were squeezed between nationalism and unionism and forced into an alliance with the Conservatives, while the Anglo-Irish were gradually excluded from the emerging sense of Irishness, and their identity of being both Irish and British ceased to be tenable.[17] An Irish patriot and an advanced reformer in the 1850s and 1860s, Monsell was, at the end of his life, regarded as part of the British hegemony and a social and political conservative. Yet, it was not his ideology that had altered but rather political circumstances had forced him, like so many of his fellow-landlords, into a more strident and self-conscious espousal of his belief in the Union and the ascendancy of the Anglo-Irish.[18] In religion, Monsell attempted to reconcile the Catholic Church to the political, intellectual and social changes of the nineteenth century. He was a Liberal Catholic at a time when both Liberals and Catholics distrusted each other, and so in the end he and his like-minded colleagues came to be distrusted by both sides. Monsell's hopes were dashed in the 1860s when the Liberal Catholics were crushed by the Pope.

While it was his *via media* that was probably the ultimate cause of his failure, there were other factors. He was of average ability, of a cautious and conservative disposition and was only an adequate public speaker. At times, he was too diffident in advancing himself. Ironically, the charge frequently levied against him of converting to Catholicism in order to further his political career was not merely false, but flew in the face of the evidence. Arguably, Monsell's Catholicism may have contributed to the considerable popularity which enabled him to stay in the Commons for twenty-six years and to his appointment to government posts as a recognised leader of the Catholic community. However, on both counts the contrary can also be asserted. While it was undoubtedly necessary for MPs representing Irish Catholic constituencies to espouse causes favourable to the Church, it was not at all necessary for them to actually convert to Catholicism, as is exemplified by the national leadership positions attained by both Butt and Parnell. On the other hand, being a Catholic was a barrier to advancement in public office within the British system. While France had a Protestant Prime Minister (Guizot) as early as 1840, Britain did not have a Catholic Cabinet minister until 1886, and has not, to date, had a Catholic Prime Minister. On the other hand, Chichester Fortescue and Lord Naas are examples of Protestant Irishmen who advanced to Cabinet rank without difficulty.

If he was not an outstanding statesman, Monsell was, nevertheless, possessed of many virtues. In private life he was a worthy figure. He was a kind and devoted husband, a loving father, a just landlord and a benevolent employer. He was pious, upright, honest and diligent. He was possessed of a very public spirit and a cosmopolitan, enlightened outlook. He made of Tervoe House one of the most celebrated residences in Ireland, with name recognition on a national scale. Under Monsell, a glittering galaxy of talent visited this house, including Cardinals Newman and Manning (the two most prominent British Catholic churchmen of the nineteenth century); the poets Manley Hopkins, de Vere and Faber (founder of Brompton Oratory and author of *Faith of our Fathers*); the architect Pugin, the statesmen Balfour, Norfolk and O'Hagan, and the prominent Irish Bishops Moriarty, Butler and O'Dwyer.[19]

In the final analysis, Monsell's enduring historical interest may rest not principally on his political impact on the affairs of state or the systems of governance of his time, nor even on his role as a local grandee among the Limerick and Irish gentry. His significance may, rather, reside in the very particular combination of religious and political views and positions that he firmly held and which represent an ideological strand in Irish political life that became virtually obliterated in the polarised world of nationalist-unionist contestation in Ireland from the intrusion of Home Rule to the settlements of 1920–3.

Catholic, Liberal and Unionist; Irishman, Briton, adopted Frenchman and European; friend of Gladstone and of Duffy, of Pope Pius IX and Newman, of Acton and Cardinal Paul Cullen, Monsell represents conjunctions of belief and loyalty that were to be eclipsed by the ideological fervour and the traumatic conflicts of the twentieth century. The fact that he was neither an O'Connell nor a Parnell should not mean that what he was and what political disposition he represented should be ignored; his political position on the spectrum of Irish politics in the Union era provides historians with a valuable vantage point from which to consider the full complexity of political life in Victorian Ireland and from which to contemplate those other political possibilities which Monsell and his contemporaries entertained, but which, in the event, were not to be realised. Perhaps the words of his old friend and mentor, Newman, may provide an appropriate epitaph for Monsell. In his *Apologia Pro Vita Sua*, Newman wrote: 'this is what the church is said to want, not party men, but sensible temperate, sober, well-judging persons, to guide it through the channel of no meaning, between Scylla and Charybdis of aye and no'.[20] Monsell was such a man for his church and for his state for nearly sixty years.

NOTES

1. *Thom's Irish Who's Who*, p.73.
2. See Gaston Monsell, *The Labour Cause in County Limerick. The Labourers and the County Council – Speech of Lord Emly – Mr A. Mackey's attack and the Labourers' Reply. The Case for Direct Labour* (Limerick: privately published, 1899) and *Speech of Lord Emly at the Annual Convention of the Irish Land and Labour Association. Held at Limerick. August 15, 1901* (Limerick: privately published, 1901)
3. *Thom's Irish Who's Who*, p.73.
4. Ibid.
5. Montgomery-Massingberd, *Burke's Irish family Records,* p.849.
6. Hanley, 'The Past Glories of Tervoe'.
7. See Stuart Ball, 'Bolton Meredith Eyres Monsell, first Viscount Monsell (1881–1969)', in *Oxford DNB.*
8. For Elinor Darwin, see Theo Snoddy, *Dictionary of Irish Artists, 20th Century* (Dublin: Wolfhound Press, 1996), pp.93–4.
9. *Munster News*, 21 April 1894.
10. Luddy, 'Angels of Mercy', pp.102–17 and Moane, 'Limerick Workhouse', pp.140–7.
11. Ensor, *England 1870–1914*, p.70.
12. Purcell, *Life of Cardinal Manning,* Vol. 2, p.162.
13. Horgan, 'Irish Catholic Whigs', *passim.*
14. Vaughan, *New History of Ireland*, Vol. 5, p.740.
15. For a recent analysis see Peter Gray, *Famine, Land and Politics : British Government and Irish Society 1843–50* (Dublin and Portland, OR : Irish Academic Press, 1999).
16. For Ulster perspectives on this process, see Alvin Jackson, *The Ulster Party: Irish Unionists in the House of Commons 1884–1911* (Oxford: Clarendon Press, 1989); James Loughlin, *Gladstone, Home Rule and the Ulster Question, 1882–93* (Dublin: Gill and Macmillan, 1986); James Loughlin, *Ulster Unionism and British National Identity since 1885* (London: Pinter, 1995); and Paul Bew, *Conflict and Conciliation in Ireland 1890–1910* (Oxford: Clarendon Press and Oxford University Press, 1987).
17. Ridden 'Making Good Citizens', pp.18–21 and 238–40.
18. Buckland, 'Southern Unionism', pp.41–4.
19. Potter, *Catholic Unionist*, pp.103–4. For Faber, see Ronald Chapman, *Father Faber* (London: Burns and Oates, 1961).
20. Partington, *Oxford Dictionary of Quotation*, p.493.

Bibliography

PRIMARY SOURCES

Manuscripts

National Library of Ireland, Dublin
- De Vere papers
- Gavan Duffy papers
- Mayo papers
- Monsell papers
- Monsell of Tervoe papers
- Smith O'Brien papers
- Journals of W.J. O'Neill Daunt
- Sir William Teeling papers

National Archives, Dublin
- Monsell papers

Library of Trinity College, Dublin
- De Vere papers

Dublin Diocesan Archives, Dublin
- Cullen papers
- McCabe papers

Limerick Diocesan Archives, Limerick
- Butler papers

Limerick City Archives, Limerick
- De Vere papers

Public Records Office of Northern Ireland, Belfast
- Dunraven papers (now in the Special Collections Department, Glucksman Library, University of Limerick, Limerick)
- O'Hagan papers

British Library, London
- Aberdeen papers
- Gladstone papers

Post Office Archives, London
Annual Reports, Postmaster-General
Tilley papers
Public Records Office, Kew, London
Board of Ordnance records
Colonial Office records
Granville papers
Russell papers
University of Southampton, Southampton
Palmerston papers
Public Records Office of Somerset, Taunton
Carlingford papers
The Oratory, Birmingham
Newman papers
Royal Archives, Windsor Castle, Windsor
Correspondence of Queen Victoria
National Archives of Scotland, Edinburgh
Dalhousie papers
Cambridge University Library, Cambridge
Acton papers

Newspapers and Journals

Freeman's Journal
Irish Times
Limerick Chronicle
Limerick Reporter
London Gazette
Munster News and Limerick and Clare Advocate
The Tablet
The Times
Vanity Fair

Parliamentary Publications

Hansards Parliamentary Debates, Third Series, Vols 1–356 (London: T.C. Hansard, 1830–91)

P.P. 1837–8 (701) VII. *Report from the Select committee on foundation schools and education in Ireland.*

P.P. 1845(20) *Evidence taken before the commissioners appointed to inquire into the occupation of land in Ireland* (Devon Commission).

P.P. 1847(6) *Report of the Select committee of the House of Lords on colonisation from Ireland; together with the minutes of evidence.*

P.P. 1848(17) *First report from the Select committee of the House of Lords on colonisation from Ireland, together with minutes of evidence.*

P.P. 1854–5(9) *Reports from the Select committee on the army before Sebastopol with minutes of evidence and appendix.*

P.P. 1854–5(32) *Army civil departments. Copy of an order of the Queen's most Excellent Majesty in council (passed on the 6th day of June, 1855) regulating the establishments of the civil departments of the army.*

P.P. 1860(7) *Report from the Select Committee on military organisation, together with the proceedings of the committee, minutes of evidence and appendix.*

P.P. 1862(8) *Report from the Select Committee on Ordnance, together with the proceedings of the committee, minutes of evidence, appendix and index.*

P.P. 1863(11) *Report from the select committee on Ordnance together with the proceedings of the committee, minutes of evidence, appendix and index.*

P.P. 1867(38) Part 1. *Report from the commissioners of the railways of Great Britain and Ireland, with minutes of evidence* (Devonshire Commission).

P.P. 1873(7) *First report from the Committee of Public Accounts, together with the proceedings of the committee, minutes of evidence and appendix.*

P.P. 1873(7) *Second report from the Committee of Public accounts, together with the proceedings of the committee, minutes of evidence and appendix.*

P.P. 1873(9) *Report from the select committee on Cape of Good Hope and Zanzibar Mail contracts; together with the proceedings of the committee, minutes of evidence and appendix.*

P.P. 1881(18) *Report from Her Majesty's Commissioners of enquiry into the workings of the Landlord and Tenant (Ireland) Act, 1870 and the Acts amending the same.* Vol. 2. *Digest of evidence. Minutes of evidence.* Part 1 (Bessborough Commission).

P.P. 1887(26) *Report of the Royal Commission on the Land Law (Ireland) Act, 1881 and the Purchase of Land (Act) 1885.* Vol. 2. *Minutes of evidence and appendices* (Cowper commission).

Printed Primary Sources

Burke, Sir Bernard, *A Genealogical and Heraldic Dictionary of the Peerage and Baronetage of the British Empire* (London: Burke's Peerage, 1887).

Gladstone, William Ewart, *The Gladstone Diaries* (edited by M.R.D. Foot and H.C.G. Matthew), 14 vols (Oxford: Clarendon Press, 1968–91).

Corish, Patrick J. (ed.), 'Irish College Rome, Kirby Papers 1862–83', in *Archivium Hibernicum,* Vol. XXX (1972), pp.29–115; Vol. XXXI (1973), pp.1–94; Vol. XXXII (1974), pp.1062.

Greville, Charles, *The Greville Memoirs; a Journal of the Reigns of King George IV, King William IV and Queen Victoria*, 8 vols (London: Longmans, Green and Co., 1874–87).

Heaney, Henry (ed.), *A Scottish Whig in Ireland 1835–38: The Irish Journals of Robert Graham of Redgorton* (Dublin: Four Courts Press in association with the National Library of Ireland, 1999).

Kimberley, John Wodehouse, 1st Earl of, *A Journal of events during the Gladstone Ministry 1868–74* (edited by Ethel Drus), in Camden Miscellany XXI (London: Camden Society, 1958).

MacSuibhne, Peadar (ed.), *Paul Cullen and his Contemporaries, with their Letters from 1820–1902*, 5 vols (Naas: Leinster Leader, 1961–77).

Montgomery-Massingberd, Hugh (ed.), *Burke's Irish Family Records* (London: Burke's Peerage, 1976).

Mungret Annual (Limerick: Mungret College, 1897 and 1907).

Newman, John Henry, *The Letters and Diaries of John Henry Newman*, 31 vols (edited by Ian Kerr, Thomas Gornall, Gerard Tracey, C.S. Dessain, Vincent F. Blehl, and Edward E. Kelly) (Oxford and London: Clarendon Press, 1961–90).

Ramm, Agatha (ed.), *The Political Correspondence of Mr Gladstone and Lord Granville 1868–1876*, 2 vols, in Camden Third Series, Vol. CXXXI (London: Royal Historical Society, 1952).

Russell, Lord John, *The Later Correspondence of Lord John Russell 1840–1878*, 2 vols (edited by G.P. Gooch) (London: Longmans and Co.,1925).

Ruvigny and Raineval, Marquis of, *The Plantagenet Roll of the Blood Royal, Being a Complete Table of all the Descendants now Living of Edward III, King of England*, 5 vols, *The Clarence Volume, Containing the Descendants of George, Duke of Clarence* (London: T.C. & E.C. Jack, 1905–11).

Somerville, Alexander, *Letters from Ireland during the Famine of 1847* (edited by D.K.M. Snell) (Dublin: Irish Academic Press, 1994).

Thom's Irish Almanac and Official Directory (Dublin: Thom, 1844–1880).

Thom's Irish Who's Who (Dublin: Thom, 1923).

Thom's Official Directory of the United Kingdom of Great Britain and Ireland (Dublin: Thom, 1881–95).

SECONDARY SOURCES

Books

Acheson, Alan, *A History of the Church of Ireland 1691–1996* (Blackrock, Dublin: Columba Press, 1997).

Acland, John E., *A Layman's Life in the Days of the Tractarian Movement. In Memoriam Arthur (Acland) Troyte* (London and Oxford: J. Parker and Co., 1904).

Akenson, D.H., *The Irish Education Experiment. The National System of Education in Ireland* (London: Routledge and Kegan Paul, 1970).

Aldous, Richard, *The Lion and the Unicorn: Gladstone vs Disrael* (London: Hutchinson, 2006).

Altholz, Joseph, *The Liberal Catholic Movement in England. The Rambler and its Contributors 1848–62* (London: Burns and Oates, 1962).

Anderson, M.S., *The Ascendancy of Europe. Aspects of European History 1815–1914* (London: Longmans, 1972).

Anderson, Olive, *A Liberal State at War. English Politics and Economics during the Crimean War*, (London: Macmillan and New York: St Martins Press, 1967).

Anonymous, *Fifty Years at Mount Saint Alphonsus, Limerick, 1853–1903* (Limerick: O'Connor and Co., 1903).

Anonymous, *Irish Roman Catholic Protest against Home Rule* (Dublin: Irish Unionist Alliance Publications, 1893).

Anonymous, *Is it opportune to define the infallibility of the Pope? Memorandum addressed to the bishops of Germany. Respectfully offered in translation to the bishops of the United Kingdom and its colonies and to the Bishops of the United States* (London: privately published, 1869).

Atkinson, Norman, *Irish Education. A History of Educational Institutions* (Dublin: Allan Figgis, 1969).

Aubert, Roger (ed.), *The Christian Centuries*, Vol. 5, *The Church in a Secularised Society* (New York: Paulist Press and London: Darton, Longman and Todd, 1978).

Auchmuty, J.J., *Sir Thomas Wyse 1791–1862, The Life and Career of an Educator and Diplomat* (London: P.S. King and Sons, 1939).

Austen, Jane, *Pride and Prejudice* (Harmondsworth: Penguin, 1933).

Bailey, William F., *Local and Centralised Government in Ireland. A Sketch of the Existing Systems* (Dublin: Hodges, Figgis and Co., 1888).

Balsan, Consuelo Vanderbilt, *The Glitter and the Gold* (London: Heinemann, 1953).

Barker, A.J., *The Vainglorious War 1854–56* (London: Weidenfeld and Nicolson, 1970).

Barr, Colin, *Paul Cullen, John Henry Newman, and the Catholic University of Ireland, 1845–1865* (Notre Dame, IN: University of Notre Dame Press, 2004).

Bateman, John (ed.), *The Great Landowners of Great Britain and Ireland* (Leicester: Leicester University Press, 1971; facsimile reprint of the

edition of 1883).
Beales, Derek, *The Risorgimento and the Unification of Italy* (London: Allen and Unwin, 1971).
Bence-Jones, Mark, *A Guide to Irish Country Houses* (London: Constable, 1988). *Life in an Irish Country House* (London: Constable, 1996). *Twilight of the Ascendancy* (London: Constable, 1987).
Bennett, Edward, *The Post Office and its Story* (London: Seeley, Service and Co., 1912).
Bew, Paul, *Conflict and Conciliation in Ireland 1890–1910* (Oxford: Clarendon Press and Oxford University Press, 1987). *Ireland: The Politics of Enmity 1789–2006* (Oxford: Oxford University Press, 2007). *Land and the National Question in Ireland 1858–82* (Dublin: Gill and MacMillan, 1978).
Biggs-Davison, John and Chowdharay-Best, George, *The Cross of St Patrick: The Catholic Unionist Tradition in Ireland* (Abbotsbrook, Bourne End, Bucks: Kensal Press, 1984).
Black, R.D. Collinson, *The Statistical and Social Enquiry Society of Ireland, Centenary Volume 1847–1947* (Dublin: Eason and Son, 1947).
Blakely, Brian L., *The Colonial Office 1868–1892* (Durham, NC: Duke University Press, 1972).
Bolton, G.C., *The Passing of the Irish Act of Union* (Oxford: Oxford University Press, 1966).
Bonham, Valerie, *A Joyous Service: The Clewer Sisters and their Work* (Windsor: Valerie Bonham and the Community of St John the Baptist, 1989). *A Place in Life: The Clewer House of Mercy 1849–93* (Windsor: Valerie Bonham and the Community of St John the Baptist, 1992).
Bowen, Desmond, *Paul, Cardinal Cullen and the Shaping of Modern Irish Catholicism* (Dublin: Gill and Macmillan, and Waterloo, Ont.: Wilfrid Laurier University Press, 1983). *The Protestant Crusade in Ireland 1800–70. A Study of Protestant–Catholic Relations Between the Act of Union and Disestablishment* (Dublin: Gill and Macmillan, 1978).
Boyce, D. George, *Nineteenth-Century Ireland: The Search for Stability* (Dublin: Gill and Macmillan, 1990).
Brady, Ciaran (ed.), *Worsted in the Game. Losers in Irish History* (Dublin: Lilliput Press, 1989).
Brogan, G.W., *The French Nation. From Napoleon to Petain 1814–1940* (London: Hamilton, 1957).
Brose, Olive, *Church and Parliament. The Reshaping of the Church of England 1828–1860* (Stanford: Stanford University Press and

Oxford: Oxford University Press, 1959).

Brown, Stewart, J. and Miller, David W. (eds), *Piety and Power in Ireland, 1760–1960 Essays in Honour of Emmet Larkin* (Notre Dame, IN: University of Notre Dame Press, 2000).

Buschkuhl, Matthias, *Great Britain and the Holy See, 1746–1870* (Dublin: Irish Academic Press, 1982).

Cannadine, David, *The Decline and Fall of the British Aristocracy* (New Haven and London: Yale University Press, 1990).

Canny, Nicholas, *From Reformation to Restoration Ireland 1534–1660* (Dublin: Helicon, 1987).

Carter, Revd T.T., *Harriet Monsell. A Memoir* (London: J. Masters and Co., 1884).

Cell, John W., *British Colonial Administration in the Nineteenth Century. The Policy-Making Process* (New Haven and London: Yale University Press, 1976).

Chapman, J.K., *The Career of Arthur Hamilton Gordon, First Lord Stanmore 1829–1912* (Toronto: University of Toronto Press, 1964).

Chapman, Ronald, *Father Faber* (London: Burns and Oates, 1961).

Cobban, Alfred, *A History of Modern France*, 3 vols (Harmondsworth: Penguin, 1961–2).

Colley, Linda, *Britons. Forging the Nation 1707–1837* (New Haven and London: Yale University Press, 1992).

Comerford, R.V., *The Fenians in Context. Irish Politics and Society 1848–82* (Dublin: Wolfhound Press and Atlantic Highlands, NJ: Humanities Press, 1985).

Conacher, J.B., *The Aberdeen Coalition 1852–55 A Study in Mid-Nineteenth-Century Party Politics* (Cambridge: Cambridge University Press, 1968). *The Peelites and the Party System 1846–52* (Newton Abbot: David and Charles, 1972).

Conroy, J.C., *A History of Railways in Ireland* (London: Longmans, Green and Co., 1928).

Cooke, A. B. and Vincent, John (eds.), *Lord Carlingford's Journal: Reflections of a Cabinet Minister, 1885* (Oxford: Clarendon Press, 1971).

Cook, Chris and Keith, Brendan, *British Historical Facts 1830–1900* (London: Macmillan, 1975).

Coolahan, John, *Irish Education, its History and Structure* (Dublin: Institute of Public Administration, 1981).

Corish, Patrick J., *The Irish Catholic Experience. A Historical Survey* (Dublin: Gill and Macmillan, 1985), (ed.), *A History of Irish Catholicism*, Vol. 5 (Dublin: Gill, 1967).

Cowell, Frank Richard, *The Athenaeum: Club and Social Life in London,*

1824–1974 (London: Heinemann, 1975).
Crossman, Virginia, *Local Government in Nineteenth-Century Ireland* (Belfast: Institute of Irish Studies, Queen's University of Belfast, for the Ulster Society of Irish Historical Studies, 1994).
Cussen, Robert, 'Caleb Powell, High Sheriff of County Limerick, 1858, sums up his grand jury', in Etienne Rynne (ed.), *North Munster studies, Essays in commemoration of Monsignor Michael Moloney* (Limerick: Thomond Archaeological Society, 1967), pp.401–25.
Daly, Mary E., *A Social and Economic History of Ireland since 1800* (Dublin: Educational Co., 1981). *The Spirit of Ernest Enquiry: The Statistical and Social Inquiry Society of Ireland 1847–1997* (Dublin: Institute of Public Administration, 1997).
Daunton, M.J., *Royal Mail. The Post Office since 1840* (London: Athlone Press, 1985).
Davidoff, Leonore, *The Best Circles. Society, Etiquette and the Season* (London: Croom Helm, 1973).
Davis, Richard, *Revolutionary Imperialist. William Smith O'Brien 1803–64* (Dublin; Lilliput Press, 1998), (ed.), *To Solitude Confined. The Tasmanian Journal of William Smith O'Brien 1849–53* (Sydney: Crossing Press, 1995).
De Vere, Aubrey, *English Misrule and Irish Misdeeds: Four Letters from Ireland addressed to an English Member of Parliament* (London; J. Murray, 1848). *Recollections of Aubrey de Vere* (London and New York: Edwin Arnold, 1897).
Denman, Peter, *Samuel Ferguson: The Literary Achievement* (Gerrards Cross: Smythe, 1990).
Dewald, Jonathan, *The European Nobility 1400–1800* (Cambridge: Cambridge University Press, 1996).
Dooley, Terence, *The Big Houses and Landed Estates of Ireland: A Research Guide* (Dublin: Four Courts Press, 2007). *The Decline of the Big House in Ireland* (Dublin: Wolfhound Press, 2001).
Duffy, Charles Gavan, *The League of North and South. An Episode in Irish History 1850–1854* (London: Chapman and Hall, 1886).
Duffy, Eamon, *Saints and Scholars. A History of the Popes* (New Haven: Yale University Press, 1997).
Duffy, Patrick J. (ed.), *To and From Ireland: Planned Migration Schemes, c. 1600–2000* (Dublin: Geography Publications, 2004).
Dunraven, Edwin Richard Wyndham-Quin, third Earl of, *Notes on Irish Architecture* (edited by Margaret Stokes) (London: G. Bell, 1875–7).
Dunraven, Windham Thomas Wyndham-Quin, forth Earl of, *Past Times and Pastimes*, 2 vols (London: Hodder and Stoughton, 1922).
Edwards, Owen Dudley and Williams, T. Desmond (eds), *The Great*

Famine – Studies in Irish History 1846–1852 (Dublin: Browne and Nolan, 1956).

Ensor, Sir Robert, *England 1870–1914,* Oxford History of England, Vol. 14 (Oxford: Clarendon Press, 1962).

Farragher, Seán P., *Père Leman (1826–1880). Educator and Missionary, Founder of Blackrock College* (Dublin and London: Paraclete Press, 1988).

Feingold, William R., *The Revolt of the Tenantry: The Transformation of Local Government in Ireland, 1872–1886* (Boston: Northeastern University Press, 1984).

Fieldhouse, D.K., *The Colonial Empires. A Comparative Survey from the Eighteenth Century* (London: Weidenfeld and Nicolson, 1966).

Finlay, James C., *The Liberal Who Failed* (Washington, DC: Corpus Books, 1968).

Fleming, Revd John, *St John's Cathedral, Limerick* (Blackrock, Dublin: Four Courts Press, 1987).

Forbes, Major General A., *A History of the Army Ordnance Services*, 3 vols (London: Medici Society, 1929).

Foster, R.F., *Modern Ireland 1600–1972* (Harmondsworth: Penguin, 1988).

Gash, Norman, *Aristocracy and People: Britain 1815–1865* (London: Edward Arnold, 1979).

Geary, L.M., *The Plan of Campaign 1886–91* (Cork: Cork University Press, 1986).

Geoghegan, Patrick M., *The Irish Act of Union. A Study in High Politics 1798–1801* (Dublin: Gill and Macmillan, 1999).

Gillard, David, *The Struggle for Asia 1828–1914. A Study in British and Russian Imperialism* (London: Metheun, 1977).

Gilley, Sheridan, *Newman and his Age* (London: Darton, Longman and Todd, 1990).

Girvetz, Harry K., *From Wealth to Welfare: The Evolution of Liberalism* (Stanford: Stanford University Press, 1963).

Gladstone, William Ewart, *The Vatican Decrees in their Bearing on Civil Allegiance: A Political Expostulation* (London: John Murray, 1874).

Gray, Peter, *Famine, Land and Politics: British Government and Irish Society 1843–50* (Dublin and Portland, OR: Irish Academic Press, 1999). *The Irish Famine* (London: Thames and Hudson, 1995).

Grubb, Alan, *The Politics of Pessimism: Albert de Broglie and Conservative Politics in the Early Third Republic* (Newark, DE: University of Delaware Press, 1996).

Gwynn, Denis, *Cardinal Wiseman* (Dublin: Browne and Nolan, 1950).

Gwynn, Stephen (ed.), *The Letters and Friendships of Sir Cecil Spring Rice, A Record*, 2 vols (Boston: Houghton Mifflin, 1929).

Hales, E.E.Y., *Pio Nono. A Study in European Politics and Religion in the Nineteenth Century* (London: Eyre and Spottisewoode, 1954).

Hall, Henry L., *The Colonial Office, a History* (London: Longmans, Green, 1937).

Hannan, Kevin, *Limerick Historical Reflections* (Limerick: Oireacht Press, 1996).

Higonnet, Patrice, *Paris: Capital of the World* (Cambridge, MA: Harvard University Press, 2002).

Hill, Judith, *The Building of Limerick* (Cork and Dublin: Mercier Press, 1991).

Hill, Roland, *Lord Acton* (New Haven and London: Yale University Press, 2000).

Hobsbawn, E.J., *The Age of Revolution. Europe 1789–1848* (London: Abacus, 1977).

Hogan, Michael, *The Seventh Number of Shawn-na-Scoob by the Bard of Thomond* (Limerick; privately published, 1876).

Hogg, Brigadier O.F.G., *The Royal Arsenal, its Background, Origin and Subsequent History*, 2 vols (Oxford: Oxford University Press, 1963).

Hoppen, K. Theodore, *Elections, Politics and Society in Ireland 1832–85* (Oxford: Clarendon Press, 1984). *Ireland since 1800: Conflict and Conformity* (London and New York: Longmans, 1989).

Hornby, William, *Factories and Plant*, History of the Second World War. United Kingdom Civil Series (London: HMSO and Longmans, 1958).

Houghton, Walter E., *The Wellesley Index to Victorian Periodicals*, 5 vols. (Toronto: Toronto University Press and London: Routledge, 1966–89).

Jackson, Alvin, *Home Rule, An Irish History 1800–2000* (London: Weidenfeld and Nicolson, 2003). *Ireland 1798–1998: Politics and War* (Oxford: Blackwell, 1999). *The Ulster Party: Irish Unionists in the House of Commons 1884–1911* (Oxford: Clarendon Press, 1989).

James, Lionel, *A Forgotten Genius, Sewell of St Colombas and Radley* (London: Faber and Faber, 1945).

Jenkins, Roy, *Gladstone* (London: Macmillan, 1995).

Johnston-Liik, E.M., *History of the Irish Parliament 1692–1800: Commons, Constituencies and Statutes 1692–1800*, 6 vols (Belfast: Ulster Historical Foundation, 2002).

Joyce, Revd P.J., *John Healy, Archbishop of Tuam* (Dublin: M.H. Gill and Son, 1917).

Keenan, Desmond J., *The Catholic Church in Nineteenth-Century Ireland. A Sociological Study* (Dublin: Gill and Macmillan and Totowa, NJ: Barnes and Noble, 1983).

Kendle, John, *Ireland and the Federal Solution. The Debate over the United Kingdom Constitution, 1870–1921* (Kingston, Montreal: McGill-Queen's University Press, 1989).

Kennedy, B.A.,'Sharman Crawford's Federal Scheme for Ireland', in H.A. Cronnie, T.W. Moody and D.B. Quinn (eds), *Essays in British and Irish History in Honour of James Eadie Todd* (London: Frederick Muller, 1949), pp.235–54.

Kenny, Terence, *The Political thought of John Henry Newman* (London: Longmans, Green and Co., 1957).

Kerr, Donal A., *A Nation of Beggars? Priests People and Politics in Famine Ireland 1846–1852* (Oxford: Clarendon Press and Oxford University Press, 1994). *Peel, Priests and Politics. Sir Robert Peel's administration and the Roman Catholic Church in Ireland 1841–1846* (Oxford: Clarendon Press and Oxford University Press, 1982).

Kerr, Ian, *John Henry Newman. A Biography* (Oxford: Clarendon Press, 1988).

Kinealy, Christine, *This Great Calamity. The Irish Famine. 1845–52* (Dublin: Gill and Macmillan, 1994).

King, Hazel, *Richard Bourke* (Oxford: Oxford University Press, 1971).

Kinzler, Bruce L., *England's Disgrace? J.S. Mill and the Irish Question* (Toronto: University of Toronto Press, 2001).

Lambert, Royston, *Sir John Simon 1816–1904 and English Social Administration* (London: Macgibbon and Kee, 1963).

Larkin, Emmet, *The Consolidation of the Roman Catholic Church in Ireland 1860–1870* (Chapel Hill, NC: University of North Carolina Press, 1987). *The Making of the Roman Catholic Church in Ireland 1850–1860* (Chapel Hill, NC: University of North Carolina Press, 1980). *The Roman Catholic Church and the Creation of the Modern Irish State 1878–1886* (Philadelphia and Dublin: Gill and Macmillan, 1975). *The Roman Catholic Church and the Emergence of the Modern Irish Political System 1874–1878* (Dublin: Four Courts Press, 1996). *The Roman Catholic Church and the Fall of Parnell 1888–1891* (Chapel Hill, NC: University of North Carolina Press, 1979). *The Roman Catholic Church and the Home Rule Movement in Ireland 1870–1874* (Chapel Hill, NC: University of North Carolina Press, 1990).*The Roman Catholic Church and the Plan of Campaign 1886–88* (Cork: Cork University Press, 1978).

Lee, David (ed.), *Remembering Limerick. Historical Essays Celebrating the 800th Anniversary of Limerick's First Charter, Granted in 1197* (Limerick: Limerick Civic Trust, 1997).

Lee, Joseph, *The Modernisation of Irish Society 1848–1918* (Dublin: Gill and Macmillan, 1973).

Lenihan, Maurice, *Limerick, its History and Antiquities* (Dublin: Hodges, Smith and Co. 1866; reprinted Cork and Dublin: Mercier Press, 1991).

Loughlin, James, *Gladstone, Home Rule and the Ulster Question 1882–93* (Dublin: Gill and Macmillan, 1986). *Ulster Unionism and British National Identity since 1885* (London: Pinter, 1995).

Lucas, Edward, *The Life of Frederick Lucas M.P. by his Brother*, 2 vols (London: Burns and Oates, 1886).

Luddy, Maria, 'Angels of Mercy: Nuns as Workhouse Nurses, 1861–1898', in Greta Jones and Elizabeth Malcolm (eds), *Medicine, Disease and the State in Ireland, 1650–1940* (Cork: Cork University Press, 1999), pp.102–17.

McCarthy-Morrogh, Michael, *The Munster Plantation: English Migration to Southern Ireland 1583–1641* (Oxford: Clarendon Press, 1986).

McCartney, Donal, *The Dawning of Democracy – Ireland 1800–1870* (Dublin: Helicon, 1987).

Macaulay, Ambrose, *Dr Russell of Maynooth* (London: Darton, Longman and Todd, 1983).

MccClelland, V.A., *Cardinal Manning: His Public Life and Influence, 1865–92* (Oxford: Oxford University Press, 1962).

McConville, Michael, *Ascendancy to Oblivion. The Story of the Anglo-Irish* (London and New York: Quartet Books, 1986).

MacDonagh, Oliver, *The Life of Daniel O'Connell 1775–1847* (London: Weidenfeld and Nicolson, 1991).

MacDougall, Hugh A., *The Acton–Newman Relations. The Dilemma of Christian Liberalism* (New York: Fordham University Press, 1962).

McElrath, Damian, *The Syllabus of Pius IX. Some Reactions in England* (Louvain: privately printed, 1964).

McMunn, Lieutenant-General, Sir George, *The Crimea in Perspective* (London: G. Bell and Sons, 1935).

Magnus, Philip, *Gladstone* (London: John Murray, 1954). *King Edward VII* (Harmondsworth: Penguin, 1964).

Magraw, Roger, *France 1815–1914. The Bourgeois Century* (London: Fontana, 1983).

Mansell, William W., *A Historical and Genealogical Account of the Ancient Family of Maunsell-Mansell-Maunsel* (London: privately published, 1850).

Matthew, Colin, Harrison, Brian and Goldman, Laurence (eds), *Oxford Dictionary of National Biography* (Oxford: Oxford University Press, 2004).

Matthew, H.C.G., *Gladstone 1809–1874* (Oxford: Clarendon Press, 1986). *Gladstone 1874–1898* (Oxford: Oxford University Press, 1995).

Moneypenny, W.F. and Buckle, G.E., *The Life of Benjamin Disraeli, Earl of Beaconsfield*, 6 vols (London: John Murray, 1910–20).

Monsell, Gaston, second Lord Emly, *The Labour Cause in County Limerick. The Labourers and the County Council. Speech of Lord Emly. Mr A. Mackey's attack and the Labourers' Reply. The Case for Direct Labour* (Limerick: privately published, 1899). *Speech of Lord Emly at the Annual Convention of the Irish Land and Labour Association. Held at Limerick, August 15, 1901* (Limerick: privately published, 1901)

Monsell, William, first Lord Emly, *A Lecture on the Roman Question delivered at Limerick December 1st, 1859, to which is added the Report of the Count de Rayneval, French Envoy at Rome* (London: privately published, 1860). *Extract from a lecture delivered to the Young Men's Society of Newcastle on the 8th December, 1861, by William Monsell, M.P., followed by some remarks by Dr Moriarty, Bishop of Kerry* (Limerick: privately published, 1861). *A Roman Catholic Liberal Peer on the Irish Home Rule Bill – Speech by Lord Emly*, Vol. 3, no. 95 (Dublin: Irish Unionist Alliance Publications, 1894).

Morley, John, *Life of William Ewart Gladstone*, 3 vols (London: Macmillan, 1903).

Morrissey, Thomas J., *Bishop Edward Thomas O'Dwyer of Limerick, 1842–1917* (Dublin: Four Courts Press, 2003). *Towards a National University. William Delaney S.J. (1835–1924)* (Dublin: Wolfhound Press and Atlantic Highlands, NJ: Humanities Press, 1983). *William J. Walsh, Archbishop of Dublin (1841–1921)* (Dublin: Four Courts Press, 2000).

Murphy, David, *Ireland and the Crimean War* (Dublin: Four Courts Press, 2002).

Murphy, Joseph, *The Redingtons of Clarenbridge. Leading Catholic Landlords in the 19th Century* (Dublin: privately published, 1999).

Newman, John Henry, *The Via Media of the Anglican Church* (Oxford: Clarendon Press, 1990). *A Letter to His Grace the Duke of Norfolk on the occasion of Mr Gladstone's Recent Expostulation* (London: B.M. Pickering, 1875).

Newsome, David, *The Convert Cardinals. Newman and Manning* (London: John Murray, 1993).

Norman, Edward R., *Anti-Catholicism in Victorian England* (London: George Allen and Unwin, 1968). *The Catholic Church and Ireland in the Age of Rebellion 1859–73* (London: Longmans, 1965).

Nowlan, Kevin B., *The Politics of Repeal. A Study in the Relations between Britain and Ireland 1841–50* (London: Routledge and Kegan Paul, 1965).

O'Brien, Grania R. and Weir, Hugh, *These my Friends and Forebears: The O'Briens of Dromoland*, (Whitegate, County Clare: Ballinakella Press, 1991).

O'Cathaoir, Brendan, *Famine Diary* (Dublin: Irish Academic Press, 1999).

O'Gara, Margaret, *Triumph in Defeat: Infallibility, Vatican I, and the French Minority Bishops* (Washington, DC: Catholic University of America Press, 1988).

O'Rourke, Revd John, *The History of the Great Irish Famine of 1847* (Dublin: J. Duffy and Co., 1902).

O'Shea, James, *Prince of Swindlers. John Sadlier M.P. 1813–1856* (Dublin: Geography Publications, 1999).

Ó Tuathaigh, Gearóid, *Ireland before the Famine 1798–1848* (Dublin: Gill and Macmillan, 1972).

Oliphant, Margaret, *Memoirs of the Count de Montalambert*, 2 vols (London: W. Blackwood and Sons, 1872).

O'Neil, Robert, *Cardinal Herbert Vaughan, Archbishop of Westminster, Bishop of Salford, Founder of the Mill Hill Missionaries* (Tunbridge Wells: Burns and Oates, 1995).

Orton, W.A., *The Liberal Tradition. A Study of the Social and Spiritual Conditions of Freedom* (New Haven: Yale University Press, 1945).

Parris, Henry, *Constitutional Bureaucracy. The Development of British Central Administration since the Eighteenth Century* (London: Allen and Unwin, 1969).

Parry, Jonathan, *Democracy and Religion. Gladstone and the Liberal Party 1868–75* (Cambridge: Cambridge University Press, 1986). *The Rise and Fall of Liberal Government in Victorian Britain* (New Haven: Yale University Press, 1993).

Partington, Angela (ed.), *The Oxford Dictionary of Quotations* (Oxford: Oxford University Press, 1992).

Pawley, Margaret, *Faith and Family: The Life and Circle of Ambrose Phillipps de Lisle* (Norwich: Canterbury Press, 1993).

Pearl, Cyril, *The Three Lives of Gavan Duffy* (Dublin: O'Brien Press, 1979).

Perry, C.R., *The Victorian Post Office: The Growth of a Bureaucracy*, Royal Historical Society Studies in History, no.64 (London: Royal Historical Society, 1992).

Pezzimenti, Rocco, *The Political Thought of Lord Acton: The English Catholics of the Nineteenth Century* (Leaminster, Herts: Gracewing, and Rome: Millennium Romae, 2001).

Pijpers, Thomas A., *Aubrey De Vere as a Man of Letters* (Nijmegen-Utrecht: Dekker and Van de Vegt, 1941).

Plumb, J.H., *The First Four Georges* (London: Batsford, 1956).

Plunkett, Horace, *Nobless Oblige – An Irish Rendering* (Dublin; Maunsel, 1908).

Poirteir, Cathal, *Famine Echoes* (Dublin: Gill and Macmillan, 1995). (ed.), *The Great Irish Famine* (Dublin and Cork: Mercier Press, 1995).

Potter, Matthew, *A Catholic Unionist. The Life and Times of William Monsell, 1st Baron Emly of Tervoe (1812–94) A Centenary Essay* (Limerick: Treaty Press, 1994). *First Citizens of the Treaty City. The Mayors and the Mayoralty of Limerick* (Limerick: Limerick City Council, 2007). *The Government and the People of Limerick. The History of Limerick Corporation/City Council 1197–2006* (Limerick: Limerick City Council, 2006). 'A Roman Catholic Francophile Anglo-Irishman: William Monsell 1812–94', in Colin Graham and Leon Litvack (eds), *Ireland and Europe in the Nineteenth Century* (Dublin: Four Courts Press, 2006), pp.77–88. 'William Monsell', in Aidan Clarke, Ronan Fanning, T.K. Hoppen, Edith Mary-Johnston-Liik, James Maguire, Maureen Murphy and James Quinn (eds), *Dictionary of Irish Biography* (Cambridge: Cambridge University Press and Dublin: Royal Irish Academy, 2009).

Purcell, Edmund Sheridan, *Life of Cardinal Manning, Archbishop of Westminster*, 2 vols (London: Macmillan, 1896).

Quinn, Dermot, *Patronage and Piety. The Politics of English Roman Catholicism 1850–1900* (Stanford, CA: Stanford University Press, 1993).

Reilly, Sr M. Paraclita, *Aubrey de Vere: Victorian Observer* (Dublin: Clonmore and Reynolds, and London: Burnes, Oates and Washbourne, 1956).

Ridden, Jennifer, *'Making Good Citizens': Irish Elite Approaches to Empire, National Identity and Citizenship*, Past & Present monograph series (Cambridge: Cambridge University Press, forthcoming).

Ridley, Jasper, *Lord Palmerston* (London: Constable, 1970).

Riviére, Marc Serge, 'In Defence of Irish Catholicism: Charles de Montalambert's aborted History of Ireland and Journal in Time', in Eamon Maher and Grace Neville (eds), *France–Ireland: Anatomy of a Relationship*, Studies in History, Literature and Politics (Frankfurt on Main: Peter Lang, 2004), pp.147–61.

Riviére, Serge and Jenny O'Connor, 'The Representation of the Irish Cultural Landscape in the Journals of Montalambert (1830) and Tocqueville (1835)', in Eamon Maher, Eugene O'Brien and Grace Neville (eds), *Reinventing Ireland through a French Prism* (Frankfurt on Main: Peter Lang, 2007), pp.41–60.

Robinson, Howard, *Britain's Post Office. A History of Development from the Beginnings to the Present Day* (Oxford: Oxford University Press, 1953).

Sainty, J.C., *Officials of the Board of Trade 1660–1870* (London: Athlone Press, 1974).

Schiefen, Richard J., *Nicholas Wiseman and the Transformation of English Catholicism* (Shepherdstown, WV: Patmos Press, 1984).

Shannon, Richard, *Gladstone*, Vol. 1, *1809–1865* (London: Hamish Hamilton, 1982).

Sheehan, John, *A Corner of Limerick* (Limerick: privately published, 1989).

Shields, Andrew, *The Irish Conservative Party, 1852–1868. Land Politics and Religion* (Dublin and Portland, OR: Irish Academic Press, 2007).

Skentelbery, Norman, *Arrows to Atom Bombs: A History of the Ordnance Board* (London: Ordnance Board, 1975).

Snoddy, Theo, *Dictionary of Irish Artists, 20th Century* (Dublin: Wolfhound Press, 1996).

Southgate, Donald, *The Most English Minister: The Policies and Politics of Palmerston* (London: Macmillan, 1966).

Spring Rice, Thomas, *An Enquiry into the Effects of the Irish Grand Jury Laws* (London: privately published, 1815).

Steele, E.D., *Irish Land and British Politics: Tenant Right and Nationality 1865–70* (Cambridge: Cambridge University Press, 1974).

Stenton, Michael, *Who's Who of British Members of Parliament*, Vol. 1, *1832–1885. A Biographical Dictionary of the House of Commons based on Annual Volumes of 'Dod's Parliamentary Companion' and Other Sources* (Hassocks: Harvester Press, 1976).

Stephen, Leslie and Lee, Sidney (eds), *Dictionary of National Biography*, 63 vols (London: Smith and Elder, 1885–1900).

Taylor, A.J.P., *Europe: Grandeur and Decline* (Harmondsworth: Penguin, 1967).

Tedder, Henry R., *The Athenaeum 1824–1924. A Centenary Record* (London: reprinted from the *Times*, 1924).

Thomson, David, *Europe since Napoleon* (London: Longmans, 1975).

Thornley, David, *Isaac Butt and Home Rule* (London: MacGibbon and Kee, 1964).

Tierney, Revd Mark, *Croke of Cashel: The Life of Thomas William Croke 1823–1902* (Dublin: Gill and Macmillan, 1976).

Touhill, Blanche M., *William Smith O'Brien and his Irish Revolutionary Companions in Penal Exile* (Colombia, MI: University of Missouri Press, 1981).

Tristam, Henry, *Newman and his Friends* (London: John Lane, 1933).

Vaughan, W.E., *Landlords and Tenants in Mid-Victorian Ireland* (Oxford: Clarendon Press, 1994). (ed.), *A New History of Ireland*, Vol. 5, *1801–1870* (Oxford: Oxford University Press, 1989).

Vidler, Alec, *Prophecy and Papacy. A Study of Lamennais, the Church and the Revolution* (London: SCM Press, 1954).

Vincent, John, *The Formation of the Liberal Party 1857–1868* (London: Constable, 1966).

Walker, Brian M. (ed.), *Parliamentary Election Results in Ireland, 1801–1922* (Dublin: Royal Irish Academy, 1978).

Walsh, Revd P.J., *William J. Walsh, Archbishop of Dublin* (Dublin and Cork: Talbot Press, 1928).

Ward, Humphrey, *History of the Athenaeum 1824–1925* (London: Athenaeum Club, 1926).

Ward, Maisie, *The Wilfred Wards and the Transition,* Vol. 2, *Insurrection vs. Resurrection* (London: Sheed and Ward, 1937).

Ward, Wilfred, *Aubrey de Vere. A Memoir. Based on his Unpublished Diaries and Correspondence* (London: Longmans and Co., 1904). *The Life of John Henry Newman,* 2 vols (London: Longmans and Co., 1912). *William George Ward and the Catholic Revival* (London: Longmans, Green and Co., 1912).

Ward, William George, *Civil Intolerance of Religious error. M. De Montalambert at Malines* (London: privately published, 1863).

White, G.K., *A History of St Columba's College 1843–1974* (Dublin: Old Columban Society, 1980).

Whyte, J.H., *The Independent Irish Party 1850–59* (Oxford: Oxford University Press, 1958).

Winter, James, *Robert Lowe* (Toronto: University of Toronto Press, 1976).

Woodgate, M.V., *Madame Swetchine (1782–1857)* (Dublin: Browne and Nolan, 1948).

Woodward, Sir Llewelyn, *The Age of Reform 1815–70*, Oxford History of England, Vol. 13 (Oxford: Clarendon Press, 1962).

Articles

Allen, Louis, 'Ambrose Phillips De Lisle 1809–78', in *Catholic Historical Review*, 40, 1 (April 1954), pp.1–26.

Altholz, Josef L., 'The Political Behavior of the English Catholics, 1850–1867', in *Journal of British Studies*, 4, 1 (November 1964), pp.89–103.

Anon, 'Madame Swetchine and her Salon', in *The Month*, 1 (July to December 1864), pp.163–76.

Barr, Colin, 'Lord Acton's Irish Elections', in *Historical Journal*, 51, 1 (2008), pp.87–114.

Fitzpatrick, David, 'Thomas Spring Rice and the Peopling of Australia', in *Old Limerick Journal,* 23, Australian edition (spring 1988), pp.39–49.

Gladstone, William Ewart,'Ritualism and Ritual', in *Contemporary Review*, 24 , 5 (October 1874), pp.663–81.

Hanley, Mary, 'The Past Glories of Tervoe', in *Limerick Chronicle* (7, 14 and 21 November 1953).

Hoppen, K. Theodore, 'Tories, Catholics and the General Election of 1859', in *The Historical Journal*, 13, 1 (March 1970), pp.48–67.

Ireland, John De Courcy, 'The French Navy at the time of the Williamite War', in *Old Limerick Journal*, 28, 1690 Siege edition (winter 1990), pp.23–6.

Kearney, Pat, 'Limerick's Campaign for a University 1838–45', in *Old Limerick Journal*, 26 (winter 1989), pp.26–35.

King, Hazel, 'Richard Bourke and his Two Colonial Administrations: A Comparative Study of Cape Colony and New South Wales', in *Journal and Proceedings*, Royal Australian Historical Society, 49, 5 (1964), pp.360–75.

McConnel, James, '"Jobbing with Tory and Liberal": Irish nationalist MPs and the politics of patronage, 1880–1914', in *Past and Present*, 188 (2005), pp.105–31.

McEldowney, John, 'Lord O'Hagan, 1812–1885', in *Irish Jurist*, 14 (1979), pp.360–77.

Machin, G.I.T., 'Lord John Russell and the Prelude to the Ecclesiastical Titles Bill 1846–1851', in *Journal of Ecclesiastical History*, 25, 3 (July 1974), pp.277–95.

Malcolmson, A.P.W., 'Speaker Pery and the Pery Papers', in *North Munster Antiquarian Journal*, 21 (1973–4), pp.33–60.

Monsell, William, 'Catholic Policy', in *The Rambler*, 5, part 13 (May 1861), pp.1–17.

'University Education in Ireland', in *Home and Foreign Review*, 2 (January 1863), pp.32–58.

'Address of the Rt. Hon. William Monsell M.P. Vice-President at the Annual meeting of the Statistical and Social enquiry Society of Ireland on 22nd January, 1869', in *Journal of the Statistical and Social Enquiry Society of Ireland,* 5, part 36 (1868/1869), pp.53–69.

'Inaugural Address of the Rt. Hon. Lord Emly 24th November, 1874', in *Journal of the Statistical and Social Enquiry Society of Ireland*, 6, part 46 (1873/1874), pp.347–65.

'Catholic Intermediate Education. St Mary's Orphanage, Blackheath', in *Dublin Review*, 26 (April 1876), pp.322–31.

Moody, T.W., 'The Irish University Question in the Nineteenth Century', in *History*, 43 (1958), pp.90–109.

Mumm, Susan, '"Not Worse than Other Girls": The Convent-Based Rehabilitation of Fallen Women in Victorian Britian', in *Journal of Social History*, 29, 3 (spring 1996), pp.527–41.

Newman, John Henry, 'Temporal Prosperity. A Note of the Church', *The Rambler*, 1 (May 1859), pp.48–58.

Nockles, Peter, 'Church or Protestant Sect? The Church of Ireland, High Churchmanship and the Oxford Movement, 1822–1869', in *Historical Journal*, 41 (1998), pp.457–93.

O'Shea, Kieran, 'David Moriarty (1814–77) III Politics', in *Journal of the Kerry Archaeological and Historical Society*, 5 (1972), pp.86–102.

Perry, Charles R., 'Frank Ives Scudamore and the Post Office', in *Albion*, 12 (1980), pp.350–67.

Potter, Matthew, 'Lord Emly and Pope Pius IX', in *Studies*, 92, 368 (winter 2003), pp.396–404.

Roantree, Dermot S., 'William Monsell and Papal Infallibility. The working of an inopportunist's mind', in *Archivicum Hibernicum*, 43 (1988), pp.118–34.

Sewell, William, 'Romanism in Ireland', in *Quarterly Review*, 67, 133 (December 1840), pp.16–28.

'Romish Priests in Ireland', in *Quarterly Review*, 67, 134 (March 1841), pp.25–40.

'Irish Peasantry' in *Quarterly Review*, 67, 135 (September 1841), pp.15–30.

Spence, Joseph, 'Isaac Butt, Nationality and Irish Toryism, 1833–1852', in *Bullán*, 2, 1 (summer 1995), pp.45–60.

Walker, Brian, 'Politicians, Elections and Catastrophe: The General Election of 1847', in *Irish Political Studies*, 22, 1 (March 2007), pp.1–34.

Woods, B.C.J., 'The Politics of Cardinal McCabe, Archbishop of Dublin 1879–85', in *Dublin Historical Record*, 26, 3 (1972–3), pp.101–10.

Entries in Oxford Dictionary of National Biography

Anon., revised K.D. Reynolds, 'Henry Fitzalan-Howard, fifteenth Duke of Norfolk (1847–1917)'.

Ball, Stuart, 'Bolton Meredith Eyres Monsell, first Viscount Monsell (1881–1969)'.

Beales, Derek, 'Ralph Bernal Osborne (1808–1882)'.

Bonham, Valerie, 'Harriet Monsell (née O'Brien) (1811–1883)'.

Champ, Judith F., revised Michael Peterburs, 'George Talbot (1816–1886)'.

Champ, Judith F., 'William Ullathorne (1806–1889)'.

Cooper, Thompson, revised G. Martin Murphy, 'Edward Henry Howard (1829–92)'.

Cooper, Thompson, revised Josef L. Altholz, 'Frederick Lucas (1812–1855)'.

Courtney, W.P, revised H.C.G. Matthew, 'William Monsell, first Baron Emly (1812–1894)'.
Cregier, D.M., 'William Joseph O'Neill Daunt (1807–94)'.
Gilley, Sheridan, 'William George Ward (1812–1882)'.
Gordon, Alexander, revised David Huddleston, 'John Jebb (1775–1833)'.
Grant, Arthur H., revised Kenneth Milne, 'Lord John George de la Poer Beresford (1773–1862)'.
Gwynn, S.L. revised Peter Gray, 'Windham Thomas Wyndham-Quin, fourth Earl of Dunraven and Mount Earl (1841–1926)'.
Huddelston, David, 'Edmond Sexton Pery, Viscount Pery, (1719–1806)'.
Larkin, Emmet, 'Paul Cullen (1803–1878)'.
Laughton, J.K., revised Andrew Lambert, 'Sir Thomas Hastings (1790–1870)'.
Lee, Elizabeth, revised M.C. Curthoys, 'Sir Stephen Edward de Vere (1812–1904)'.
Lee, Sidney, revised Alan O'Day, 'William Sherman Crawford (1781–1861)'.
McEldowney, John F., 'Thomas O'Hagan, first Baron O'Hagan (1812–1885)'.
Matthew, H.C.G., 'Chichester Samuel Parkinson-Fortescue, Baron Carlingford and second Baron Clermont (1823–1898)'. 'Frederic Rogers, Baron Blachford (1811–1889)'.
Norgate, G. Le G., revised Alan O'Day, 'Charles Owen O'Conor (known as the O'Conor Don) (1838–1906)'.
Norgate, G. Le G., revised Michael Herity, 'Edwin Richard Windham Wyndham–Quin, third Earl of Dunraven and Mount Earl (1812–1871)'.
O'Brien, R.B. revised Brigette Anton, 'Sir Charles Gavan Duffy (1816–1903).'
O'Donoghue, D.J., revised Leon Litvack, 'John Samuel Bewley Monsell (1811–1875)'.
Parkes, S.M., 'Sir Patrick Joseph Keenan (1826–1894)'.
Pawley, Margaret, 'Ambrose Lisle March Phillipps de Lisle (1809–1878)'.
Paz, D.G., 'Sir Thomas Wyse (1791–1862)'.
Perry, C.R., 'Frank Ives Scudamore (1823–1884)'. 'Sir John Tilley (1813–1898)'.
Skinner, S.A., 'William Sewell (1804–1874)'.
Steele, David, 'John Francis Maguire (1815–1872)'. 'Roundell Palmer, first Earl of Selbourne (1812–1895)'.
Sutherland, Gillian, 'Ralph Robert Wheeler Lingen (1819–1905)'.
John Sweetman, 'Fox Maule, second Baron Panmure and eleventh Earl of Dalhouisie (1801–1874)'.

Todd, E.M., 'James Henthorn Todd (1805–1869)'.

Wasson, Ellis Archer, 'Thomas Spring Rice, first Baron Monteagle of Brandon (1790–1866)'.

Welch, Robert, 'Aubrey Thomas de Vere (1814–1902)'.

Unpublished Theses

Bew, J.P.A., 'The Dilemmas of Liberal Unionism' (M. Phil., University of Cambridge, 2002).

Buckland, Patrick James, 'Southern Unionism 1888–1922 with special reference to the period after 1914' (Ph.D, Queens University Belfast, 1969).

Farragher, Rev. Sean P., 'Peré Leman. A French Contribution to Ireland' (Ph.D, University College Galway, 1985).

Feingold, William Leo, 'The Irish Boards of Poor Law Guardians. 1872–86. A Revolution in Local Government' (Ph.D, University of Chicago, 1974).

Hoppen, K.T., 'William George Ward and Nineteenth–Century Catholicism' (unpublished Ph.D, University of Cambridge, 1966).

Horgan, David Thomas, 'The Irish Catholic Whigs in Parliament 1847–74' (Ph.D, University of Minnesota, 1975).

Jupp, P.J., 'Irish Parliamentary Representation 1801–20' (Ph.D, University of Reading, 1966).

Malcolm, B.D., 'Educational Reform at the Royal Military Academy Woolwich and the Royal Military College Sandhurst, 1854–1874' (M.Phil., Kings College, University of London, 1985).

Moane, Damien Jude, 'The Limerick Workhouse: 1841–1861' (unpublished MA, Mary Immaculate College, University of Limerick, 2002).

Morrissey, Thomas J., 'Some Jesuit Contributions to Irish Education' (Ph.D, University College Cork, 1975).

Murphy, Charlotte Mary, 'The Life and Politics of Thomas Spring Rice, 1st Baron Monteagle of Brandon 1790–1866' (MA, University College Cork, 1991).

O'Callaghan, Rev. Edward, 'Bishop Edward Thomas O'Dwyer and the Course of Irish Politics 1870–1917' (MA, University College Galway, 1976). 'English Catholics and the Irish Question 1870–1893' (Ph.D, University College Galway, 1983).

O'Doherty, M., 'Patrick Keenan, Educator and Administrator: A Study of the Influence of Sir Patrick Keenan on Key Developments in Nineteenth-Century Education' (M.Ed., University College Dublin, 1998).

O Dubhtaigh, Fiacra S., 'A Review of the Contribution of Sir Patrick Keenan (1826–1894) to the Development of Irish and British Colonial Education' (M.Ed., Trinity College Dublin, 1974).

O'Ferrall, R.F.B., 'The Growth of Political Consciousness in Ireland

1823–1847: A Study in O'Connellite Politics and Political Education' (Ph.D, Trinity College Dublin, 1978).

Potter, Matthew , 'A Catholic Unionist: The Life and Times of William Monsell, first Baron Emly of Tervoe 1812–1894' (Ph.D, National University of Ireland, Galway, 2001).

Ridden, Jennifer, '"Making Good Citizens": National Identity, Religion and Liberalism among the Irish Elite c. 1800–1850' (Ph.D, University of London, 1998).

Roantree, Dermot S., 'William Monsell, M.P., and the Catholic Question in Victorian Britain and Ireland' (Ph.D, University College Dublin, 1990).

Spence, Joseph, 'The Philosophy of Irish Toryism, 1833–52: A Study of Reactions to Liberal Reformism in Ireland in the Generation between the First Reform Act and the Famine, with Especial Reference to Expressions of National Feeling among the Protestant Ascendancy' (unpublished Ph.D, University of London, 1991).

Spillane, Michael, 'The Fourth Earl of Dunraven, 1841–1926: A Study of his Contribution to the Emerging Ireland at the Beginning of the Twentieth Century' (Ph.D, Mary Immaculate College, University of Limerick, 2002).

Tyler, Warwick Perceval Newell, 'Sir Frederick Rogers, Permanent Under-Secretary at the Colonial Office 1860–1871' (Ph.D, Duke University, 1963).

Index